CORE
JAVA™ Media
Framework

ISBN 0-13-011519-3

90000

9 780130 115195

PRENTICE HALL PTR
CORE SERIES

CORE

JAVA™ Media Framework

Linden deCarmo

Prentice Hall PTR, Upper Saddle River, NJ 07458

www.phptr.com

Library of Congress Cataloging-in-Publication Data

deCarmo, Linden.
    Core Java media framework / Linden deCarmo.
        p.   cm.
    ISBN 0-13-011519-3
    1. Java (Computer program language) 2. Multimedia systems.
    I. Title.
    QA76.73.J38D428   1999   99-21037
    006.7'6--dc21   CIP

Editorial/production supervision: *Vincent Janoski*
Acquisitions editor: *Mark Taub*
Marketing manager: *Dan Rush*
Manufacturing manager: *Alexis Heydt*
Editorial assistant: *Audri Bazlan*
Cover design director: *Jerry Votta*
Cover designer: *Talar Agasyan*

©1999 by Prentice-Hall

Published by Prentice Hall P T R
Prentice-Hall, Inc.
Upper Saddle River, NJ 07458

Prentice Hall books are widely used by corporations and government agencies for training, marketing, and resale.

The publisher offers discounts on this book when ordered in bulk quantities.
For more information, contact: Corporate Sales Department, Phone: 800-382-3419; Fax: 201-236-7141;
E-mail: corpsales@prenhall.com; or write: Prentice Hall P T R, Corp. Sales Dept.,
One Lake Street, Upper Saddle River, NJ 07458.

TRADEMARKS: Sun, Sun Microsystems, Java, JavaBeans, JavaSound, and Solaris are trademarks or registered trademarks of Sun Microsystems, Incorporated in the United States and other countries. Microsoft, Windows 95, Windows 98, and Windows NT are registered trademarks of Microsoft Corporation. Macintosh and QuickTime are registered trademarks of Apple Computer, Incorporated. RealPlayer and RealAudio are trademarks of RealNetworks, Incorporated.

Display quotations by Yogi Berra are printed by permission of Yogiltd@aol.com. All display quotations designated "NIV" are taken from the Holy Bible New International Version, copyright 1978 by the New York International Bible Society, and used by permission of Zondervan Bible Publishers.

All products or services mentioned in this book are the trademarks or service marks of their respective companies or organizations.

Printed in the United States of America
10 9 8 7 6 5 4 3 2 1

ISBN 0-13-011519-3

Prentice-Hall International (UK) Limited, London
Prentice-Hall of Australia Pty. Limited, Sydney
Prentice-Hall Canada Inc., Toronto
Prentice-Hall Hispanoamericana, S.A., Mexico
Prentice-Hall of India Private Limited, New Delhi
Prentice-Hall of Japan, Inc., Tokyo
Prentice-Hall Singapore Pte. Ltd., Singapore
Editora Prentice-Hall do Brasil, Ltda., Rio de Janeiro

Contents

CHAPTER 2

CHAPTER 3

CHAPTER 4

CHAPTER 18

CHAPTER 19

CHAPTER 20

CHAPTER 21

Preface

The Java Media Framework (JMF) is the most exciting addition to the Java Family of APIs since the introduction of Swing. No longer are you restricted to passive dialogs and silent windows. Now you can use JMF to spice up your applications with audio and visual effects. JMF is divided into three phases: media playback, media capture and conferencing. This book concentrates on the media playback portion of JMF, the Java Media Player API, and how you can use it in real-world scenarios.

Who Should Read This Book?

Multimedia has transitioned from an exotic feature used by few applications to a core feature of Web sites, databases, games and virtually all business applications. As a result, anyone who programs in Java needs to read Core JMF.

Core JMF is targeted at serious programmers who don't want a warmed-over version of Sun's JMF's documentation. It not only clarifies the confusing areas in Sun's documentation, but it also provides unique insights to the inner working of the JMF classes and interfaces. Throughout the text, you'll find honest evaluations of JMF's strengths and weaknesses and advice on how to work around bugs.

Core JMF does not assume that the entire world revolves around Microsoft and its Win32 API. You'll discover how to leverage JMF's cross-platform capabilities on Microsoft Windows 95, Windows 98, Windows NT, Sun Solaris and other flavors of UNIX. You'll see comparisons of how JMF runs on each platform and how to avoid platform specific issues so that your applications are portable.

Core JMF does not contain fluffy example programs that show you how to make noise or play video in a window. Rather, you'll encounter example programs that solve real-world multimedia problems. Some of sample programs will show you how to:

- Enhance your applets with multimedia.
- Integrate JMF with a Swing file chooser dialog.
- Create multimedia beans.
- Use JMF objects with native C/C++ programs.
- Create a CD Player.
- Synchronize text with an audio CD.
- Stream multimedia content over the Internet.

This book assumes you have a solid knowledge of Java programming concepts. However, you do not have to be a multimedia expert to read it. You'll find thorough explanations of each multimedia acronym or term.

If you already are a multimedia aficionado and are familiar with environments such as QuickTime, MCI, or DirectShow, this book will show you how each component of JMF compares to the API you already know, so you can rapidly transition to JMF programming.

About This Book

Core JMF covers the core JMF classes and interfaces that you will use in your programs. If you are looking for an exhaustive overview of every JMF API, you should read Rob Gordon and Stephen Talley's *Essential JMF*. After you've finished reading Core JMF, you'll have thorough knowledge of the following JMF topics:

- Multimedia Applets.
- Synchronization.
- Player Design and Development.

- Real-time streaming over the Internet.
- Enhancing other Java API's such as Swing, JavaBeans, and JNI with multimedia.
- Cross platform multimedia development and issues.

The book is not a disjointed set of unrelated example programs. Rather, it is a cohesive unit. Each chapter builds on the lessons learned in previous chapters. As a result, you'll be able to create sophisticated Java applications and objects without being overwhelmed with details.

Here are some highlights of what you'll learn in each chapter:

Chapter 1: Multimedia Evolution. Chapter 1 explains why the Java Media Framework (JMF) was created and why you'll want to use it in your programs. It starts with a digital audio primer that defines how analog audio waveforms are captured and stored in the digital realm. Readers who are familiar with digital audio and Video can jump directly to the "Audio Woes" section of the chapter.

The chapter then explores the primitive audio features found in JDK 1.0.2 and explains why they are inadequate for non-trivial programs. We then uncover an undocumented audio interface present in JDK 1.x and explain how to use it.

You'll be introduced into Sun's Java Media and Communication APIs, the most exciting of which is JMF. Finally, you'll discover three key reasons why you should incorporate JMF into your Java programs.

Chapter 2: JMF's Growing Pains. This chapter examines how JMF operates on platforms such as Solaris, Microsoft Windows 95 and 98, Windows NT and the Apple Macintosh. We reveal the companies that have been involved in developing JMF runtimes and uncover why JMF was a crucial component of the United States Justice Department's lawsuit against Microsoft.

You'll also discover the challenges that developers face when they port JMF to environments, such as QuickTime and DirectShow, and how these challenges affect your JMF programs.

We then instruct you how to install JMF on your operating system and set up your development tools so you can compile and test the JMF programs we'll create in subsequent chapters.

Chapter 3: Everything Revolves Around Time. This chapter introduces you to the two core components of JMF: the **Player** interface and the **Manager**. You'll learn about the variety of media formats used by a **Player** and how to differentiate between a **TimeBase** and **MediaTime**. You'll also discover a clock's states (or phases) and how clocks affect synchronization.

Chapter 4: Taking Control of the Situation. Chapter 4 examines **Controllers** and their impact on the utilization of multimedia resources in your programs. You'll learn what a **Controller** is, its modes of operation and why this model is superior to the older multimedia architectures.

We'll also show you the most efficient techniques to manipulate Controller states and explain how to monitor a **Controller**'s status by listening for events.

Chapter 5: Origins. This chapter explores **DataSources** and how they are used by the **Manager** and the **Player**. You'll learn why a **DataSource** removes all input/output responsibilities from a **Player** and how this makes the **Player** more flexible.

We'll discover the differences between a Push and Pull **DataSource** and explain why the Pushed multimedia content will play a larger role in the future. Finally, we'll introduce you to **MediaLocators** and show you how they can be used to connect a **DataSource** to a Player.

Chapter 6: AlohaJMF: A JMF Applet. In this chapter, you'll leverage all the information learned in Chapters 1 through 5 to write your first JMF Applet. We'll explain the similarities between the Applet interface and the JMF's Player interface and explain how to use Player methods in your applets. We'll also give you tips to make your JMF enhanced applets more user-friendly.

Chapter 7: Getting Control Over Your Applications. Chapter 7 will show you why Controls are a crucial part of the **Player** and why every application must use them. You'll learn the three types of controls that a Player can surface and the most efficient means to obtain these controls. Finally, we'll show you how to incorporate the most popular controls in your applications and squeeze the best performance from them.

Chapter 8: Multimedia Swing Set. Swing and JMF can be a dangerous combination and Chapter 8 teaches you how to safely mix JMF in Swing-based applications. First, you'll find out how to enhance Swing's **JFileChooser** class with multimedia previewing capabilities. Then, you'll discover how to simultaneously handle JMF and Swing events. Finally, we'll explain the problems you'll encounter in Swing multimedia development and show you how to avoid these pitfalls.

Chapter 9: The Next Generation: JavaBeans and JMF. Chapter 9 introduces you to the JavaBeans object model and how it can be used to create multimedia objects. You'll learn what an object model is and how JavaBeans compares to other object models. We'll then take the multimedia chooser created in Chapter 8 and create a JavaBean from it.

While we're creating this multimedia object, we'll reveal guidelines for converting a general purpose multimedia class into a multimedia bean and give you specific examples of how to use these guidelines.

Chapter 10: Going Native. Chapter 10 teaches you how to reuse JMF objects in your C or C++ programs with the Java Native Interface (JNI). You'll discover how to start the Java virtual machine in C++ and learn how to avoid serious performance bottlenecks present in JNI.

You'll then find out how to launch and use the JavaBean from Chapter 9 in a C++ program. We'll show you the most efficient means to access Java constants, member variables and methods and how to optimize your JNI code.

Chapter 11: The Art of Synchronization. In Chapter 11 you'll learn what synchronization is and why it is a vital feature of all multimedia platforms. We'll use the timing concepts you learned in Chapter 3 to explain how JMF synchronizes multiple **Player**s. You'll learn about the complexities involved with manually synchronizing two or more **Player**s and find out about **Controller** methods which make synchronizing Players simple and fun.

We'll also teach you the things you shouldn't try with synchronized **Player**s and the catastrophic results if you ignore these warnings. Finally, you'll learn how synchronization affects event reporting and how to respond intelligently to events from a synchronized **Player**.

Chapter 12: Journey to the Center of the Player. Chapter 12 introduces you to the mysteries of **Player** creation. We shatter the myth that **Player** development is an arduous task and explain why you'll want to create your own **Player**s. You'll learn how to install a JMF Player and discover how the JMF **Manager** locates installed Players and associates them with **DataSource**s.

We'll show you how to find out what kind of content a **DataSource** is transporting and whether the **DataSource** is cramming the content into one stream or separating its output into multiple streams. We then explain how Players retrieve media from the **DataSource**'s streams and play this content.

Finally, in order to illustrate synchronization, we create a real world synchronization example program. Over the next five chapters, we create a Caption Player and CD Audio Player and an application that shows you how to synchronize text to the music on a CD.

Chapter 13: The Multimedia Caption DataSource. In Chapter 13 you'll learn how to create a **DataSource** that processes multimedia captions. You'll find out about the Multimedia Caption Markup Language (MCML) and why it is ideal for synchronizing text to audio/visual content.

We then review how the MCML is used inside our **DataSource**. You'll learn why this **DataSource** has multiple output streams and how these output streams are important for multiple language support.

Chapter 14: MediaHandler Primer. Chapter 14 provides the infrastructure necessary to create robust **Player**s. You'll be provided with a **Player** shell that you can use to build your **Player**s. Then, we'll tell you why certain methods must be performed on threads and explain the side-effects of improper thread usage.

You'll learn how to properly divide the **Player**'s workload so that client applications are responsive to user input. Finally, you'll discover when to clean up multimedia resources so your **Player** can gracefully shut down.

*Chapter 15: The **Caption MediaHandler**.* We'll show you how to write a MCML Player using the principles revealed in Chapter 14. You'll parse MCML streams, decode the captions and present it via Swing.

You'll learn how to create a **ControlPanel** component to start, pause, stop and search within a caption stream. You'll find out how to use a **VisualControl** within a **Player**. We'll also explain how threads improve the interactivity of the **Player**.

We'll discuss the techniques **Player**s should use to report events and the dangers of reporting events on worker threads. You'll also find out how to create custom events that let you enhance applications that use your **Player**. Throughout the chapter, you'll receive valuable debugging tips that will save you hours of development and debugging.

Chapter 16: Grapling with the CD. This chapter uncovers a gaping hole in the JMF architecture and shows how you can work around it. Since JMF prevents you from writing non-streaming **Player**s, we'll show you a secret technique to work around the problem. You'll also learn how to leverage this technology to create a CD **Player** that doesn't use JMF's streaming model.

This chapter advises you when you should enhance a **Player** with native code. It also guides you through the minefield of Windows multimedia development and shows you how to safely integrate a JMF **Player** with native Windows' multimedia calls.

Chapter 17: The Ultimate Synchronization: The Marriage of Players. This is the concluding chapter in the synchronization series. You'll discover how to combine and synchronize the CD Player created in Chapter 16, with the MCML Player and **DataSource** created in Chapters 13 through 15. In addition, we'll review the responsibilities a Player must assume in order to synchronize with other Players and point out problem areas in synchronized **Player** development.

Chapter 18: Meddling in a Player's Business With a MediaProxy. Chapter 18 introduces you to the **MediaProxy** interface. You'll learn how a **MediaProxy** modifies content after it leaves a **DataSource** but before it reaches the **Player**. We'll also provide realistic examples of when you want to use a **MediaProxy**.

We'll show you how to create a **MediaProxy** by modifying the MCML **DataSource** to transmit a single stream of caption content. Then, we'll use a **MediaProxy** to transform the single caption stream into the multi-stream format expected by the **Player** we created in Chapter 15.

Chapter 19: Real-time Streaming. This chapter provides a thorough explanation of real-time streaming on the Internet and shows you how they are used in JMF. You'll learn about technologies such as RTP and RTSP and how they are superior to HTTP or FTP for transporting multimedia content over the Internet Protocol.

We'll also introduce you to the RTSP-based RealNetwork's RealPlayer G2 and show you how to exploit the custom RealPlayer methods and events in your programs.

Chapter 20: A Real-Time Hybrid. Chapter 20 will examine Sun's mysterious RTP architecture and show you how to use RTP in your applets and applications. You'll discover how Sun uses a **MediaProxy** to bridge the chasm between their RTP-specific **DataSource** and generic **MediaHandlers**. We'll also show you how the RTP **Depacketizer** provides data type independence and enables you to stream custom media types.

You'll learn how to create RTP applets. We'll show you where to find RTP servers or create your own RTP conferences in order to test the RTP applet.

Chapter 21: Where Is JMF Headed? We conclude the book by examining the current strengths and weaknesses in JMF and preview how future JMF releases will address these weaknesses. You'll learn about Pure JMF 1.1, the first version of JMF that runs on all Java platforms. We'll also examine the web server version of JMF that dramatically simplifies the installation and usage of JMF applets.

Then we'll review JavaSound: the API that gives you finer control over audio and MIDI hardware. Finally, we'll take a peek at JMF 2.0. This release promises to provide evolutionary new functions such as the Plug-in API. The Plug-in API will let you create and dynamically insert special effect routines into Players.

Appendices

The Appendices give you additional details on error conditions, file formats and sources for additional information on the Internet.

Feedback

All books will contain unforeseen errors in the text and bugs in the example programs, and this book is no exception. If you'd like to report a bug, e-mail comments and other feedback at lindend@pandasys.com.

Conventions

Table P-1 shows the coding conventions used in this book.

Convention	Example
Class names have initial Capital letters	`public class Handler` `implements MediaProxy`

Method names have an initial low-ercase letter and the rest of the words start with a capital letter.°	`public DataSource getData-`
	`Source() throws IOException,`
	`NoDataSourceException`

Variable names have an initial low-ercase letter and the rest of the words start with a capital letter.	`protected byte [] timebuffer;`
static variables begin with an underscore.	

°**Note:** methods are always referred to without their associated parameters.

Table P-2 shows the typographic conventions used in this book.

Typeface or Symbol	Description
`courier`	Used in source code, command-line entries, and other technical terms.
italics	Refers to definitions, quotes, emphasis, book title or a variable.

MULTIMEDIA EVOLUTION

We shall not flag or fail. We shall go on to the end...we shall never give up.

Winston Churchill, Hansard, June 4, 1940

And the most glorious exploits do not always furnish us with the clearest discoveries of virtue or vice in men; sometimes a matter of less moment, an expression or a jest, informs us better of their characters and inclinations, than the most famous sieges, the greatest armaments, or the bloodiest battles whatsoever.

Plutarch, *Life of Alexander*

Chapter 1

J ava's future was at stake. Its dramatic growth had become threatened by its poor interactive capabilities. Java became popular because Web sites could use it to create interactive programs that ran on a multitude of platforms. As the Internet increased in popularity, these Web pages had to offer background music, digital video, and digital audio to attract visitors. Since the initial Java Developments Kits (JDKs) were only capable of primitive audio playback, each site was forced to either concoct a different scheme for advanced multimedia support or use an undocumented Java audio interface.

These schemes required users to download plug-ins, ActiveX objects, and proprietary Java code augmented by native methods. Not only were these utilities incompatible and redundant, but each was tied to a specific platform (such as Win32 or Solaris). As a result, Sun created the Java Media Framework (JMF). JMF is an object-oriented architecture designed for multimedia presentation, capture, and conferencing that will not only satisfy the needs of Webmasters, but any Java developer.

Why JMF Anyway?

To appreciate JMF, it's important to understand the limitations imposed by the JDK 1.0.2 multimedia interface. The primary problem with the initial

1

JDKs is that they were digital audio-centric and ignored important media types such as digital video and Musical Instrument Digital Interface (MIDI). Furthermore, these interfaces were playback only and could not record any media format. Finally, they could only play an extremely limited subset of digital audio content.

Digital Audio Primer

If you dust off your old high school physics book, you'll remember that the sounds we hear are actually analog waveforms (or waves). The sounds produced by these waves are controlled by their frequency, wavelength, and amplitude (or volume) (see Figure 1-1). If you are interested in the mechanics of analog sounds, I recommend Ken Pohlmann's *Principles of Digital Audio* (Howard W. Sams & Company).

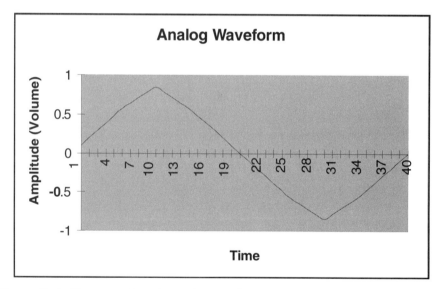

Figure 1-1   Illustration of analog audio waveform.

Digital audio content is the digital representation of an analog audio wave. The quality of digital audio is influenced by its sampling rate and resolution. Sampling is the process of capturing the position of an analog wave at specific points in time (Figure 1-2). The sampler then must interpolate (or perform an educated guess) the position of the analog wave between the sample points.

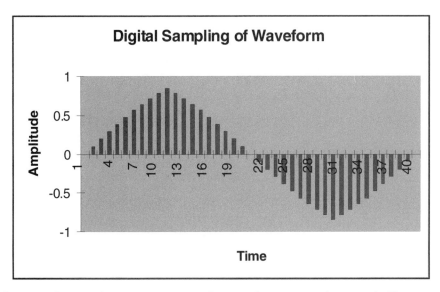

Figure 1–2 Sampling measures an analog waveform at periodic intervals. The more samples you take, the closer the digital waveform will represent the original analog waveform.

If you use a higher sampling rate, the distance between sampling points is reduced, thereby increasing the accuracy of the interpolation. Consequently, digital audio files with high sampling rates are more pleasing to the ear. For example, compact discs use a sampling resolution of 44Hz to obtain high-fidelity sound. However, a high sampling rate is not necessary for all occasions. For example, speech can be sampled at 8KHz. In general, higher sampling rates are necessary for music, while lower sampling rates are acceptable for speech.

Core Tip

If you are unsure of the sampling rate you should use for recordings, Nyquist's theorem may help. It states that you must sample at twice the frequency of the content you are trying to capture or you will not be able to adequately represent the waveform. For instance, if you are recording a voice waveform that ranges between 0 and 4Hz, you should sample at 8Hz.

The second factor affecting audio quality is the size of the storage unit for each sample. If larger storage units are used, you can track the movements of the analog wave more accurately. For example, if you store each sample in a bit, the digital representation of the wave can be either 0 or 1. By contrast, if you use 16 bits to store the sample, each sample can be one of 65,536 potential values, and consequently, more closely approximate the original analog wave (contrast Figure 1-2 with Figure 1-3). Speech typically only requires 8 bits of capture resolution, while advanced audio formats can use 24 bits or more of resolution.

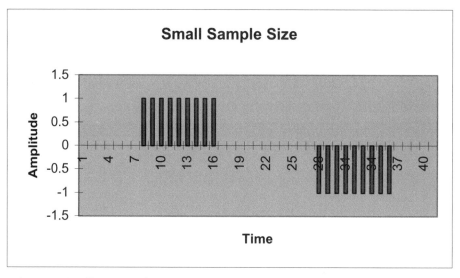

Figure 1-3   Illustration of capture size importance. The analog waveform in Figure 1-1 was fed into a sampler with only one bit of resolution. As a result, considerable information was lost.

One significant difference between an analog waveform and a digital stream is that you can easily write algorithms (called signal processors) to manipulate the digital stream (or signal, in electrical engineering terms). For instance, you can create a chipmunk-type effect (i.e., high pitched squealing voices) by throwing out every other sample in the stream. By contrast, analog streams must be converted by a special hardware device called an Analog/Digital (A/D) converter before you can perform signal processing.

Time to Squeeze the Charmin™?

As we've discovered, higher sampling rates and capture resolution result in superior audio quality. However, they have a significant side effect: tremendous storage consumption. To explain, digital audio is captured via a technique called Pulse Code Modulation (PCM). The formula below describes the space requirement for each second of digital audio:

Storage space = *Capture size* X *sampling resolution* X *channels*

If you plug in the numbers for CD-quality audio into the formula (44KHz, or 44,100 samples per second x 16 bits per sample x 2 channels), you'll discover that it eats up approximately 166K per second. Since the storage and throughput requirements for PCM are prohibitive, most multimedia developers use compression techniques in their programs and Web pages.

The compression techniques use COmpressor/DECompressors (CODECs) to reduce storage requirements. The compressor runs an algorithm on the PCM data and outputs digital audio. The decompressor transforms the compressed audio into PCM that can be played on any sound card. Each CODEC has audio characteristics (or side effects), and all offer trade-offs between compression ratios, processing power required, and audio quality.

Applications that focus on speech tend to use μ-law, A-law, or TrueSpeech μ-law and A-law take advantage of the fact that words can be sampled at 8KHz to produce acceptable output. In fact, these technologies are used outside the computer realm. μ-law is used by North American phone lines, while A-law is used by European telephony products.

TrueSpeech variants have been adopted by the International Telecommunications Union (ITU) as the preferred compression technology for speech. It is heavily used by Internet-based video conferencing products and is the preferred solution for many digital answering machines.

Although μ-law, A-law, or TrueSpeech excel at speech compression, they are not as adept at compressing music and other sounds that require high fidelity. As a result, techniques such as Dolby Digital (AC-3) and Digital Theater Sound (DTS) are used to reproduce high-fidelity audio. For example, AC-3 is able to compress five channels plus a bandwidth-limited sixth channel of high-quality audio into a bit-stream of only 284kbs per second while simultaneously retaining much of the original quality. Although there are a number of other competing audio compressors, these CODECs dominate the consumer high-fidelity market.

The first version of Java only supported μ-law content wrapped in the .au file format (popular on Solaris and the Internet). If you desired to play back a clip that was stored in PCM, TrueSpeech, or another CODEC, or if the file was stored in another format (such as .WAV files for Windows and .AIFF files on the Macintosh), then you had to run a converter, which would translate the digital audio into μ-law and store it in a .au file before it could be played.

Core Tip

Besides being inconvenient, converting audio will likely degrade audio quality. If you decide that you must change file formats or audio compressors, be sure to use a program (such as SOX) that minimizes the damage by intelligently converting sampling rates and compressors.

Audio Woes

Once you overcome the limited digital audio compressor and file format support in JDK 1.0.2, it is shocking to see how few methods are available to manipulate these files. Beginning multimedia developers can use the **Applet.play()** call shown in Listing 1.1 to load and play an .au file.

Listing 1.1 **Applet.play()** illustration.

```java
public class PrimitiveAudio extends java.applet.Applet
{
   public void init()
   {
     play( getCodeBase(), "alarm.au" );

     try
     {
       // we have NO clue how long this will take
       // so we will sleep and hope that we can guess
       // how long it will take....
       Thread.sleep( (long) 5000 );
     }
     catch (InterruptedException e)
     {
       System.out.println("Someone woke us up unexpected-
ly...");

     }
   }
}
```

Although **Applet.play()** is easy to use, you'll quickly outgrow it as you develop your audio programs. For instance, **Applet.play()** is like a car without brakes; once you issue the call, there's no way to stop it from playing.

As a result, if your program loads a 20-minute file and starts playing, there's no way to abort it without exiting the program!

Another serious limitation with **Applet.play()** is that it offers no means to create loops (or play the same sound repeatedly). Therefore, you'll quickly want to transition to the **AudioClip** interface.

Table 1.1 Definition of **AudioClip** Interface

Method	Description
Void loop()	Starts playing audio clip in a loop.
void play()	Starts playing audio clip.
void stop()	Stops playing audio clip.

After you glance at the methods of the **AudioClip** interface (Table 1.1), you'll probably gather that it addresses the main weaknesses in **Applet.play()**—the inability to stop or create effects with loops. However, there is a hidden advantage to using **AudioClip**. Unlike **Applet.play()**, **AudioClip** does not begin playback immediately if it knows the resource (or URL) it needs for playback.

```
audioClip1 =  getAudioClip( getCodeBase(), "clock1.au" );
```

As a result, you can have multiple **AudioClip** objects lying around and play and control them at your convenience. By contrast, **Applet.play()** is forced to process one file at a time. Listing 1.2 illustrates how you can exploit multiple **AudioClip** objects. It creates two clips, causes them to loop, starts playback, and sleeps for a couple of seconds. It then stops playback of the first clip, sleeps for an additional second before stopping the clip, and quits.

Listing 1.2 Playing multiple files with **AudioClip**.

```
import java.applet.AudioClip;

public class LessPrimitive extends java.applet.Applet
{
    AudioClip audioClip1;
    AudioClip audioClip2;

    // Applet role
    public void init()
```

Listing 1.2 Playing multiple files with `AudioClip`. (continued)

```
    {

        // create two audio objects

        audioClip1 =  getAudioClip( getCodeBase(),
"clock1.au" );
        audioClip2 =  getAudioClip( getCodeBase(),
"clock2.au" );

        // play two audio files in loop mode

        audioClip1.loop();
        audioClip2.loop();

            try
        {
        // we still have NO clue how long these files will
take
            // if we want to play them one time
            // however, we put them in loop mode, so they will
play forever
            Thread.sleep( (long) 2000 );
        }
        catch (InterruptedException e)
        {
            System.out.println("Someone woke us up unexpected-
ly...");

        }

            // stop the first clip after 2 seconds

            audioClip1.stop();

        try
        {
            // we still have NO clue how long these files will
    take
            // if we want to play them one time
            // however, we put them in loop mode, so they will
play forever
            Thread.sleep( (long) 7000 );
    }
        catch (InterruptedException e)
        {
```

Listing 1.2 Playing multiple files with `AudioClip`. (continued)

```
      System.out.println("Someone woke us up unexpected-
ly...");

    }

    // stop the 2nd after another 7 seconds

    audioClip2.stop();

  }
}
```

Another advantage of the **AudioClip** interface is that it streams its output to an audio mixer. Mixers combine multiple audio streams into a single output that can be played on any audio card. Mixers also let multiple **AudioClip** objects play simultaneously.

Core Tip

Sophisticated audio mixers have cross-process mixing capabilities (i.e., they are able to mix audio streams from multiple processes). As a result, you can start any application without concern that it will prevent subsequent applications from using an audio device.

There is one drawback to using cross-process mixers: they must be written as a device driver or they must access shared memory. Device drivers operate in a separate context from applications and are permitted to read audio buffers from any process. Since device driver code cannot be written in Java, this option is not portable.

If cross-process mixing is done outside a device driver, the mixer must have access to cross-process shared memory. When a given application streams content into the shared memory region, the mixer is awoken, and it merges the application's audio stream into the final audio output stream. The disadvantage to this approach is that a context switch is necessary for every buffer that must be mixed.

All known Java multimedia Application Programmer Interface (APIs) use in-process mixers and do not support cross-process mixing. As a result, you can play multiple audio files inside a given Virtual Machine (VM), but two VMs cannot mix audio streams.

Alas, **AudioClip** also has serious deficiencies. As Listing 1.2 illustrates, there's no mechanism to determine when a clip has finished playing. Therefore, we had to guesstimate when each clip completed by sleeping an arbitrary amount of time. If you know the exact length of each file you will be playing, this hack isn't too frustrating. However, if your application must play content of unknown length, this solution clearly is not palatable.

Furthermore, even if you know the length of a given audio file, **AudioClip** has no status methods or events. Thus, you cannot determine the amount of audio that has been played. As a result, it is impossible to write a simple media player-type application that tracks the amount of time left to play in a file.

Sneaking Through the Audio Backdoor

Lurking under the covers of almost every Java Runtime Environment (JRE) is an officially undocumented internal package called **sun.audio**. It is used by both **Applet.play()** and **AudioClip** and provides many of the features we've been demanding: the ability to determine the length of an audio file and the capability to control where playback begins in the audio stream.

Core Tip

*Since **sun.audio** is an officially undocumented internal package, theoretically it does not have to be included in a JRE. As a result, if you use this package, your Java application will not be considered pure, since it may not run on every VM.*

*Although it is risky to use this package, the default implementations of **Applet.play()** and **AudioClip** are dependent on it, and a multitude of Java audio programs must use it to obtain functional audio capabilities. Therefore, by virtue of its huge installed base of users, **sun.audio** is a defacto "core" API.*

*Since **sun.audio** is undocumented, it is difficult to locate commented documentation on how to use it. Fortunately, HTML documentation for **sun.audio** is included on the CD that accompanies this book.*

Everything in **sun.audio** revolves around the **AudioPlayer** class. **AudioPlayer** operates on its own thread and provides methods to start and stop playback of an audio stream. Although these methods appear similar to **AudioClip**, there is one significant difference: Each method is passed an **InputStream** class as a parameter.

InputStreams represent the flow of data into an object, and sun.audio contains two **InputStream** subclasses: **ContinuousAudioDataStream** and **AudioDataStream**. **AudioDataStream** extends **ByteArrayInputStream,** and streams an **AudioData** object for its clients. The **AudioData** object represents an array of bytes of digital audio data; this array can only contain 8 KHz, μ-law data. If you're using a different format (such as PCM), it must be converted to 8 KHz, μ-law before it can be streamed from memory. The **ContinuousAudioDataStream** extends **AudioDataStream** to support continous playback (i.e., it loops the **AudioStream** indefinitely).

Besides being stream-oriented, the player doesn't assume that you always want to restart playback at the beginning after stopping a stream. Rather, when you call **AudioDataStream.start()**, it resumes playback at the place where you last stopped it. If you need to restart the stream at the beginning, you should call **AudioDataStream.reset()**.

Streaming Through the Backdoor

The BackDoor applet shows how to use the **sun.audio** package. The first thing this applet does is create a **FileInputStream** for the audio file we intend to play. Once this object is created, we use the **AudioStream** class to convert this stream into a format that our **AudioPlayer** can understand (i.e., an **AudioData** object). This **AudioData** object is then used to construct a **ContinuousAudioDataStream** and an **AudioDataStream**.

```
FileInputStream fis = new FileInputStream( new File(
"clock1.au") );

    AudioStream as = new AudioStream( fis );

    AudioData ad = as.getData();
```

The player first attempts to play the **ContinuousAudioData-Stream** for five seconds (the player will loop until our thread wakes up). It then plays 500 milliseconds worth of the **AudioDataStream** and stops playback.

Next, the player resumes playback at the point where we stopped, plays for 2000 milliseconds, and stops again. Finally, it calls the **AudioDataStream reset()** method to seek back to the start of the stream and plays the file from the beginning for another four seconds. You can test Backdoor on the **appletviewer**, but don't try it with Netscape Navigator or the Internet Explorer, since they will throw an exception when running it.

```
public class Backdoor extends java.applet.Applet
{
    // AudioPlayer instantiated to force run of static ini-
tializers.
    AudioPlayer audioPlayer = AudioPlayer.player;
    AudioDataStream audioDataStream;
    ContinuousAudioDataStream continuousAudioDataStream;

    // Applet role
    public void init()
    {
        try
        {
        // Get sound from file stream.
        FileInputStream fis = new FileInputStream( new File(
"clock1.au") );
        AudioStream as = new AudioStream( fis );
        AudioData ad = as.getData();
        audioDataStream = new AudioDataStream( ad );
        continuousAudioDataStream = new ContinuousAudioDataS-
tream( ad );

            System.out.println( "Data file len " +
as.getLength() );

        audioPlayer.start( continuousAudioDataStream );
        try
        {
          Thread.sleep( (long) 5000 );
        }
        catch (InterruptedException e)
        {
        }
```

```
audioPlayer.stop( continuousAudioDataStream );

  audioPlayer.start( audioDataStream );

  try
{
  Thread.sleep( (long) 500 );
}
catch (InterruptedException e)
{
}

audioPlayer.stop( audioDataStream );
try
{
  Thread.sleep( (long) 2000 );
}
catch (InterruptedException e)
{
}

audioPlayer.start( audioDataStream );
try
{
   Thread.sleep( (long) 1000 );
}
catch (InterruptedException e)
{
}

  audioDataStream.reset();
audioPlayer.start( audioDataStream );
try
{
   Thread.sleep( (long) 4000 );
}
catch (InterruptedException e)
{
}

}
catch(IOException e)
{
}
}
}
```

Although **sun.audio** exists on most VMs, it can be a challenge to use it inside a browser such as Netscape Navigator or Internet Explorer. For instance, Netscape 4.06 reports the following error if you try to run the original version of the Backdoor applet:

```
at java.lang.Throwable.<init>(Compiled Code)
at java.lang.Exception.<init>(Compiled Code)
at java.lang.RuntimeException.<init>(Compiled Code)
at java.lang.SecurityException.<init>(Compiled Code)
at netscape.security.AppletSecurityException.<init>(Compiled
Code)
at netscape.security.AppletSecurityException.<init>(Compiled
Code)
at netscape.security.AppletSecurity.checkRead(Compiled Code)
at netscape.security.AppletSecurity.checkRead(Compiled Code)
at java.lang.SecurityManager.checkRead(Compiled Code)
at java.io.FileInputStream.<init>(Compiled Code)
at java.io.FileInputStream.<init>(Compiled Code)
at Backdoor.init(Compiled Code)*
at netscape.applet.DerivedAppletFrame$InitAppletEvent.dis-
patch(Compiled Code)
at java.awt.EventDispatchThread$EventPump.dispatchEvents(Com-
piled Code)
at java.awt.EventDispatchThread.run(Compiled Code)
at netscape.applet.DerivedAppletFrame$AppletEventDispatch-
Thread.run(Compiled Code)
```

If you closely examine this stack dump, you'll see that this exception was caused by the **FileInputStream** we were trying to feed into the **Audio-Stream** object. Even though we requested that the Netscape VM give us permission to read from the file system, it refuses to let us access our audio file. Consequently, we'll work around this apparent bug by creating a generic **InputStream** object from a URL. Since the **AudioStream** object is equally happy with an **InputStream** as with a **FileInputStream**, this modified version of BackDoor (called ScreenDoor on the CD) will run on all browsers.

```
InputStream InStream = null;
URL m_url = null;
try
{
        m_url = new URL(getCodeBase(), "clock1.au");
}
catch(Exception e)
{
};

try
```

```
{
  InStream = m_url.openStream();
}
catch (Exception e)
{
}

  // Get sound from file stream.
  // Netscape doesn't seem to like applets touching the file
  // system, so we'll use a generic input stream object
  // instead......
  //FileInputStream fis = new FileInputStream( new File(
"clock1.au") );
  //AudioStream as = new AudioStream( fis );

  AudioStream as = new AudioStream( InStream );
```

Don't Leave the Backdoor Open

The **sun.audio** package addresses some of the limitations in **AudioClip**, and introduces exciting new features such as streaming audio from memory buffers. However, **sun.audio** is still shackled by the fact that it can only play 8 kHz, μ-law data, and it offers no API to determine the current playing position of the media. Furthermore, since Sun has never officially acknowledged its existence, it is unlikely that these shortcomings will ever be addressed.

Ultimately, all of these problems in **sun.audio** will be fixed when Sun releases its JavaSound API. JavaSound will not only let you stream from memory buffers, but it will remove the restrictions on audio formats (see Chapter 21 for more information on JavaSound).

JMF to the Rescue!

Sun realized that the current multimedia API was unacceptable and began to design an object-oriented, feature-rich, multimedia architecture that could not only handle audio playback, but all forms of multimedia processing. Sun calls this architecture the Java Media and Communication APIs.

- **Java 2D API.** Leverages the Abstract Windowing Toolkit (AWT) to provide advanced support for arbitrary shapes, text, and images and the ability to rotate and scale these objects. It also provides font and color capabilities.

- **Java 3D API.** Enables applications to manipulate 3D objects.
- **Java Advanced Imaging API.** Gives programmers access to image processing features such as image tiling, regions of interest, and deferred execution.
- **Java Media Framework API.** Defines a comprehensive environment for the presentation, capture, and conferencing of time-based multimedia data streams (a stream is the flow of multimedia content from one location to another).
- **JavaSound API.** Is a lower-level audio API that gives you access to a 32-channel mixer and MIDI synthesis engine.
- **Java Speech API.** Lays the foundation for speech recognition and text-to-speech capabilities.
- **Java Telephony API (JTAPI).** Provides the functionality to incorporate telephony equipment into Java-enabled Web pages and other applications.

Because of the magnitude of the task of developing these APIs and the importance of creating a true cross-platform solution, Sun has collaborated with other companies that are domain experts in each field to design the APIs. For example, the initial release of JMF was created by the triumvirate of Intel, Silicon Graphics, and Sun. Each company participated in the design and released runtime environments for their respective platforms.

Although many of these APIs are intriguing, you can't count on them being part of every VM. Sun divides APIs into two categories: core and standard extension. Core APIs must be available on every licensed VM. The only exceptions to this rule are the versions of Java that run on embedded environments (Personal Java and Embedded Java). These environments scale back the number of core APIs since they have strict memory and performance constraints.

The second type of API is the standard extension. These APIs are defined and published by Sun. If a vendor implements one of these, it must conform to Sun's specification. As an individual API becomes popular, it, or portions of it, may migrate from a standard extension to a core API. However, you have no guarantee that any extension will ever be made part of the core API.

All of the Java Media and Communication APIs are considered standard extensions and are contained in a package prefixed with **javax**. As a result, if your program uses JMF or any of the multimedia APIs, you'll need to find a way to ensure that support for the extension is installed before your application can run (see Chapter 5 for installation instructions). If you want multimedia functionality, but only want to use core APIs, you'll have to live with the primitive **AudioClip** interface.

Is JMF Worth the Risk?

Given that JMF is not a core API, why should you bother using it? There are four significant reasons for using JMF: rich media type support, functionality, extensibility, and portability.

The primary advance of JMF is that it releases the Java programmer from the digital audio dungeon. You can now incorporate digital video, MIDI, and advanced audio compression algorithms into your applets and applications. Unlike the decision to restrict the **AudioClip** class to a file format native to Solaris, JMF is file format-independent. As a result, the first runtime ships with support for the most popular video file formats: MPEG-1, QuickTime, and Video for Windows.

JMF also opens the door to MIDI files. MIDI is particularly intriguing to Internet programmers because the file sizes are minuscule and the sound can be impressive as long as the user has the correct MIDI playback engine (or synthesizer). Unlike digital audio, these files do not sample audio waves. Rather, they store musical notes that a synthesizer transforms into analog sounds. Consequently, they excel at representing musical content, but are poor choices for speech or nonmusical content.

Core Tip

Although JMF lets you write multiplatform MIDI applications, it doesn't solve MIDI's major weakness: each platform plays the content differently. MIDI defines the instruments that a player must support, but it doesn't mandate how they should sound. The low-level MIDI devices on each operating system use different techniques to represent the instruments in the file and this causes each environment to have a slightly different sound quality.

> *Sun's JavaSound engine contains a wave-table MIDI synthesis engine that plays identically across all operating systems. Because JavaSound runs on the same platforms as JMF, JavaSound will ultimately provide identical MIDI playback on all JMF environments.*

JMF also supports new digital audio media types. You can now play .WAV files with a variety of compression types (such as TrueSpeech), without having to convert the files into the .au format. Furthermore, JMF lets you play compressed MPEG audio files (or .MP3 files).

JMF also provides a rich set of APIs for these additional media formats. Not only does it address every weakness in the JDK 1.0.2 library, but it also provides advanced APIs to boost performance and synchronize multiple data streams.

Another important advance is JMF's extensibility. To play a media format or compression technology not supported by JMF, you can write your own Java layer for the new technology and seamlessly incorporate it into JMF. As a result, your programs will always be able to handle the latest multimedia content.

The last improvement of JMF is its consistency and portability. Proprietary Java APIs that offer similar functionality to JMF have always existed. However, they were never designed to run on a multitude of platforms. Furthermore, they were typically designed to address a particular need and aren't part of a consistent multimedia architecture.

Summary

Multimedia is flooding the Internet, and as the Internet becomes more consumer-centric, this trend will only increase. To stay ahead of competing interactive technologies, Java must not only be able to perform all of the tasks found in native environments, but it must also be able to rapidly support new technology as it is released.

The existing multimedia support in Java was woefully deficient and could not support any of these requirements. It supported a limited subset of digital audio content and lacked rudimentary capabilities found on most computing platforms.

Sun recognized the need for comprehensive multimedia capabilities and created the Java Media and Communication APIs. Although all of the Java Media and Communication APIs are media-centric, we're going to focus on those APIs that impact interactivity the greatest: the Java Media Framework and JavaSound.

Now that you understand why JMF is necessary, it's time to examine some runtime implementations of JMF and evaluate how closely they follow the specification.

JMF'S GROWING PAINS

Far better it is to dare mighty things, to win glorious triumphs, even though checkered by failure, than to take rank with those poor spirits who neither enjoy much nor suffer much, because they live in the grey twilight that knows not victory nor defeat.

Theodore Roosevelt, Chicago, April 10, 1899

It is not the critic who counts. Not the man who points out how the strong man stumbled or where the doer of deeds could have done better. The credit belongs to the man who is actually in the arena, whose face is marred by dust and sweat and blood; who strives valiantly; who errs and comes short again and again; who knows the great enthusiasms, the great devotions; who spends himself in a worthy cause. Who, at the best, knows in the end the triumph of high achievement, and who at the worst, at least fails while daring greatly, so that his place shall never be with those timid souls who know neither victory nor defeat.

Theodore Roosevelt, *The Strenuous Life: Essays and Addresses*

Chapter 2

J ava is suffering from an identity crisis. Sun originally envisioned Java as a "write once, run anywhere" platform. Developers embraced this philosophy and created programs that—theoretically—were plat-form-independent. This explosion in developer activity caused companies such as Netscape, Microsoft, and Apple to tune the Java Virtual Machine for their respective hardware and software products. Unfortunately, programmers discovered that their programs ran differently on each VM due to bugs in the VM's implementation or because of vagueness in the Java specification. Hence, the saying "Write once, test everywhere" was born.

The inconsistent behaviors between VMs (not to mention financial realities) have resulted in a shakeout in the VM provider market. Netscape exited the VM market and created an API called the Open Java Interface, which software vendors can use to plug custom VMs into their Navigator. Apple joined with Microsoft to create a unified VM for the Macintosh. As a result, Sun, IBM, and Microsoft are the last major players in the Java VM market for PCs.

These changes should not be considered a slowdown of the Java market. Rather, companies are focusing on their strengths and finding unique niches for their products. Hewlett Packard's (HP's) embedded version of a Java VM has created considerable publicity due to its small footprint. Other vendors have tailored VMs for particular embedded environments or for freeware markets. This activity has not only created VMs for a variety of platforms, but has also ensured that the few PC-based VMs that exist are robust and meet the Java specifications.

Growing Pains

JMF is also undergoing an identity crisis. Conceived by the powerful triumvirate of Intel, Silicon Graphics, and Sun, its purpose was to enable multiplatform multimedia applications. Each vendor focused on optimizing JMF for its respective operating platforms. Intel dedicated their efforts to enabling JMF on the Win32 platforms (Windows 9x and Windows NT), Sun concentrated on Solaris, and Silicon Graphics owned the IRIX development.

The first public draft of JMF documentation was made available for external comments in February 1997 (see http://java.sun.com/products/java-media/mail-archive/Framework/0001.html). Shortly thereafter, Intel released the first JMF runtimes for Win32. Sun and Silicon Graphics soon followed with beta implementations for their platforms.

The final JMF specification was frozen in September 1997 (see http://java.sun.com/products/java-media/mail-archive/Framework/0440.html).
Intel was once again the first to ship a runtime for Win32 based on this platform. Sun released its 1.0 version of Java in April 1998 (see http://java.sun.com/products/java-media/mail-archive/Framework/1125.html).

Unfortunately, even before the final release of the JMF specification, signs of trouble were brewing in the JMF family. Each company had its own agenda for developing JMF runtimes. Silicon Graphics wanted to maintain its dominant position in the high-end graphics and multimedia markets. Intel needed to ensure that JMF was optimized for MMX™ in general, and the Pentium II in particular, so that they could sell processors. Sun needed to promote a cross-platform multimedia environment that could effectively compete with the Microsoft Windows monopoly and would also promote Solaris.

Although Silicon Graphics released a .96 beta version of JMF, development was frozen at that level. Silicon Graphics has been refocusing on core businesses and is unlikely to resume development of this product since they decided to divest themselves of Cosmo, the division responsible for JMF development.

An even bigger shock was unleashed by Intel in July 1998. Intel stated that due to changing Java market conditions, they were exiting JMF development in early 1999. Since Intel's product had earned a reputation for stability and compatibility, many developers on the JMF mailing lists and newsgroups became distraught about the future of the API.

There are many potential explanations why Intel made this decision. One possible rationale could be extrapolated from a similar decision Intel made in the software DVD market. Intel developed DVD audio and video software decoders that were optimized for the Pentium II processor. Before the product could ship, at least three other companies released equivalent DVD decoders. Since Intel wrote their software to create demand for their processors, and other companies were fulfilling this role, Intel withdrew its products, since their goals were accomplished.

The JMF runtime, like the software DVD product, was released so that the Intel processor had a best-of-breed Java multimedia platform. Because Intel understands the Pentium family processors better than anyone does, they were able to release Pentium optimized versions of JMF before either of their partners. This enabled Win32 running on Intel processors to become the dominant platform for JMF development.

Although many people assumed that Sun would focus on the Solaris version of JMF, the company eventually released a Win32 version. This parallels the evolution of Java VMs on Intel processors. Sun originally relied on Microsoft to create a Win32 Java VM. However, the Wintel market was too important for Sun to be dependent on another company to provide the primary Java VM (especially on a company whose commitment to cross-platform support was dubious at best). Therefore, Sun released their own VM for Win32 and associated browsers.

Sun's Win32 version of the JMF runtime had a similar architectural design as the Intel version and added a few extra features. With Sun supplying high-quality Intel-based Win32 runtimes, one can surmise that Intel no longer felt a pressing need to continue with this product.

Core Tip

Although Sun's Win32 JMF runtime has narrowed the gap between itself and the Intel runtime, it still is not as robust nor as performance-tuned as Intel's solution. If you develop on the Win32 platform and experience strange problems with the Sun alternative, the problems may not be your fault. Therefore, it is advisable to test on both runtimes to separate problems in your application from runtime bugs.

A more sinister explanation for Intel's decision to drop JMF development may be found in the documentation associated with the antitrust case filed by the U.S. Justice Department against Microsoft Corporation. According to CNET:

> *"in early 1997, one Microsoft executive pinpointed Intel's work on Java multimedia technology as 'the area of most contention [between the two companies] since Intel does not see their work with Sun and others as bad for the overall PC space, only as good for Intel.' Over the coming days, another Microsoft executive continued 'to engage' on the matter, encouraging it to curtail the work, or at the very least to carry it out 'less visibly.'"*

CNET News.com, September 23, 1998

Based on this documentation, one could logically assume that Intel was forced to drop their JMF runtimes to salvage their relationship with Microsoft. Regardless of Intel's true reason for ceasing Java multimedia development, Sun needed a partner to help it give JMF a sense of legitimacy and true cross-platform capabilities.

Core Tip

Additional background material concerning the conflicts between Microsoft, Sun, and Intel can be found at the following Web sites:

http://www.news.com/News/Item/0,4,26706,00.html?st.ne.ni.lh

http://www.news.com/SpecialFeatures/0,5,26707,00.html

On October 7, 1998, Sun announced that IBM had decided to partner with them to design the JMF 2.0 release. Among the features that IBM and Sun have promised for JMF 2.0 include the ability to capture media and perform real-time signal processing on digital media streams. Additional details on the 2.0 release can be found in Chapter 21.

Little Guys to the Rescue?

As the Java VM shakeup created opportunities for enterprising developers and companies, so the disintegration of the JMF three enabled developers to exploit unique niches for JMF runtimes. For example, Brian Griffith created "WhippedButter," a JMF runtime that operates on top of Quicktime 3.0. Since Quicktime itself is cross-platform, WhippedButter is not only the only Mac JMF runtime, but it also works on Win32 platforms.

Core Tip

WhippedButter is included on the CD that accompanies this book. You can also find out more about WhippedButter by emailing Archipelago Productions (bagrif@mbay.net).

Examination of JMF Ports

Sun created lofty goals for the JMF API: a cross-platform multimedia platform capable of supporting a variety of media types. To determine if these claims are realistic, we'll need to examine how JMF interacts with existing multimedia environments and look at the robustness of each implementation.

Sun is quite emphatic that it wants Java application developers to write 100% pure Java programs can run on any compliant Java VM. However, this edict has never applied to Java VM developers. When you create a Java VM, the overriding mandate is performance. Therefore, VMs contain large quantities of native code that exploit specific features of a given platform.

Likewise, when you port JMF to a given platform, you must interface the hardware with native code; the only exception to this would be a platform that ran Java as its native language. If the operating environment is already in existence, porting JMF involves interfacing JMF to the existing multimedia infrastructure available on the platform (see Figure 2-1). If the particular platform lacks essential features, it is the responsibility of the programmer porting JMF to compensate for these weaknesses.

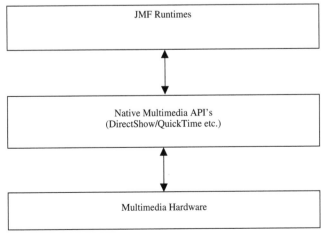

Figure 2-1 Generic block layout for a JMF port.

If the hardware or operating system is still under development, implementing JMF is less problematic. If required features are missing, the infrastructure or associated hardware can be modified, instead of having to hack the ported JMF code. As a result, these newer environments should have more robust and compatible versions of JMF than older platforms. In fact, if the JMF API is used as the native API, performance will improve, since it is unnecessary to map JMF objects to native objects.

Core Tip

Sun has managed to squeeze enough performance out of Java to create a Pure Java JMF runtime in its 1.1 release. Although the Pure Java version is not as feature-rich as the native runtimes, it proves that fast processors and optimized Java runtimes can support Pure Java multimedia. See Chapter 21 for additional information on the Pure Java runtime.

DirectShow

Since Windows 95/98 (and its corresponding API, Win32) dominates computing, its multimedia platform, DirectShow, has spawned the most JMF ports. These ports utilize DirectShow because it is 32-bit, thread-safe, object-oriented platform, and it is architecturally similar to JMF.

JMF runtime developers are attracted to DirectShow because they can use modern operating system features such as semaphores and threads. Furthermore, since it is a 32-bit API, they can use familiar tools such as Visual C++.

DirectShow's object-oriented nature also facilitates the creation of JMF Player objects. DirectShow uses small objects (called filters) to manipulate multimedia data. A JMF port can dynamically compose Players by connecting two or more filters. This enables JMF/DirectShow to instantly support new media types as they become available (see Figure 2-2).

Finally, DirectShow is architecturally similar to JMF. DirectShow has a special category of filter, the source filter, which is similar in concept to a DataSource. DirectShow's Renderer filters work like a JMF MediaHandler.

And, DirectShow offers the Filter graph manager that performs a supervisory role just like JMF's Manager.

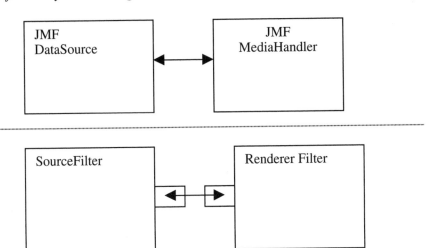

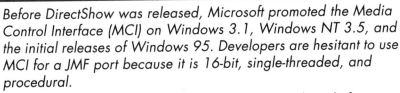

Figure 2–2 Illustration of Player construction using a DirectShow filter. In this illustration, the DataSource creates a DirectShow Source Filter, and the MediaHandler creates a DirectShow Renderer filter. When the manager connects the Player to the DataSource, the underlying Source and Renderer filters are connected.

Core Tip

Before DirectShow was released, Microsoft promoted the Media Control Interface (MCI) on Windows 3.1, Windows NT 3.5, and the initial releases of Windows 95. Developers are hesitant to use MCI for a JMF port because it is 16-bit, single-threaded, and procedural.

Although you could theoretically port JMF to such a platform, it would require an inordinate amount of work. Since Microsoft has preannounced MCI death, the viability of such a product is questionable.

For additional insights on the DirectShow architecture, see my article, "A New Architecture for Multimedia," in the January 6, 1998, issue, *PC Magazine* (also available online at http://www.zdnet.com/pcmag/pctech/content/17/01/os1701.001.html).

Core Tip

If you wish to access DirectShow functionality from within Java, Microsoft provides J/Direct. J/Direct enables Java programs to call COM-based subsystems such as DirectShow. Unfortunately, use of J/Direct shackles you to the Win32 platform.

It should now be clear why Microsoft was (allegedly) so anxious for Intel to cease JMF development. If Microsoft can lure Java multimedia developers into using J/Direct and DirectShow, these developers will inadvertently perpetuate their Win32 monopoly.

Intel Versus Sun

Both Intel and Sun build their Win32 JMF products using DirectShow. Intel was the first to announce that they would use DirectShow (or ActiveMovie, as it was previously called). At the time of this announcement, this was a high-risk option. Although architecturally interesting, ActiveMovie was unproven technology.

However, ActiveMovie had significant advantages. Since it was a 32-bit multithreaded environment, the Pentium II family would run multimedia applications faster than the 16/32-bit hybrid model used by MCI. Furthermore, ActiveMovie's flexible architecture would enable Intel to exploit the MMX features found in their processors.

Sun was more secretive about what multimedia technology was used for the Intel port, and many developers on the JMF newsgroups debated whether it used DirectShow or MCI. However, once the runtime was released, a Sun representative indicated that they too were using DirectShow as the Win32 infrastructure.

Because both products are built on DirectShow, their feature set and performance is similar. Intel had a considerable head start in the Win32 environment, so there was an implicit understanding among developers that it was the stabler of the two solutions. However, with each successive point release, the Sun product becomes more robust.

One significant difference between the two runtimes is how they interface to native code. The Sun product uses the Java Native Interface (JNI), while the Intel version comes in two flavors: one that supports JNI and another that uses a concoction from Microsoft called the Raw Native Interface (RNI). JNI is the official mechanism for Java programs to interface with native methods, while RNI is Microsoft-specific and proprietary to Windows Java VM.

Although this may seem like another meaningless tussle between Sun and Microsoft, it has significant impact for the JMF developer. Microsoft's Java VM (used by the Internet Explorer) only supports RNI, and as a result, is not compatible with the Sun JMF product. Fortunately, Sun offers the Java plug-in that brings true Java and JMF compatibility to the Internet Explorer.

Core Tip

After a lengthy battle in court, a judge decided that Microsoft's failure to support JNI was a violation of their contract with Sun. Furthermore, the judge ordered Microsoft to add JNI support to their Java runtimes and clean up Visual J++ so it is easier to develop pure Java applications. As a result, if you download the latest Internet Explorer or Visual J++ updates, you will be able to develop JNI-based JMF applications with Microsoft tools.

Although Microsoft released this update only a few weeks after the judge's order, the JNI performance is surprisingly good. In fact, in many tests, it performs better than Sun's JDK 2 JNI support.

Therefore, if you or your users decide to use Sun's JMF and also use Internet Explorer, you'll need to install Sun's Java plug-in addition to the JMF runtime. For more details on interfacing to native code, I suggest you read Rob Gordon's excellent book, *Essential JNI*.

By contrast, since Intel offers packages with both JNI and RNI support, any package can be used without modification by both Netscape and Internet Explorer. As long as Microsoft continues to promote their noncompliant RNI, Intel will retain a significant advantage in the Win32 market.

Quicktime

Quicktime was the first large-scale multimedia environment. It ushered in the digital media age. Besides being the first to market, Quicktime is a flexible architecture. Apple incorporated new technologies such as QuickTimeVR and MPEG-2 video by extending, and not replacing, Quicktime's object-like architecture.

Quicktime is popular among broadcast professionals because of its emphasis on controlling time-based media with separate tracks. Unlike other media platforms, Quicktime is not file-oriented; rather, it uses a high level description of the media, called a track, which contains pointers (or references) to one or more media files.

Each track instructs Quicktime where to find content and when it should be played (see Figure 2-3). As a result, multiple tracks are more powerful than a corresponding .AVI file, since they can reference content from multiple locations.

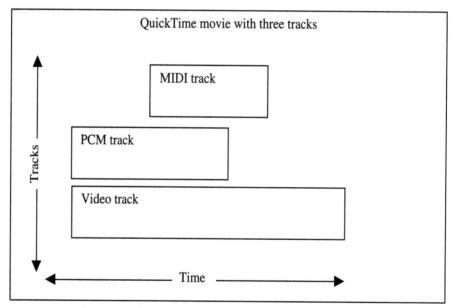

Figure 2–3   Illustration of Quicktime tracks.

Furthermore, a QuickTime file (or .MOV file) can simultaneously support the presentation of multiple tracks. Because each track contains instructions about when content should be presented, QuickTime can synchronize seemingly incompatible forms of media such as a MIDI file and a movie. This feature, in particular, is popular among media professionals, since they typically create multiple tracks of content and must synchronize them during playback.

To present tracks, QuickTime uses components. Components abstract hardware details from the programmer and enable it to support a variety of hardware and even multiple operating systems. QuickTime has three categories of components: **MediaHandlers**, data processors, and utilities.

MediaHandlers are similar to JMF **DataSource**s. They create file format independence for QuickTime and enable it to adapt to new file formats as they are released. Data processors are roughly equivalent to **Player**s. They are responsible for the decompression and presentation of multimedia content.

Utility components are storage locations for routines that must be accessed by other components. For instance, QuickTime has a clock component that provides real-time clock information based on a hardware source to all other components in the system. Like JMF, QuickTime has the concept of a continuously running clock and a clock that is interruptible. However, QuickTime uses the opposite naming convention from JMF (i.e., **TimeBases** are interruptible in QuickTime nomenclature).

Finding and connecting the correct components can be a complex process, so QuickTime provides the Component Manager to abstract these details from the programmer. It is the equivalent to JMF's Player Manager, since it helps to assemble components.

QuickTime is more than just an environment to port JMF. Its .MOV file format was chosen by the International Organization for Standardization (ISO) as the file format for streaming MPEG video (MPEG-4). In particular QuickTime was chosen because of its network protocol independence and its flexibility as a file format. Since Sun announced support for MPEG-4 in a future release of JMF, the QuickTime file format has become the preferred solution for JMF applications.

Solaris

Solaris is Sun's flagship operating system, so it is no surprise that Sun optimized the JMF runtime for this environment. Although UNIX does not provide a multimedia API as comprehensive as DirectShow or QuickTime, each UNIX implementation provides the fundamental building blocks necessary to implement a JMF runtime. The Solaris version exploits the native hardware-accelerated video scaling and decoding features provided by XIL and XLIB X-Windows components to enhance video playback.

For audio support, the Solaris port communicates with the /dev/audio device. All audio streams are converted to 22KHz (approximately half the CD audio 44 kHz sampling rate). Therefore, don't be shocked if you try to play 44 kHz audio and the sound quality isn't up to CD standards.

Core Tip

Sun has revealed that they open the /dev/audio device exclusively in write-only (i.e., O_WRONLY) mode once a Player becomes realized. As a result, no other non-JMF application can use the device while there is at least one JMF Player prefetched. To share the device with non-JMF applications, be sure to deallocate every Player (deallocation forces JMF to close all exclusive resources such as the /dev/audio device). This principle also applies to the Win32 version of JMF.

Runtime Summary

JMF already runs on the most popular operating systems, and this number will increase with Java's popularity and the need for cross-platform multimedia (see Table 2.1). Unfortunately, each JMF runtime will have a unique set of bugs. If these instabilities are major, programmers will be tempted to compensate for these problems by either avoiding problematic APIs or by attempting to detect the specific platform their JMF application is running and write workarounds for the bugs.

Since JMF's purpose is to create robust binary compatibility across platforms, forcing developers to avoid buggy methods or to write special code for a particular platform defeats the entire purpose of JMF. Therefore, the onus is on Sun to create a certification program to ensure that each release meets a specific quality standard.

Table 2.1 Performance Comparison of JMF Runtimes with .MOV Files

Functional Comparison

Feature	JMF	DirectShow	QuickTime	MCI (OS/2)	MCI (Win32)
Object-oriented	Yes	Yes	Yes	Yes	No
Thread-based	Yes	Yes	No	Yes	No
Thread-safe	Yes	Yes	Yes	Yes	No
Stream-oriented	Yes	Yes	Yes	Yes	No
Media Track Support	Yes	Yes	Yes	Limited	Limited
Synchronization	Yes	Yes	Yes	Yes	No
CODEC Support	No	Yes	Yes	Yes	Yes
Real-time Signal Processing Filters	No	Yes		No	No

JMF Performance Comparison

JMF method	Solaris (Sparc)	NT (intel)	Win98
Create Player	361 milliseconds	1122 milliseconds	550 milliseconds
Realize/Prefetch	482 Milliseconds	1482 milliseconds	1530 milliseconds
Stop	150 Milliseconds	10 milliseconds	0 milliseconds
Deallocate	10 Milliseconds	100 milliseconds	50 milliseconds
Close	25 Milliseconds	60 milliseconds	60 milliseconds

Solaris version tested on Sparc Ultra 10 with 300 MHz Sparc processor.
Solaris machine had no audio card.
NT/98 version tested on 400 MHz Pentium II processor.
NT clock granularity is 10 milliseconds.

You're Only as Good as Your Tools

Since JMF is a new environment, there are a number of issues that you will encounter if you use Java development tools to create JMF applets and applications.

To test your JMF application with a Visual development environment (i.e., Visual Café or Visual J++) you must do one of the following: add the directory containing the **jmf.jar** file to your **CLASSPATH** environment variable, or update the class search path in your Visual development program.

The following is an illustration of changing the **CLASSPATH** variable in Win32 environments: Note that you must specify the entire pathname of the **jmf.jar** file (including **jmf.jar**!) for the Java class loader to find the JMF libraries.

```
Set CLASSPATH=%CLASSPATH%;jmf.jar;
```

The following is an illustration of the UNIX **CLASSPATH** variable that includes **jmf.jar**. PC users should be aware that UNIX separates paths with a colon (**:**).

```
CLASSPATH=/usr/jdk1.1/lib/classes.zip:/home/ldecarmo/
JMF1.02/lib/jmf.jar:.
```

```
setenv JMFHOME /home/someuser/JMF1.02
setenv CLASSPATH /usr/jdk1.1/lib/classes.zip:/home/ldecarmo/
JMF1.02/lib/jmf.jar:.
```

Once the **CLASSPATH** variable is correctly initialized, you'll need to tell the operating system where it can locate the native libraries needed by the JMF classes.

On NT or Windows 95, you should update the **PATH** variable to point to the location where the JMF libraries are stored:

```
Set PATH=%PATH%;g:\jmfinstalldirectory\lib;
```

On Solaris, **LD_LIBRARY_PATH** must be changed to include the directory where the JMF libraries are stored:

```
setenv LD_LIBRARY_PATH $JMFHOME/lib:${LD_LIBRARY_PATH}
```

Under most circumstances, if you choose to update the **CLASSPATH** variable, your development environment will automatically inherit the system settings and be able to use the JMF classes. If you choose not to update the **CLASSPATH** variable, you will have to manually update the class search path for every project.

Core Tip

Since JMF installation requires only a **CLASSPATH** *update and an update to the binary search path, it is possible to keep multiple versions on the same machine. This feature is particularly important if you must perform regression testing of your Java applications on older JMF releases.*

If you switch between different revisions of JMF, be sure to update both the **CLASSPATH** *and* **PATH** *variables. Many people remember to update* **CLASSPATH***, but forget to change the binary search path. This results in JMF native binaries trying to communicate with incompatible JMF Java classes. If you see an exception similar to the following being written to Standard Error, you have a native binary/class mismatch.*

```
Could not load library jmutil
Exception occurred during event dispatching:
java.lang.NoSuchMethodError: pause
at com.sun.media.jmf.audio.AudioMixer.doneUsingAudio
Device(AudioMixer.java:90)
at com.sun.media.renderer.audio.AudioRenderer.abort-
Prefetch(AudioRenderer.java:347)
at com.sun.media.MediaController.deallocate(MediaCon-
troller.java:729)
at com.sun.media.MediaPlayer.abortPrefetch(Compiled
Code)
at com.sun.media.MediaController.deallocate(MediaCon-
troller.java:729)
```

Symantec Visual Café Setup

Café does not inherit the **CLASSPATH** variable from the system; rather, it uses the **SC.INI** file in the bin directory under the directory where you installed Café to configure Java libraries. If you want JMF capabilities in all your projects, update the **CLASSPATH=** variable in the **SC.INI** file (see the following for a sample).

```
CLASSPATH=g:\runtimes\swing-1.1beta2\SWINGALL.JAR;g:\run-
times\jmf\lib\jmf.jar;
```

Core Tip

If you have a version of Café earlier than 3.0, download the latest Swing package from java.sun.com and update **CLASSPATH= statement** *to point to the new Swing location. We will be creating JMF programs that require Swing 1.1 support.*

You can also add the **jmf.jar** library to individual projects by selecting the *Project* menu, and then the *Options* element. This will display a notebook with tabs. Click on the *Directories* tab, then select *Classes* (see Figure2-4). Click on the new class path and enter the entire pathname for the **jmf.jar** file.

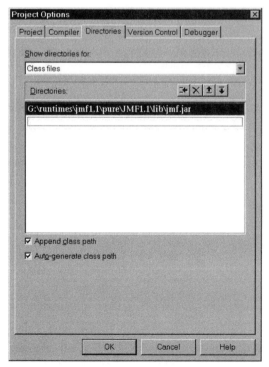

Figure 2–4   How to set class path in Café on a per project basis.

Visual J++

Although many Java purists consider native code an evil almost on par with the "goto" statement, Sun has always offered programmers access to native methods. Native methods are especially important to multimedia programmers, since they often must supplement their Java applications with high-performance native code.

Although native code locks your JMF program into a specific platform, there are circumstances when it is necessary. For instance, in the latter chapters of this book, we extend JMF to support new types of Players. The only mechanism to write such Players is to use native methods. Additional reasons for native code are time-sensitive signal processing routines or methods that must take advantage of processor-specific multimedia commands (i.e., AltiVec on the PowerPC or MMX on x86 processors).

Visual J++ is probably the best environment to write 100% pure Java code. However, there are certain risks associated with using it. The most dangerous is RNI. Microsoft's documentation doesn't warn you that RNI is incompatible with the Java specification or non-Microsoft VMs.

Even more insidious is Microsoft's attempt to blend Win32 APIs into the Java environment. For instance, Microsoft provided a mechanism whereby you can access DirectShow functions from within Java applets and applications. This enables you to use powerful, high-performance DirectShow features that may have no JMF equivalents.

Unfortunately, Microsoft does not alert you to the fact that some of their Java APIs will bind you to Win32. As a result, you may think you're writing a 100% pure JMF program, but in reality, you may be writing a Windows-specific application. We will not use any Windows-specific Java multimedia APIs in this book.

Core Tip

VJ++ is hopelessly incompatible with Sun's JMF Win32 runtimes. This tragic situation arose because VJ++ is dependent on the Microsoft Java VM, which is RNI only and doesn't support JNI. If your JMF programs mysteriously fail to run inside VJ++, you should examine the debug output window. If you see an error similar to the following, you have a JNI/RNI conflict:

```
Could not load library jmutil
  java.lang.UnsatisfiedLinkError: jmfaudio.dll cannot
load because RNIGetCompatibleVersion export not found
(new behavior.)library: jmfaudio
```

*Given the magnitude of the incompatibilities between the VJ++
and Sun JMF runtime, VJ++ users either must utilize the Intel JMF
runtimes or switch to a different Java IDE.*

Installation Woes

Because JMF is a standard extension and not a core API, installing your
applet or application can be a complicated procedure. You not only must
install the applet, but the associated runtime. Furthermore, you'll need a
strategy for running inside the Internet Explorer.

Sun does not provide an elegant a solution to install JMF runtimes on the
client machine. If you have created a JMF application, Sun permits you to
include the associated JMF runtime install program with your application.
Unfortunately, this option will not work if you need to run on multiple operating systems.

Since applets cannot modify local resources such as path settings, etc., they
also cannot use Sun's JMF install program. Rather, you will have to point
potential users to Sun's JMF Web site, request that they download the JMF
runtimes, then run your applet.

Core Tip

*JMF 1.1 dramatically simplifies the process of installing JMF
on a client machine. It offers a pure Java runtime, so you no
longer need to update native binaries on the client machine. This
release and associated installation information is discussed in
Chapter 21.*

Summary

To develop a cross-platform JMF binary, it is important to understand the
variety of hardware and software environments JMF must interact with.

Although Sun has defined a standard, each JMF platform has a unique set of quirks that you must investigate and debug. If you utilize the correct development environment and intelligent install routines, it is possible to achieve binary compatibility across JMF runtimes.

Now that you understand the JMF architecture and runtime considerations, it's time to dig underneath JMF and discover how it works.

EVERYTHING
REVOLVES
AROUND TIME

I wasted time, and now doth time
waste me.

William Shakespeare, *Richard II*

"It is well known, that time once past never
returns; and that the moment which is lost
is lost for ever. Time therefore ought,
above all other kinds of property, to be
free from invasion and yet there is no man
who does not claim the power of wasting
that time which is the right of others."

**Samuel Johnson, Idler #14,
July 15, 1758**

If time be of all things the most precious,
wasting time must be, as Poor Richard
says, the greatest prodigality, since, as he
elsewhere tells us, lost time is never found
again, and what we call time-enough, always proves little enough.

Benjamin Franklin, *The Way to Wealth*

Chapter 3

T ime, and the passage of time, influences every aspect of JMF. Just as clocks represent and manipulate time, JMF uses the Player interface to track and manage time when playing a media stream. These Players can only operate on time-based media, so if you ever encounter a multimedia data stream that is time-independent (i.e., a stream that can enter and leave the time dimension at will), you're out of luck!

As we discovered earlier, JMF supports a plethora of multimedia file formats and CODECs. Since these media streams have dramatically different file structures, performance characteristics, and decoding requirements, each must have a unique Player object that is tailored to handle a specific type of content.

This proliferation of Players necessitates a Manager (or supervisor) to track the location and responsibilities of each Player installed in the system (see Figure 3-1). This Manager is like a genie: it's always around, waiting to find and create a Player on your behalf. Without it, you could never be positive that the Player you created could handle your media stream.

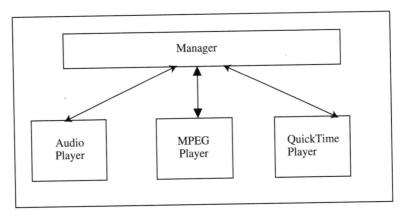

Figure 3–1   The Manager and Player relationship.

Because of our benevolent Manager, it is trivial to create a Player. Simply construct a URL object, and build the Player with that URL (see Listing 3.1).

Listing 3.1 Creating a Player with a URL.

```
mrl = new MediaLocator(mediaFile)
player = Manager.createPlayer(mrl);
```

Although this code appears simple, behind the scenes, the Manager and Player create a slew of additional objects on your behalf. In fact, each Player extends the following interfaces: **Clock**, **Controller**, **Duration**, and **MediaHandler**.

This chapter will focus on the **Clock** interface and how it influences the behavior and capabilities of a Player.

Time Is Unrecoverable

All watches monitor the passage of time, and the **Clock** interface is no exception. Sun refers to this passage of time as a **TimeBase**. A **TimeBase** is an uninterruptible flow of time from a known starting point that increases at a predictable frequency. For instance, Greenwich Mean Time qualifies as a **TimeBase**, since its starting point is defined and it increases in a predictable fashion without interruption.

JMF's default **TimeBase** is the number of nanoseconds consumed since a starting point in time that you define. By default, this Clock is driven by the operating system's Clock. As a result, if you're running JMF on an operating system with poor system Clock resolution (such as OS/2), you may notice that the default Clock floats (reports times that are slightly inaccurate).

Fortunately, Sun realized that the system Clock might not be accurate enough in every environment, so JMF permits Players to override the default **TimeBase**. For example, an audio Player could use its own hardware Clock that has finer granularity than nanoseconds for a **TimeBase**.

To examine a Clock's **TimeBase** in greater detail, your only option is to call its **getTimeBase()** method. This will return a **TimeBase** object. Unfortunately, all you can do with this method is query the current time in nanoseconds (**getNanoseconds()**). One method that **TimeBase** is missing is the ability to query the frequency of **TimeBase** ticks. This would enable you to determine whether the underlying Clock is accurate enough for your needs. Table 3.1 lists the approximate accuracy of the Clock on several popular operating systems.

Table 3.1 Accuracy of the Operating System Time Clock for Specific Platforms

Operating System	Java System Clock Granularity
Windows NT	10 milliseconds
Windows 95/98	10 milliseconds
OS/2	32 milliseconds

If you're unhappy with **TimeBase**'s resolution, or if you wish to synchronize multiple Clocks to the same **TimeBase,** you can set a Clock's **TimeBase** via **setTimeBase** (see Listing 3.2).

Listing 3.2 Manipulating a **TimeBase**.

```
// get a Time object from the controller
timeBaseTime = controller.getTimeBase().getTime();

// get the current # of seconds
timeBaseTime.getSeconds();

// give the controller a new TimeBase
controller.setTimeBase( tb );
```

The first line of this listing reveals the final method available in a **Time-Base:getTime()**. **getTime()** returns a **Time** object. **Time** objects serve two purposes: They increment and report the consumption of time. You can construct them in seconds, or if you need finer granularity, in nanoseconds.

Better than a Timex?

Besides monitoring the continuous flow of time, a Clock also has stopwatch capabilities that are exploited by a time format called media time. Media time represents the time consumed within a given stream, and unlike a **Time-Base**, media time is interruptible and can flow backwards. For example, as you play a .WAV file, the media time gradually increases. Once you stop the playback of the .WAV file, the media time ceases advancement and remains suspended until the .WAV file resumes playback.

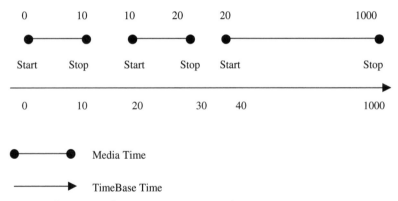

Figure 3–2   Illustration of **TimeBase** versus media time. **TimeBase** times are continuous, whereas media times are interruptible.

Media times and **TimeBase** times appear to pull the Clock in different directions. Media times are interruptible and bidirectional, while a **Time-Base** is continuous and everincreasing. Thus, a Clock is always striving to reconcile the differences between competing time formats. As a result, Clocks use the formula below to morph (or transform, in Sun terminology) the current **TimeBase** time into a media time.

Current **MediaTime** = ((**TimeBase** Start Time + Current **TimeBase** Time) °
Clock Rate)+ **MediaStart** Time

The current **MediaTime** is the actual amount of time that has been played in the media stream. It is calculated by adding the starting time for the **Time-Base** to the amount of time since the **TimeBase** started. This value is then multiplied by the speed and direction of the Clock. This number is added to the starting time for the media stream and results in the current **MediaTime**.

Although this formula transforms **TimeBase** time into media time, it cannot account for the fact that the **TimeBase** time is continuous while media time isn't (i.e., when playback is stopped, media time should not increase). As a result, Clocks are either in **Stopped** or **Started** state. Clocks become **Stopped** when they don't have enough information to perform a transformation, and become **Started** when this information becomes available. By default, a Clock is in **Stopped** state.

To enable a transformation, you need to ensure that it knows the Clock rate and Media Start Time. The Clock rate is set by the Clock's **setRate()** method, and describes the scaling factor between media time and **Time-Base**. By default, a Clock assumes a rate of 1.0. Positive rates greater than 1.0, or negative values less than -1.0, cause the media time to increase (or decrease) faster than the **TimeBase** time (i.e., fast-forward and fast-reverse, respectively). By contrast, positive values less than 1.0 and negative values less than –1.0 cause the media time to increase (or decrease) slower than the **TimeBase** time (i.e., slow-forward or slow-reverse, respectively).

```
Float scalingrate = myplayer.setRate( 4.5);
```

Use **setRate()** with caution: The scaling factor used with **setRate()** is only a suggestion to the Clock. A Clock is only required to support a rate of 1.0 and can internally adjust whatever rate you suggest to a rate it supports. For instance, you may request a rate of 8.3528, but the Player may only support 1.0 and 1.5, so it will pick the nearest rate (1.5) to your request. Thus, it is essential to check the return code from **setRate()** to verify the actual rate that the Clock will use (see Listing 3.3).

Since setting the rate of the Player is always unpredictable, you never know if the rate you request will work. You may have to go through several cycles until you find an acceptable value. A more elegant solution would be for Sun or the Player developer to extend the **Clock** interface to report which rates are available on the active device.

Listing 3.3 Illustration of proper Clock rate control.

```
Float scalingrate = myplayer.setRate( 4.5);
if (scalingrate != 4.5 )
{
   System.out.println( "the clock refused my request!!!!");
}
```

The second half of the information required by the Clock is the Media Start Time. The Media Start Time informs the Player of the position in the media to start streaming. This information is communicated by passing a **Time** object to the Clock's **setMediaTime()** method (see Listing 3.4).

Listing 3.4 Attaching a starting media time to a Clock.

```
Time newtime = new Time( (double) 100 );
controller.setMediaTime( newtime );
```

Once you've primed the Clock, it can be started by issuing the **sync-Start()** call with a **TimeBase** time as a parameter. The Clock synchronizes the **TimeBase** time parameter to the current media time, sets its **TimeBase** start time member variable, and begins the media time counter.

```
Time startmenow = myplayer.getTimeBase.getTime();

// commence playback immediately
myplayer.syncStart( startmenow );
```

The Clock will remain running until either the Clock's **stop()** method is issued or the end of the media stream is encountered. When you invoke **stop()**, the Clock returns to **Stopped** state and ceases synchronizing the media time to the **TimeBase**.

CORE TIP

*JMF programmers normally do not interface directly with raw **Clock** objects. Rather, they use convenience objects (such as Players) that extend the **Clock** interface. These convenience objects not only relax the restrictions on Clock usage, but also provide simpler access to **Clock** methods. For instance, the Player's **start()** method shields you from the complexities of the Clock's **syncStart()** method. It correlates the **TimeBase** and media time on your behalf and commences playback at the correct point in time.*

The other means of stopping a Clock is to set a specific stopping point in the media. The Clock can be stopped at a specific time in the presentation by calling **setStopTime()** with the desired media stopping time.

It is your responsibility to keep track of a Clock's state. If you forget and call a **Clock** method while in an invalid state, a **ClockStartedError** exception will be thrown (see Table 3.2). Although well-designed objects report their state, there is no **getState()** method in the **Clock** interface. Fortunately, the Player interface adds layers of abstraction on top of the base **Clock** interface, so you'll only run into these restrictions on those rare occasions when you must use the raw **Clock** interface.

Table 3.2 Valid methods for each Clock state.

Clock State	Valid Methods	Potential Exception
Stopped	syncStart()	ClockStartedError
	setTimeBase()	ClockStartedError
	setMediaTime()	ClockStartedError
	setRate()	ClockStartedError
Started	mapToTimeBase	ClockStoppedException

After discovering all of the complexities involved with managing two different time formats, you may wonder why any of this is necessary. In fact, two time formats are wasteful if you're only going to play one file at a time. Fortunately, Sun realized that synchronization of multiple Players would be impossible without using compatible time systems (i.e., the same **TimeBase**). We will explore the ramifications of **TimeBase**s on synchronization in Chapter 11.

Summary

JMF uses the **Player** interface to track and manipulate the management of time within a media stream. Because there are a plethora of Players installed in most JMF environments, the **Manager** interface is responsible for finding and utilizing the correct Player for a given media stream.

Each Player extends several interfaces. This chapter explored the inner workings of the **Clock** interface. Clocks support two time formats: **TimeBase** and media time. **TimeBase** tracks continuous time from a known starting time. By contrast, media time can start and stop or even flow backward. Because these formats are diametrically opposed, the majority of the functionality in a Clock involves the transformation of **TimeBase** times to media times.

Next, we'll examine a second interface that the Player extends: the **Controller**.

TAKING CONTROL OF THE SITUATION

The mind is its own place, and in it self
Can make a Heav'n of Hell, a Hell of Heav'n.
What matter where, if I be still the same,
And what I should be, all but less than he
Whom Thunder hath made greater? Here at least
We shall be free; th'Almighty hath not built
Here for his envy, will not drive us hence:
Here we may reign secure, and in my choyce
To reign is worth ambition though in Hell:
Better to reign in Hell, than serve in Heav'n.
Milton, _Paradise Lost,_ 1667

Chapter 4

Besides managing time, a Player is responsible for the system resources it consumes. For instance, video playback requires the Player to use processing power on a sound card and to use screen real estate. If multiple Players try to use the same resource (i.e., a hardware decoder on a sound card), an error will result. Thus, to control these resources, the Player extends the **Controller** interface.

A **Controller** is a clock on steroids. It not only integrates the consumption of resources into the clock architecture, but it also provides a mechanism for you to track resource usage and turbo-charge performance by caching multimedia content.

Break with Tradition

As the previous chapter revealed, a Clock cannot enter **Started** state until all the transformation information is available. The **Controller** expands the limitations on when a clock may start. **Controllers** can only enter the **Started** state when the resources required are available. Furthermore, because acquiring resources is a complex process, the **Controller** breaks the **Stopped** state into five substates: **Unrealized**, **Realizing**, **Realized**, **Prefetching** and **Prefetched** (see Figure 4-1).

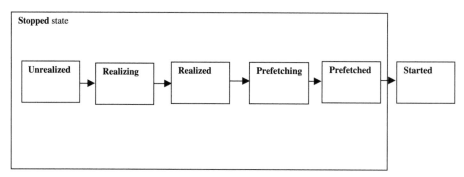

Figure 4–1   `Controller` states.

The fine granularity of **Stopped** states exists because Sun learned from the limitations of other multimedia environments. Older multimedia architectures (such as the MCI interface defined by OS/2 and Windows 3.1 and Windows 95), are notorious for poor error handling and reporting. In these environments, if an error occurred while you were trying to acquire resources (or open a device), it was hard to determine the exact cause of the error. For instance, it was difficult to distinguish between failures because of too many Players competing for the same hardware resources or because of malfunctioning hardware.

By contrast, the **Controller**'s multi-state architecture eliminates ambiguity in error handling. Since each state has a specific set of error conditions, JMF error and exception handling should be considerably more robust than older multimedia programs.

Because a **Controller** offers a multitude of new states, it provides the **getState()** method that enables you to determine its current state. It is strange that Sun placed this method in the **Controller** and not the **Clock**, since this method is equally applicable to both objects. However, since we'll be interfacing primarily with Players and **Controllers**, the omission from the **Clock** class will not affect us.

Equilibrium

Controllers seek a sense of equilibrium. A **Controller** is in balance when its current and target states are identical. When you request that a **Controller** transition into a new (or target) state, its current state is no longer the same as its target state. Consequently, it performs all duties necessary to restore the current and target states to the same value. (See Listing 4.1 for an example of state information.)

Listing 4.1 Illustration of current and target state transitions. When a state transition event is received, you can query it to determine the `Controller`'s current, previous, and target states.

```
if ( event instanceof TransitionEvent)
{
    TransitionEvent transitionevent = (TransitionEvent)
event;
    System.out.println("Current state: " + transition-
event. getCurrentState() );
    System.out.println("Old state: " + transitionevent.
getPreviousState () );
    System.out.println("Target state: " + transitionevent.
getTargetState () );
}
```

Once you call the **syncStart()** method, a Clock transitions instanta-neously from **Stopped** state into **Started** state. By contrast, **Control-ler**s must acquire resources that may not be readily available, so state transitions can be lengthy procedures. For instance, on certain systems, com-pressed audio files require microcode (low-level, hardware-specific software) to be downloaded to the audio processor before the presentation can com-mence. Thus, if **Controller** state transitions operated like **Clock** transi-tions, your thread would be held hostage until the microcode setup process completed.

Controllers alert you to potential lengthy state transitions by using two types of state transfers: synchronous and asynchronous. Synchronous state transfers occur instantaneously, while asynchronous transfers can take an indeterminate amount of time (see Figure 4-2). Since synchronous transfers occur so rapidly, the **Controller** can immediately change its current state to the desired target state when you request a state change.

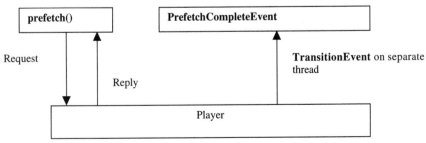

Figure 4-2 How asynchronous requests are processed by a Player.

Core Tip

In computer science, a synchronous call completes before it returns to the caller and there are no time restrictions placed on call completion. By contrast, "synchronous" in JMF terminology means that a call must complete its work quickly and return to the caller.

Because asynchronous transfers can have an indeterminate length, the **Controller** must wait for a transition to complete before equalizing the current and target states. When the asynchronous transfer completes, it also notifies your application via a state transition event. Without this event, you would have to needlessly poll the **Controller**'s state via the **getState()** method to obtain this information. Fortunately, JMF enables you to monitor these transitions via the **ControllerListener** interface.

Are You Listening to Me?

The **ControllerListener** interface is like a conference call: Multiple listeners can log in and receive a snapshot of the inner workings of the **Controller** (such as state transitions and media errors). The system communicates with the **ControllerListener** by sending it events.

Core Tip

*Since all JMF events are derived from **java.util.EventObject**, JMF complies with the JDK 1.1 event model. Consequently, if you're familiar with how other JDK 1.1 subsystems (such as JavaBeans or AWT) handle events, you already know how to respond to JMF events. The only new wrinkle is the name of the event handler, which changes from **propertyChange()** to **ControllerListener()**.*

Events are the lifeblood of any modern multimedia environment. Primitive multimedia platforms (such as Windows 3.1 MCI interface) are single-threaded and primarily synchronous, so the application controls the environment's state. By contrast, JMF may use multiple threads and asynchronous state transitions, so your application is dependent on the system to inform you about the Player's status (see Table 4.1).

The most important use of the **ControllerListener** interface is monitoring state transitions. When you request an asynchronous action (such as **Realize()**, **Prefetch()**, or **Start()**), the Player will do some busy work, then signal your **ControllerListener** when the state transition is complete.

Table 4.1 Transition Events	
Event	*Caused By*
`RealizeCompleteEvent`	`realize()`
`PrefetchCompleteEvent`	`prefetch()`
`StartEvent`	`start()`
`StopEvent`	`stop()` or an error condition

A nice feature of these **TransitionEvents** is their state information methods: **getPreviousState()**, **getCurrentState()**, and **getTargetState()** (see Listing 4.1). If you've lost track of the Player's state, you can use this feature to reorient yourself.

To create a **ControllerListener**, you must implement the **ControllerListener** interface in your target class. You inform the **Controller** that you wish to join the interested parties list by calling the **Controller**'s **addControllerListener()** method as follows:

```
myController.addControllerListener( this );
```

JMF sends events to your **ControllerListener** through the **controllerUpdate()** method. The **Controller** passes a generic **ControllerEvent** parameter to this method. It's your responsibility to determine the instance (or type) for that event before you can process it. Typically, this is accomplished by a series of **if** and **else if** statements (see Listing 4.2).

Listing 4.2 Using **ControllerListener** to monitor state transition events.

```
public synchronized void controllerUpdate(ControllerEvent
event)
{

        // When the Player is Realized, get the visual
        // and control components and add them to the Applet


        if (event instanceof StartEvent)
        {
            System.out.println("controller started....");


        }

            else if ( event instanceof StopByRequestEvent ||
```

Listing 4.2 Using `ControllerListener` to monitor state transition events. (continued)

```
                        event instanceof RealizeCompleteEvent  ||
                        event instanceof PrefetchCompleteEvent   )
         {
             System.out.println("State transition....");
         }
}
```

Proper programming techniques demand that a program remove itself from the **Controller**'s listener list if it no longer wishes to receive notifications. Although the Java garbage collector will clean up orphaned listeners, this only occurs when the object goes out of scope. During this period, the **Controller** will needlessly send events to your listener method.

Evolution of a Controller

The progression of states in a **Controller** parallels the growth stages of a human. Newborn babies are unaware of the resources necessary for survival. Likewise, a **Controller** in **Unrealized** state is ignorant of the content it must play or the physical resources necessary to create the presentation.

As a baby grows, it learns how to formulate primitive thoughts and acquire simple objects. Similarly, as a **Controller** transitions from **Unrealized** to **Realized** state, it calculates the basic resources it needs for presentation and immediately acquires all nonexclusive resources.

A nonexclusive resource permits simultaneous access by multiple users. By contrast, an exclusive resource has limited availability and usually only supports access by a single user. For instance, a 256-channel audio mixer could be considered nonexclusive since approximately 256 users can play audio streams on it. An exclusive resource is an audio device that supports only one stream at a time.

Core Tip

In general, exclusive devices are a bad idea and you should avoid them if possible. If a program uses an exclusive device, it can never be assured that it will be able to open and use it. This uncertainty confuses users and causes software support problems.

All of the JMF Players and programs contained in this book use nonexclusive devices.

When you issue the **realize()** call, the **Controller** synchronously transfers into **Realizing** state. This state is just a pseudo-state to alert you that the **Controller** is asynchronously transitioning into the **Realized** state. When the necessary nonexclusive resources have been obtained, the Player enters the **Realized** state and notifies all listeners about the state transition via a **RealizeComplete** event.

Once it is realized, a Player can enable visual controls such as the *Play*, *Stop*, and *Pause* buttons.

Core Tip

If you're used to synchronous programming in multimedia environments such as Win32's MCI, it may take a while to adjust to JMF's asynchronous programming model. In the Win32 multimedia world, by default, each call blocks inside the multimedia subsystem until the action is completed.

By contrast, JMF calls return instantly and you must wait on an asynchronous event to inform you of task completion. This programming model is radically different from the one to which many people are accustomed. Never assume that the associated action is completed because a JMF method returns to your application.

The listing below illustrates the trap that synchronous programmers fall into when they first start using JMF. Instead of waiting for the Player to notify the application that **realize()** *has completed, the application assumes the* **realize()** *call is synchronous and proceeds on to a subsequent call even though the Player is still trying to* **realize()**.

```
myplayer.realize();
myplayer.prefetch();
myplayer.start();
```

Core Tip

Since a **Realized** *Player doesn't use exclusive resources, theoretically, you can have an unlimited number of* **Realized** *Players active. If the Player doesn't access an exclusive resource, you can even start an unlimited number of that category of Player. However, if the Player acquires an exclusive resource during the prefetch process, no other instance of that Player can enter the* **Started** *state.*

Swimming Downstream

Playback latency (or the response time between requesting playback and the commencement of the presentation) is a problem with which all digital multimedia environments must grapple. Latency issues arise because digital multimedia data must be retrieved and decompressed by a decompression engine before it can be presented by the presentation engine.

Because many compression techniques use variable compression ratios, it may be impossible to determine exactly how long this process will take. By contrast, the presentation engine operates under strict real-time constraints: specific amounts of data must be available at predefined points of time. If decompressed audio and video data are not available at specific time intervals, the presentation engine will stall, and the user will experience audio/visual breakups.

To prevent potential stalls, most environments attempt to insulate the retrieval and decompression process from the real-time requirements of the presentation engine by caching (or buffering) data. The process of buffering data creates a pool of excess decompressed data before playback begins. These excess buffers ensure that the presentation engine doesn't stall if the decompression engine temporarily fails to supply it with enough data for whatever reason (such as variable compression ratios or input/output difficulties).

It is the responsibility of the decompression engine to ensure that the buffer pool remains full or approximately full. Should the pool be too small, or should the decompression engine be too slow, the presentation engine will eventually catch up to the decompression engine and break up (i.e., audio pops or dropped video frames) will result (see Figure 4.3).

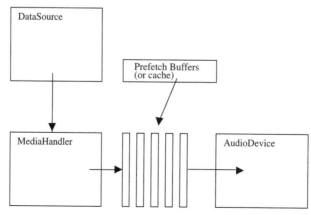

Figure 4–3 Illustration of multimedia cache. The cache insulates the audio hardware device from fluctuations in transmission speed between the **MediaHandler** and the **DataSource**.

Users expect no latency or minimal latency. If you are using a single-purpose device (such as a set-top box or a DVD Player), you can achieve minimal latency by using a small cache of buffers. Since the device has optimized its input and output architecture to deliver a particular media type, very little caching is required.

However, a small cache size is impractical on a multitasking, multimedia platform. Because these environments run multiple tasks, the decompression engine has no assurance that it can use all of the processing resources on the system or that it will receive regular time slices. Furthermore, multitasking platforms normally use a general-purpose input/output subsystem, so it is not possible to achieve the same throughput levels as a dedicated device. As a result, these environments require a larger cache to offset the additional constraints.

Cache size and latency are inversely related. Larger caches require more time to prefetch, or fill, and therefore, increase latency. Fortunately, there are tricks you can use to decrease latency when using a large multimedia cache. One of these techniques is prefetching.

Prefetching is the process of filling the multimedia cache before the user actually begins playback. After the prefetch fills the multimedia cache, the presentation can begin with minimal latency. Typically, multimedia applications preload during startup, so that playback can immediately commence when the user hits the Play button.

To prefetch, you issue the **prefetch()** call on a **Realized** Player. This causes the **Controller** to synchronously transition into **Prefetching** state. Once in **Prefetching** state, the **Controller** acquires all resources necessary for immediate playback. This includes acquiring exclusive resources, prefilling the media cache, and performing any device or media-specific actions necessary to initiate playback.

After this process is complete, the **Controller** sends a **PrefetchCompleteEvent** to your **ControllerListener** and officially enters **Prefetched** state. At this point, the Player has been primed, and if you issue **start** (or the equivalent, **syncStart()** from the **Clock** interface), the Player will enter **Started** state and begin playback. When the presentation begins, the Player will send a **StartCompleteEvent** to your listener.

Our investigation of the effects of latency has been limited to a theoretical discussion. Fortunately, the **Player** interface offers performance-metric APIs that can graphically illustrate the latency difference between a **prefetched** and a non-**Prefetched** Player on a given platform. **getStartLatency()** is supposedly intelligent enough to report the latency differences between **Prefetched** and non-**Prefetched** state.

Unfortunately, Sun permits Players to return **LATENCY_UNKNOWN**. It is much easier to return this error message than to perform latency calculations, so poorly written Players may arbitrarily choose to report the error, thereby limiting the usefulness of **getStartLatency()**.

Are You a Good Citizen?

Multimedia applications are resource-intensive. They often use megabytes of memory and exclusive hardware decoders and require considerable processing power. Once your JMF program enters **Prefetched** state, the exclusive-use resources it owns may prevent other JMF programs from running. If you are using a true operating system (such as UNIX or DirectShow on Windows NT) on a powerful machine with excess memory, JMF can acquire these resources, and occasionally fail to release them without affecting other programs. Yet, releasing resources on a resource-constrained environment (i.e., Windows 3.1 or Windows 95), can be catastrophic.

Since JMF is portable and must run on resource-constrained platforms (ultimately, including embedded platforms), the **Controller** offers the **deallocate()** method. **deallocate()** forces the **Controller** to jettison all exclusive-use resources and minimize nonexclusive resources. Sun's documentation also recommends that the Player release its multimedia caches when you call **deallocate()**, although it is not required to release this memory until it is closed. As a result, even if your JMF programs are properly written, you may notice that their memory consumption varies greatly from platform to platform.

deallocate() is only valid while in **Stop** state, and it behaves differently depending on the **Controller**'s substate. For example, if the **Controller** is **Prefetched** or **Prefetching**, **deallocate()** will cause the Player to roll back to the **Realized** state. Deallocating while in **Realizing** state causes the Player to send listeners the **DeallocateEvent** and return to the **Unrealized** state. However, once you arrive at the **Realized** state, it is permanent. You cannot return to the **Unrealized** state without closing the Player and constructing a new one (see Table 14.5 for deallocate state transition rules).

Once you call **deallocate()**, the **Controller** sends a **DeallocateEvent** to all interested **ControllerListeners**. Since **deallocate()** is asynchronous, this event is used to notify you that resource reclamation is in progress and you've lost access to the given resource. The **DeallocateEvent** does not imply that state transition has finished. You must wait for the appropriate state transition event (i.e., **RealizedCompleteEvent**) for final state indication.

A Closer Examination of Events

So far, we've limited ourselves to using events for tracking state transitions. **Controller**s also send events to indicate additional stop conditions, media shutdown, errors, and stream changes.

Once the Player enters **Started** state, you can cause it to temporarily leave and reenter **Started** state. For instance, issuing **setMediaTime()** with a distant future starting time may force the Player to refill its multimedia cache before playback can continue. As a result, the Player sends you a **RestartingEvent** to indicate exit and likely reentry of **Started** state, drops back into **Prefetching** state, fills up the cache, and then reenters **Started** state.

JMF also provides utility events that ease multimedia programming. For example, you can use the **CachingControlEvent** to monitor media download speed and present visual feedback to the user. We will explore these events in greater detail in Chapter 6, when we create our first JMF applet.

During playback, a Player can encounter a variety of conditions that will asynchronously force it into **Stopped** state. The most common are:

- **EndOfMediaEvent**. If the Player runs out of data, it will send an **EndOfMediaEvent** event.
- **StopAtTimeEvent**. If you inform the Player of the desired stopping point via **setStopTime()**, the Player issues a notification when it encounters this point in the media.
- **DataStarvedEvent**. This event is reported when the **Controller** has no more data to process. This can be caused by slow or unreliable transport mechanisms (such as HTTP) or by the Player using too small a cache.

When the **Controller** encounters a fatal action, or if you call the **close()** method on a **Controller**, it notifies your application of a **ControllerError** event and then terminates. These catastrophic errors include:

- **ResourceUnavailableEvent**. A vital resource is unavailable, so the **Controller** can't function. For example, the audio Player sends this event if the sound card is being exclusively used by another application.

- **ConnectionErrorEvent**. The Player can't connect to the source of multimedia content. For instance, a movie Player would report this if you were trying to play a movie over the FTP protocol and your computer could not connect to the FTP server.
- **InternalErrorEvent**. This event is a catch-all for all other errors that can't be classified because they are device-specific. Players typically override this event with a Player-specific error class. Therefore, if you know the type of Player you are using, you can analyze the error in depth. See Appendix A for more information.

Core Tip

If you've created multimedia programs in DirectShow on Win32 or the Stream Programming Interface (SPI) on OS/2, you can quickly adjust to JMF events. All three environments are multithreaded and report asynchronous events to applications. DirectShow uses a queue and events semaphores, while SPI implements a callback routine that is similar in concept to the **ControllerListener**.

Finicky Controller

The **Clock** interface throws exceptions if you call a method while in the wrong state. Since a **Controller** extends the **Clock** interface to handle resources, it is even more restrictive about which methods can be used in particular states. For instance, a **NotRealized** error is thrown if you try to manipulate the **TimeBase** on an **Unrealized Controller** (see Table 4.2). Similarly, calling **syncStart()** on a non-**Prefetched** Player will result in a **NotPrefetchedError**.

Table 4.2 APIs that are Invalid for Specific States

API	State	Result
getTimeBase()	Unrealized	NotRealizedError
setTimeBase()	Unrealized	NotRealizedError
setMediaTime()	Unrealized	NotRealizedError
setRate()	Unrealized	NotRealizedError

Table 4.2 APIs that are Invalid for Specific States   (continued)

`setStopTime()`	`Unrealized`	`NotRealizedError`
`getStartLatency()`	`Unrealized`	`NotRealizedError`
`syncStart()`	`Realized`	`NotPrefetchedError`
`syncStart()`	`Started`	`ClockStartedError`
`setTimeBase()`	`Started`	`ClockStartedError`
`setMediaTime()`	`Started`	`ClockStartedError`
`setRate()`	`Started`	`ClockStartedError`
`deallocate()`	`Started`	`ClockStartedError`

If you try to restart a **Player** (via **syncStart()** or **deallocate()**), or change the playback rate (using **setRates**) when it is started, the **Player** will throw a **ClockStartedError**. For instance, you can **stop()** the **Started** Player and then issue a **deallocate()** to release memory.

In addition, the Player implementation of the **Controller** interface relaxes the restrictions on methods that can be used on a **Started** Player. Both **setRate()** and **setMediaTime()** are legal on a **Started** Player; changing the playback rate allows you to dynamically fast-forward or rewind.

The Dangers of a Used Car Lot

Used car salesmen have earned a reputation for selling you more car than you need. Similarly, the functionality we've uncovered in JMF may be more multimedia than you require. While the **AudioClip** interface is far too primitive for serious multimedia development, the intricate details of states and events may make JMF too complicated for the average programmer. Fortunately, JMF offers shortcuts so that the casual programmer can comfortably use it.

JMF shortcuts enable you to perform multiple state transitions with a single call. For example, if you call **start()** while in **Unrealized** state, the Player will automatically call **realize()**, **prefetch()**, and **start()** on your behalf (see Figure 4-4). Similarly, if you call **prefetch()** while in **Unrealized** state, the Player will automatically call **realize()** and **prefetch()** (see Figure 4-5).

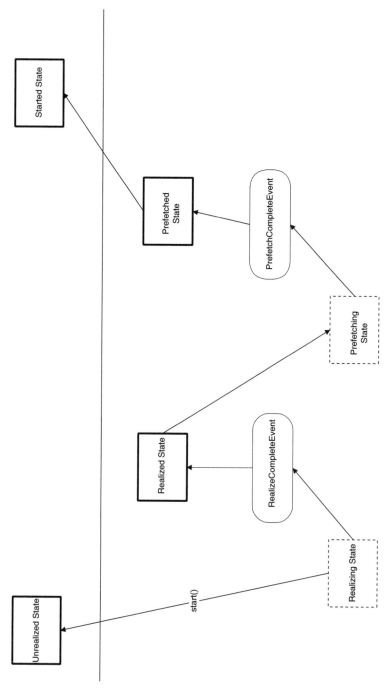

Figure 4–4 Calling **start()** while in **Unrealized** state.

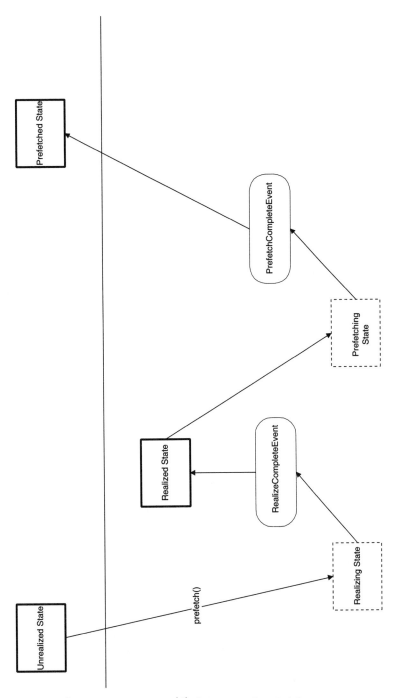

Figure 4-5 Calling **prefetch()** while in **Unrealized** state.

The **Controller**'s **start()** method may have side effects. Since the Player is transitioning states on your behalf, you cannot react to unforeseen occurrences. For instance, if you issue **start()** on an **Unrealized** Player and later decide that you don't want playback to start, the Player will transition to **Started** state anyway. By contrast, if you control state transitions yourself, you can abort playback after any event.

Core Tip

Advanced programmers normally shy away from shortcut methods provided by multimedia environments such as MCI since they lose control over a device and the shortcuts are often slower than performing the steps manually. While it is true that you lose control when you use JMF shortcuts, they actually improve performance since the Player is able to make multiple state transitions without having to communicate with your application.

How Long Does This Last Anyway?

The last feature a **Controller** offers is the implementation of the **Duration** interface. This interface addresses a significant weakness in the old **AudioClip** class: the inability to figure out a media's playing time. The interface's only method is **getDuration()**, and it reports the currently loaded media object's playing time when played back at normal speed (i.e., a rate of 1.0).

If you call **getDuration()** when the Player is unsure of its resources, it returns **DURATION_UNKNOWN**. This error is a signal that your application should wait until the Player becomes **Realized** before attempting to make this call again.

Core Tip

__DURATION_UNKNOWN__ is often reported by Players using the HTTP and FTP protocols, since some of these servers cannot determine media length.

Simple media types such as .WAV or .au files always have a determinate length. By contrast, formats such as .MOD files can contain loops, resulting in files that will play infinitely. In these scenarios, a **Controller** returns **DURATION_UNBOUNDED** to indicate that it is unable to calculate the media's length (see Listing 4.3).

Listing 4.3 Determining the length of a Player's media.

```
if ( myPlayer.getDuration() == DURATION_UNBOUNDED )
{
        // print warning
}
```

Summary

By extending the **Controller** interface, JMF gives you explicit control over when resources are consumed and released. Advanced programmers can exploit these features to improve performance. Casual programmers can bypass these details and immediately start playback via the Controller's **start()** method.

In the next chapter, we'll explore the remaining **Player** interfaces.

ORIGINS

"This most beautiful system of the sun, planets, and comets, could only proceed from the counsel and dominion of an intelligent and powerful Being."

Sir Isaac Newton, *Mathematica Principia*, 1686

To suppose that the eye, with all its inimitable contrivances for adjusting the focus to different distances, for admitting different amounts of light, and for the correction of spherical and chromatic aberration, could have been formed by natural selection, seems, I freely confess, absurd in the highest possible degree.

Charles Darwin, *The Origin of Species*

Chapter 5

A ll multimedia devices share one common feature: They must be supplied with data from an external source. Furthermore, most video and audio decoders have to be fed huge quantities of content in a timely manner. Every Player has a **MediaHandler** object that enables it to meet these requirements.

Why a MediaHandler?

The focus of early multimedia platforms (such as MCI on Windows 3.0) was performance. These environments were not object-oriented and they closely coupled input/output routines to the decoding of multimedia content in a single runtime module (or driver). This architecture maximized performance, since there was no overhead in transmitting data from one section of the driver to another.

The designers quickly discovered that tight coupling had significant disadvantages. First, the entire driver had to be rewritten if someone wanted to play the file using a new protocol (i.e., HTTP versus disk I/O). Second, maintenance was difficult, because file format dependencies were interwoven throughout the driver.

The next generation of multimedia platforms (SPI on OS/2 and Direct-Show on Win32) learned from these mistakes and removed input/output responsibilities from multimedia decoders. As a result, a single multimedia driver could support multiple media formats. For example, the same OS/2 .WAV driver could handle .WAV, .AIFF, .IFF, and .MOD content.

Being Pushy Isn't All Bad

The Internet has become embroiled in a war between Push and Pull technologies. Browsers became popular because they allowed users to cruise the Internet and retrieve (or pull) interesting information from Web sites. The next phase of Internet evolution focused on sending (or pushing) this information directly to their mailbox or browser without users having to search for it. However, companies such as Netscape, Microsoft, and Pointcast have conflicting and incompatible visions of how push technology should operate and evolve, thereby delaying its acceptance.

While JMF is not directly involved in the Push and Pull battle, it must be able to provide multimedia content using either technique. Since JMF separates data input objects from multimedia decoders, it is able to provide this functionality by creating two categories of input objects (or **DataSources** in JMF terminology): **Push** and **Pull**.

Pull **DataSources** are currently the dominant mechanism to transport multimedia content. They are initiated and controlled by consumers of multimedia data. For example, when you request to view a movie or listen to an audio file, you are pulling data toward the multimedia decoders (the file can exist on your local computer or a remote network).

The user has complete control over a Pull **DataSource**. Data transfers commence when you request that the Player **prefetch** or **start()**. You also dictate when the stream should pause and where in the media stream playback should commence. When the player enters the **Stopped** state, transfers cease.

By contrast, **Push DataSource**s are like riding a wild bull: You have minimal control over their direction and no influence over your final destination (see Figure 5-1). Typically, they are initiated by a remote location (i.e., a server). Unlike a Push **DataSource**, Pull **DataSource**s continue to transmit even if the Player is in **Stopped** state. As a result, consumer objects are responsible for processing content even when they are not ready to accept it.

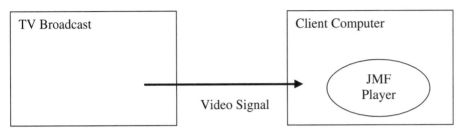

Figure 5-1   How pushed content operates.

Although Push is in its infancy, the emergence of digital media technologies and the Internet will gradually shift focus to Pushed multimedia. Consumers are transitioning from analog media formats (such as analog terrestrial [or earth-bound] broadcasts) towards digital broadcast content (such as satellites, cable, and eventually HDTV), which is Push-oriented. Furthermore, an increasing number of Internet sites offer live video broadcasts that are Pushed toward the end-user. The combination of these factors will accelerate the acceptance of Pushed content.

Return of the Manager

Since the data source is a separate object from the Player, it requires assistance to connect. As we discovered in Chapter 3, the **Manager** object is responsible for assembling a Player on your behalf, and part of this responsibility is connecting the Player with a data source.

The first step in constructing a Player is creating a **MediaLocator**. This object describes the content's location and the protocol necessary to process this content. For example, Listing 5.1 shows how you can construct a **MediaLocator**.

Listing 5.1 Associating a **MediaLocator** with a URL.

```
try
{
    url = new URL(getDocumentBase(), mediaFile);
    mediaFile = url.toExternalForm();
    // Create a media locator from the file name
    if ((mrl = new MediaLocator(mediaFile)) == null)
      Fatal("Can't build URL for " + mediaFile);
}
catch (MalformedURLException e)
{
    Fatal("Invalid media file URL!");
}
catch (IOException e)
{
    Fatal("IO exception creating player for " + mrl);
}
```

A **MediaLocator** is similar to conventional Java URL objects. In fact, you can obtain the URL associated with the **MediaLocator** via the **getURL()** method. The primary difference between the two objects is that **MediaLocator**s can be constructed without a **URLStreamHandler**. This distinction is important since JMF lets you write multimedia-specific input routines, which alleviate the need for a large **URLStreamHandler**.

The **Manager** calls the **MediaLocator's getProtocol()** method to determine the protocol necessary to transfer the data. It then assembles a list of **DataSources**, which potentially may support this protocol. The **Manager** runs an algorithm to determine the correct **DataSource** to use with this file.

Once this data source is obtained, the **Manager** is responsible for attaching it to a **MediaHandler**. Since all Players extend the **MediaHandler's** interface, this process implicitly links a **DataSource** to a Player. After the **DataSource** is associated with the Player, it is possible to stream content.

Summary

All multimedia devices must process data from an external source. Modern, object-oriented multimedia environments such as JMF separate data consumption from data production to enable file format and protocol independence in the decoding engine. JMF extends this separation concept by classifying **DataSources** as Push or Pull. Since Pull sources behave far differently from Push **DataSource**s, Players must be intelligent enough to adjust the feature set available with each technique.

Because the **DataSource** and Player are independent objects, a supervisory object is required to facilitate communication between the two entities. Therefore, JMF uses the **Manager** object to facilitate the connection of the source to a Player. The use of an independent **Manager** object ensures that a given Player can connect with multiple sources and that a given source can supply multiple Players (or **MediaHandler**s).

Now that you understand the JMF architecture and runtime considerations, let's write a JMF applet.

ALOHAJMF: A JMF APPLET

Toiling,—rejoicing,—sorrowing,
  Onward through life he goes;
Each morning sees some task begin,
  Each evening sees it close;
Something attempted, something done,
  Has earned a night's repose.

Thanks, thanks to thee, my worthy friend,
  For the lesson thou hast taught!
Thus at the flaming forge of life
  Our fortunes must be wrought;
Thus on its sounding anvil shaped
  Each burning deed and thought.
Henry Wadsworth Longfellow, *The Village Blacksmith*

Chapter

Since a Hello World-type applet is usually the first Java code people write, we will design a primitive JMF applet called AlohaJMF (see Figure 6-1). This approach is advantageous because it enables us to illustrate core JMF principles without GUI layers getting in the way. You'll also be able to lift the source from this applet and place it directly on your Web site.

Benefits of Object-Orientation

When you create your first JMF applet, you'll notice the similarities between the applet methods and JMF methods (see Table 6.1). This synergy exemplifies the benefits of a well-designed object-oriented interface. If you choose core methods carefully, these methods can be inherited by child objects, and they also can be reused by seemingly unrelated objects.

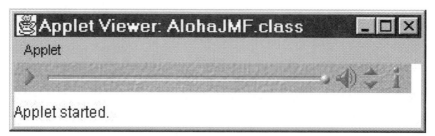

Figure 6–1   Appletviewer running AlohaJMF on Win32 platform.

Table 6.1 Comparison of Core Feature Set for Applets and JMF

Applet Method	*JMF Method*
`init()`	`realize()`
	`prefetch()`
`start()`	`start()`
`stop()`	`stop()`
	`deallocate()`
`destroy()`	`close()`

Applets 101

The first step in creating our applet is to create a spartan HTML page. The only important tag in this code is:

```
<APPLET  CODE = AlohaJMF.class WIDTH = 320 HEIGHT = 270 >
<PARAM  name=file value="alohameansgoodbye.wav">
</APPLET>
```

Core Tip

This book assumes a thorough knowledge of HTML. If you would like to read a book which covers HTML fundamentals, examine Core Web Programming *by Marty Hall.*

When a browser encounters the applet tag, it loads our AlohaJMF.class, and invokes the Applet **init()** method. Because **Applet.init()** is essentially a constructor for the applet, we'll use it to perform setup operations such as constructing a Player and attaching a listener to the Player (see Listing 6.1).

Listing 6.1 AlohaJMF's **init()** method is responsible for constructing a Player.

```
try
{
        player = Manager.createPlayer(mrl);
        // Add ourselves as a listener for a player's events
        player.addControllerListener(this);
}
catch (NoPlayerException e)
{
        System.out.println(e);

}
```

Although we compared the applet's **init()** to a constructor, there are some important differences between the two. First, a constructor should never fail since the object ceases to exist and there is no mechanism to retry. Consequently, you should never create a Player in a constructor, since Players can throw exceptions for a myriad of reasons.

Second, a constructor can only be called once. If you locate your JMF player creation code in the constructor, it will be impossible to recreate the Player later. By contrast, it is possible, although unlikely, that **init()** may be called more than once. For instance, if the browser decides to flush its applet cache and the applet is needed again, the browser will be forced to call **init()** a second time.

Core Tip

Java programs rely on try-catch blocks to handle error situations. The compiler will force you to wrap methods that generate exceptions in a try block, but you must also be alert enough to place calls dependent on these exception generating methods in a try block. If these dependent calls are outside the try block, they will cause an unhandled exception when errors occur.

The listing below illustrates what happens if you forget to place a sensitive section of code in a try block. Although the creation of the

*Player is performed inside a try-catch block, this code snippet attempts to perform a **addControllerListener()** outside of the scope of the try-catch block. Since **addControllerListener()** does not throw an error, the compiler will not issue a warning. However, at runtime, if player construction fails, the code will gracefully catch the exception, but then go down in flames when it tries to call **addControllerListener()**, since the player object is **null**.*

```
try
{
        player = Manager.createPlayer(mrl);
}
catch (NoPlayerException e)
{
        System.out.println(e);
        Fatal("Could not create player for " + mrl);
}

// Add ourselves as a listener for a player's events
// if player is null, this call will cause an exception
// therefore, it should be in a try block

player.addControllerListener(this);
```

Zealous first time JMF programmers may be tempted to shove too much functionality in the **init()** method. If you call **start()** before you attach a **ControllerListener**, you may miss state transition events. Furthermore, good programming practice dictates that you limit **init()** to initialization functions.

Core Tip

For AlohaJMF to work, your Java VM must be able to access local files. If you see a file access exception being thrown in the debugger, you'll need to enable the local file access option for your VM.

After **init()**, the **start()** method is invoked. **start()** is normally called immediately before **paint()** or after the applet has been stopped and restarted. Both scenarios require that the Player either be started or restarted. Therefore, we commence playback in **Applet.start()** by issuing **alohaPlayer.start()**.

Core Tip

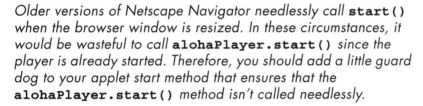

Older versions of Netscape Navigator needlessly call **start()**
*when the browser window is resized. In these circumstances, it
would be wasteful to call* **alohaPlayer.start()** *since the
player is already started. Therefore, you should add a little guard
dog to your applet start method that ensures that the*
alohaPlayer.start() *method isn't called needlessly.*

```
// older versions of Navigator will send bogus start()
messages
// to our applet. This check will ensure that we don't
needlessly
// try to restart the player......

if ( alohaPlayer.getState() != Controller.Started )
{
alohaPlayer.start();
}
```

Because this is our first JMF applet, we're going to use **aloha-
Player.start()** to simplify state transition processing. **aloha-
Player.start()** will implicitly **realize**, **prefetch**, and **start** our
Player. However, our **ControllerListener** must still monitor state transition events or we won't know when it is safe to display GUI widgets. Consequently, we'll track the receipt of the **RealizeCompleteEvent**. This
event, notifies our applet that we can safely add visual components to our
applet panel (see Listing 6.2).

Listing 6.2 A minimal **ControllerListener**.

```
public synchronized void controllerUpdate(ControllerEvent
event)
{
      // If our player died, bail out of here.
      if (player == null)
          return;

      // When the player is Realized, get the visual
      // and control components and add them to the Applet
      if (event instanceof RealizeCompleteEvent)
      {
          if (controlComponent == null)
             if (( controlComponent = player.getControl-
PanelComponent()) != null)
```

Listing 6.2 A minimal `ControllerListener`. (continued)

```
            {
                controlPanelHeight = controlComponent.get-
PreferredSize().height;
                panel.add(controlComponent);
                height += controlPanelHeight;
            }
        if (visualComponent == null)
            if (( visualComponent = player.getVisualCompo-
nent())!= null)
                {
                panel.add(visualComponent);
                Dimension videoSize = visualComponent.get-
PreferredSize();
                videoWidth = videoSize.width;
                videoHeight = videoSize.height;
                width = videoWidth;
                height += videoHeight;
                visualComponent.setBounds(0, 0, video-
Width, videoHeight);
                }

        panel.setBounds(0, 0, width, height);
        if (controlComponent != null)
            {
            controlComponent.setBounds(0, videoHeight,
                                    width, controlPanel-
Height);
            controlComponent.invalidate();
            }
    }
    else if (event instanceof ControllerErrorEvent)
    {
        // bad things have happened, we've got to quit….
        player = null;
    }
    else if (event instanceof ControllerClosedEvent)
    {
        //panel.removeAll();
    }
}
```

Core Tip

Be sure to issue a **validate()** *after you add your components in* **controllerUpdate()**, *or you'll spend many fruitless hours trying to figure out why the Player's controls don't paint.*

Table 6.2 Execution Sequence in JMF Applet

Applet Method	JMF Functions
init()	Manager.createPlayer()
	Player.addControllerListener()
start()	Player.start()
controllerUpdate()	RealizeCompleteEvent
stop()	Player.stop() Player.deallocate()
destroy()	Player.close()

Core Tip

You may notice that Table 6.1 indicated that the **applet.init()** *method closely correlated with the Player constructor. However, Table 6.2 reveals that we never explicitly call the Player constructor. This inconsistency is resolved when you understand that* **Manager.createPlayer()** *actually constructs a Player on your behalf.*

Nothing is more irritating than leaving a Java-enabled Web page and having the background audio continue to play. This problem is further aggravated by the fact that there are no longer any GUI controls for the user to click on to stop playback. Therefore, it is imperative that your code stop the Player when the applet's **stop()** method is called. Failure to do so may have unpredictable results, one of which may be uncontrollable audio.

Besides stopping playback, a well-behaved JMF applet should release resources associated with the Player. If you fail to do this, subsequent JMF applets may not be able to function, since your applet still has these resources locked up.

Applet.stop() is not the appropriate place to close your Player objects. **Applet.stop()** warns the applet that it is being suspended, and that it may be restarted at a later time using **start()**. If you make the mistake of closing the Player in **stop()**, you'll need to recreate the Player when **start()** is called. This would force the Player to **realize** and **prefetch** before starting, thereby dramatically slowing performance.

The correct place to close the Player is the applet's **destroy()** method, since you can be assured that the applet is permanently unloaded.

Juicing Up the Applet

Although our AlohaJMF applet baptized you into the world of JMF, it is missing some important features. For example, if you run the applet on a local machine, downloading and preloading is virtually instantaneous. By contrast, if the same file is accessed over a slow modem connection, the applet will not be responsive during the download and many users will be convinced that it is hung. To avert this problem, we'll add support for a caching control to monitor download progress in our second applet, AlohaJr (see Listing 6.3).

Listing 6.3 Caching control use.

```
if (event instanceof CachingControlEvent)
{
    if (player.getState() > Controller.Realizing)
      return;
    // Put a progress bar up when downloading starts,
    // take it down when downloading ends.
    CachingControlEvent e = (CachingControlEvent) event;
    CachingControl cc = e.getCachingControl();

    // Add the bar if not already there ...
    if (progressBar == null)
    {
        if ((progressBar = cc.getControlComponent()) !=
null)
        {
           panel.add(progressBar);
           panel.setSize(progressBar.getPreferredSize());
                validate();
        }
    }
}
```

Although you can quickly code a caching control, it is difficult to debug it inside an applet, since local files load too quickly. To test the control, we need to load the content from a remote source with slower throughput. Unfortunately, applets cannot access resources outside the server where they were loaded. This prevents you from loading multimedia content from an HTTP server if your HTML code resides on a local machine.

Core Tip

Here's one technique for debugging applets that must access content from remote sites. Store the HTML page on the remote HTTP server. However, specify that you want to load the class file from your local machine. This enables you to load local debug class files while retaining permission to access files on the server. The syntax to accomplish this is illustrated below:

```
<APPLET code=AlohaJMF.class
codeBase=file://G:\jmf\ height=320 width=240>
<PARAM NAME="file" VALUE="http://www.myserver.com/
aloha.wav">
</APPLET>
```

Proper **CachingControl** support requires you to manually transition states and not rely on **Player.start()**. Without this functionality, visual components may be displayed and playback will commence before the download completes (we will solidify AlohaJr's caching control in the next chapter).

AlohaJr also contains the framework for robust error handling. For instance, once a **ControllerErrorEvent** is received, all references to the Player are erased, since it has become dysfunctional. Failure to do this will result in an exception when other methods try to use the **Player** object.

Finally, properly written JMF applets should watch for the **ControllerClosedEvent**. After this event is received, the Player has terminated, and it is safe to remove any controls you've added. Theoretically, all Java runtimes should perform this cleanup; however, you can never be sure that every runtime is bug-free. Therefore, if you clean up after yourself, you won't be dependent on others.

Summary

The similarities between the applet interface and the Player interface permits anyone familiar with Java programming to rapidly create a multimedia-enhanced Web page.

Robust applets should also monitor download progress so that the user doesn't think that the applet is hung. They should also smoothly process **ControllerErrorEvents** to prevent exceptions. When the Player is destroyed, it should remove any visual controls users have added to the panel.

It's now time to take control over your JMF applets and applications.

GETTING
CONTROL OVER
YOUR APPLICATIONS

The desire of power in excess caused the angels to fall; the desire of knowledge in excess caused man to fall.

Sir Francis Bacon, *Of Goodness*

To clear up which, I endeavoured to give some ideas of the desire of power and riches; of the terrible effects of lust, intemperance, malice, and envy. All this I was forced to define and describe by putting cases and making supposi-tions. After which, like one whose imagination was struck with something never seen or heard of before, he would lift up his eyes with amaze-ment and indignation. Power, government, war, law, punishment, and a thousand other things, had no terms wherein that language could express them, which made the difficulty almost insuperable, to give my master any conception of what I meant.

Jonathan Swift, *Gulliver's Travels*

Chapter 7

The Player interfaces we've discussed so far are like the engine in a sports car; it has plenty of performance, but minimal usefulness by itself. Although car fanatics get pumped about the performance characteristics of an engine, a car's body allows the engine to show its potential. Similarly, each Player provides user interface objects that make the Player useful.

These objects, or controls, are GUI objects (or AWT Components) that you can embed in your applications or Web pages to control features in a Player. These controls present a default user interface over the functionality embedded in a Player's controllers. Most Players contain controls that can play, pause, and stop. Other players supply controls over exotic audio and video features.

Getting a Driver's License

A neophyte driver doesn't learn how to drive with a Corvette; they simply cannot control one. Similarly, most JMF programmers are ignorant of the advanced features in a given Player and are unable to create an acceptable user interface for this functionality. As a result, it is advisable to rely on a Player's controls for feature control.

For instance, if the mythical SoupedUpVideo, Inc., releases a revolutionary Player that can simultaneously play forward and backward, your existing GUI may implode when it tries to support it. Yet, if you use the control associated with the Player, your application will smoothly support the SoupedUpVideo, Inc., product and all other future Players.

Although this approach is flexible and convenient, most programmers are hesitant to relinquish control of their user interface to an unknown Player. Unfortunately, this is the inherent risk of using an object-oriented system. JMF defines the architecture for creating controls, but provides no assurance that the control's user interface will meet your quality standards. For the vast majority of Players, the benefits outweigh the costs. However, if you are strongly opposed to using another person's user interface, you can ignore the Player's controls and provide your own.

Sticks and Stones May Break My Bones, but Names Will Never Hurt Me

A Player can contain three types of controls: named, prepackaged, and anonymous. Named controls are uncovered by requesting a specific control's name from the Player. Simply call the Player's **getControl()** method with the name of the desired control and the Player will return the control object associated with the name (see Listing 7.1). If the Player doesn't support the specified control, **getControl()** will return NULL.

Listing 7.1 Retrieving a control by name from a Player.

```
String controlName = "MyCustomControl";
MyCustomControl mycontrol = null;
Control control = player.getControl(controlName);
if ( control != null && control instanceof MyCustomControl)
{
    System.out.println("able to obtain control!");
}
else
{
    System.out.println("Unable to obtain control!");

}
```

Although searching for a control by name is convenient, it is pointless if you don't know the naming convention used by **getControl()**. Fortunately, **getControl()** uses a simple nomenclature to query for a control: the full class or interface name.

Core Tip

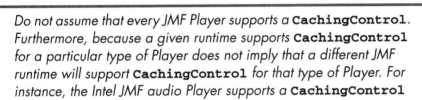

Do not assume that every JMF Player supports a **CachingControl**. *Furthermore, because a given runtime supports* **CachingControl** *for a particular type of Player does not imply that a different JMF runtime will support* **CachingControl** *for that type of Player. For instance, the Intel JMF audio Player supports a* **CachingControl** *object, while the 1.0.x Sun JMF Player does not.*

Our AlohaJMF applet in Chapter 6 waits until a **CachingControlEvent** is received before displaying a progress bar, since it never knows if the content is being loaded locally or remotely. However, if you know that the content will always be loaded from a remote site, you may want to display the progress bar immediately. Listing 7.2 illustrates the proper procedure to grab a **CachingControl** object.

Listing 7.2 Proper technique to obtain a **CachingControlEvent**.

```
if (event instanceof CachingControlEvent)
{
        //if (player.getState() > Controller.Prefetching)
        //    return;

        // Put a progress bar up when downloading starts,
        // take it down when downloading ends.
        CachingControlEvent e = (CachingControlEvent)
event;
        CachingControl cc = e.getCachingControl();
}
```

Core Tip

CachingControl *is a cross between a named control and a prepackaged control. Although the Player doesn't contain a dedicated method to return a* **CachingControl** *interface, the* **CachingControlEvent** *contains a* **getCachingControl()** *method, which gives direct access to the associated* **CachingControl** *interface.*

If you constantly use a control, searching for it by name is considerably slower than simply obtaining a reference to the object. To explain, requesting an object name causes the Player to compare the names of the controls it contains with your request until it find a matching String. By contrast, if you were able to call a method whose sole purpose was to supply references to a specific control, performance would improve since no comparisons would be necessary.

Prepackaged controls improve upon named controls by offering dedicated access methods that return specific control objects. Every Player has at least one dedicated prepackaged control method: **getGainControl()**.

Core Tip

Although every Player contains a **getGainControl()**, *this does not imply that each Player must support* **GainControl**. *For instance, if you were using a bitmap viewer Player, that Player's* **getGainControl()** *would return* **NULL**, *since it has no audio capabilities.*

Gaining Control Over Your Player

The **GainControl** is one of the most popular prepackaged controls. It functions like a software amplifier: You can use it to boost or dampen the amplitude of an audio signal.

GainControl can process data in one of two forms: deciBels (dB) or level. dBs describe the relative levels of two electrical voltages. Positive dB values boost the signal, whereas negative values attenuate the signal. Since dB operates on a logarithmic scale, it requires exponentially larger values to affect the audio waveform.

$$Value = pow(10.0, gainDB/20.0)$$

Core Tip

The deciBel is aimed at digital audio professionals who need explicit control over audio devices. It is popular in this environment because the dB logarithmic scale closely models the perception of sound by the ear (the ear perceives sounds in a logarithmic fashion). Unless you thoroughly understand all of the formulas necessary to calculate dBs, you should avoid use of this scale.

Because this logarithmic dB scale can be difficult to interpret and use, most programmers communicate with the **GainControl** in a simpler data format: gain level. A gain level may range between 0.0 (no amplification) and 1.0 (maximum amplification).

By default, the control uses no amplification, since there can be no assurance that all digital audio hardware devices can support this feature. You can verify the current level setting by calling **getLevel()** (see Listing 7.3).

Listing 7.3 Use of **getLevel()** to obtain the **GainControl**'s current level setting.

```
// grab a reference to a gain control object
// this can ONLY be done on a realized Player!!!!!
GainControl gain = player.getGainControl();
float level = gain.getLevel();
```

Core Tip

*Although the JMF documentation doesn't mention any limitations on when **getGainControl()** may be used, it can only be called on a **Realized** Player. If you try to use this method on an **Unrealized** Player, you'll be thrown a **NotRealizedError**.*

To change the gain level, call the **GainControl**'s **setLevel()** method. Simple programs may try to set a specific value and assume that it will operate identically on all audio devices. Unfortunately, there are wide variations in how hardware devices interpret **setLevel()** requests. Therefore, it is imperative that you examine the return code from **setLevel()**, since the Player may not be able to honor your request. For instance, if the device has minimal amplification capabilities, it will return the maximum gain value it supports in the return code.

Core Tip

You can exploit the return code produced by **setLevel()** *to test the sensitivity of a given Player implementation. Issuing* **setLevel(1.0)** *will cause the Player to return the maximum useful gain value (the Player will treat values greater than the return code as 1.0). Similarly,* **setLevel(0.0)** *will return the minimum useful gain value (values less than this will be treated as 0.0).*

Once you know the sensitivity of a control, you can tweak your application to minimize its limitations. For example, if a control indicated that its useful range was 0.0 to 0.5, it would be pointless to use a slider that ranged between 0.0 and 1.0, since the Player would ignore half of the settings.

Core Tip

Warning: Both **GainControls** *and* **CachingControls** *are exceptions to the* **getControl()** *naming convention. Neither can be returned by* **getControl()** *if you pass the class name in as a* **String**. *Unfortunately, no logical explanation for this contradiction is known.*

For those circumstances where you need to instantly silence audio, but leave the gain setting intact, the **GainControl** offers **setMute(true)**. You turn the mute state off by issuing **setMute(false)**. **setMute(false)** automatically restores the gain setting in effect before **setMute(true)** was called.

Sophisticated audio applications are not satisfied with simply changing the **GainControl**'s level or dB setting or muting the device. Rather, they also need to monitor all changes to the Player's audio status. For instance, a thread in that application may set the gain to 0.8. A separate thread may subsequently change the level to 0.4. The first thread may want to be notified of this change so it can update its sliders. For these scenarios, you should register a **GainChangeListener** (see Listing 7.4).

Listing 7.4 Proper technique to add a **GainChangeListener** to a Player.

```
// grab a reference to a gain control object
// this can ONLY be done on a realized Player!!!!!
GainControl gain = player.getGainControl();

// add a listener for gain events (we will only get
// gain events on this listener, not normal events...)
gain.addGainChangeListener( this );
```

Core Tip

Environments such as OS/2 and Windows have system-wide objects that notify applications when a global setting (such as system gain) has changed. Unfortunately, this is not possible with Java, since Java programs may potentially run in separate VMs whose objects cannot easily intercommunicate. Thus, when you register a **GainChangeListener***, it will only notify you when the object in that VM changes, and not when a program outside that VM changes the system-wide gain setting.*

Inside your **GainChangeListener**, you'll need to create a **gainChange()** method to process **GainChangeEvent**s (see Listing 7.5). **GainChangeEvent**s are read-only objects that inform you of the current dB and level settings.

Listing 7.5 Illustration of `GainChangeListener` implementation.

```
public void gainChange(GainChangeEvent event)
{
        System.out.println("Gain level is: " +
event.getLevel() );
}
```

Even a Broken Clock Is Right Twice a Day

In some situations, you won't know the name of every control stored in a Player and the Player won't offer a prepackaged method to access every control. In these circumstances, you have to manually retrieve each control from the Player and interrogate it to see if it has visual controls (see Listing 7.6). If controls are available, you can incorporate them into your application.

Listing 7.6 Illustration of interrogating a Player for controls.

```
Control[] controls = player.getControls();
int totalControls = controls.length;

for ( int loop = 0; loop < totalControls; loop++ )
{
                        Component aControl = con-
trols[loop].getControlComponent();

                        if ( aControl != null )
                        {
                            // dump out the controls
name.......
                            System.out.println( aCon-
trol.toString() );
                        }
}
```

Summary

Controls enable you to manipulate specialized features on a controller. Because it is impossible for your application to anticipate every feature by all current and future controls, they may contain a user interface that you can use in your application to manipulate these options.

There are three types of controls: named, prepackaged, and anonymous. Each requires a different technique to access them from inside a Player. However, the prepackaged option is preferred, since it is the most efficient.

In the next chapter, we'll take advantage of these controls to create a Swing component that enables you to preview multimedia content inside the **File Open** dialog.

MULTIMEDIA SWING SET

Before me there were no created thing,
Only eterne, and I eternal last.
All hope abandon, ye who enter in!"
Dante, *Divine Comedy, The Inferno*

So saying, her rash hand in evil hour
Forth reaching to the Fruit, she pluck'd, she eat:
Earth felt the wound, and Nature from her seat
Sighing through all her Works gave signs of woe,
That all was lost

Milton, *Paradise Lost,* 1667

Chapter 8

When we built AlohaJMF in Chapter 6, we encountered several problems whose solutions were beyond the scope of a simple applet. These problems included minimal utilization of the caching control, weak state management, and difficulty debugging remote multimedia content. You'll learn to address these problems in Audio-Preview, a multimedia enhanced Swing file dialog (see Figure 8-1).

(a)

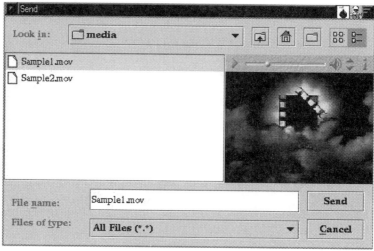

(b)

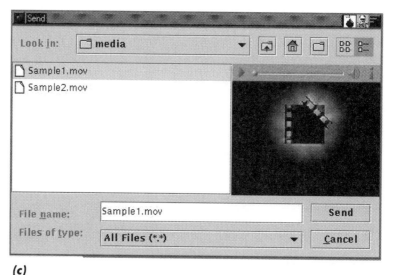

(c)

Figure 8-1   (a) AudioPreview dialog running on Windows NT; (b) AudioPreview dialog running on Solaris; (c) AudioPreview dialog running on Compaq UNIX.

AudioPreview is similar to Sun's Swing FileChooserDemo sample, but it lets you sample audio content rather than preview bitmaps. AudioPreview offers intelligent state management and proper caching control. Furthermore, since it is an application, it can access files from any location, so debugging is simplified.

Core Tip

This book assumes familiarity with Swing, otherwise known as the Java Foundation Classes, or JFC. If you would like additional background material on Swing, I suggest you examine Core Java Foundation Classes, Graphic Java: Mastering the JFC, *or http:// java.sun.com/products/jfc/index.html.*

The Pain of Configuration

In this project, we'll use Swing 1.1 (beta 3 and later) to create AudioPreview. First, you will need to ensure that the JFC 1.1 **swingall.jar** is in your class search path.

In addition, Swing 1.1 needs JDK 1.1.6 or higher to be stable. If you try to run this applet on any JDK older that 1.1.6, the results are unpredictable. For example, although Swing 1.1 appears to work with the JDK 1.1.5 in Visual-Cafe 2.5, it exhibits mysterious crashes during debugging that do not occur with JDK 1.1.6.

Building Blocks

The core object in AudioPreview is the **JMFFileChooser** class, and it is the first object invoked by the **main()** routine. It immediately creates a button and attaches a listener to the button. Then it constructs an output area that will be used to notify the user of selection requests (see Listing 8.1).

When the user clicks on the **AudioPreview** button, the listener's **actionPerformed()** method is invoked. This method is responsible for creating the enhanced **JfileChooser** dialog and cleaning up the dialog when the user closes it. The first step in this process is to create a generic **JfileChooser** dialog. Then, we'll spice up the dialog with the following features: a file filter, file viewer, and a previewer.

> **Listing 8.1** The **JMFFileChooser** constructor is responsible for creating user interface elements necessary to launch the multimedia chooser.

```
public JMFFileChooser()
{
        super("JMFFileChooser");

        JButton sendButton = new JButton("AudioPreview");
        sendButton.addActionListener(new SendListener());

        log = new JTextArea(5,20);
        log.setMargin(new Insets(5,5,5,5));
        JScrollPane logScrollPane = new JScrollPane(log);

        Container contentPane = getContentPane();
        contentPane.add(sendButton, BorderLayout.NORTH);
        contentPane.add(logScrollPane, BorderLayout.
CENTER);
}
```

Filtering Out the Riff-Raff

After creating the dialog, the Player passes a custom **MultimediaFilter** object to the **addChoosableFileFilter()** method to screen out non-audio files. **JfileDialog** calls the **MultimediaFilter**'s **getDescription()** method to determine the name attached to the filtering method. In this example, we use "Digital Audio", but you can use any descriptive name you wish. The name we return is added to the "files of type" list box in the dialog.

```
filechooser.addChoosableFileFilter(new MultimediaFilter());
```

The core of this class can be found in the **accept(File f)** method. The system retrieves every filename in the directory and passes them to the **MultimediaFilter**'s **accept()** method. If the file is a directory or if it is an audio file, **accept()** returns **true** to indicate that the file should be viewed, else it will reject the file and eliminate it from the view by returning **false**.

Core Tip

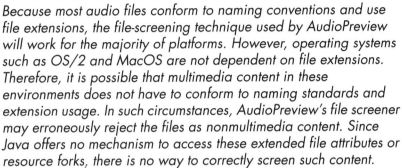

Because most audio files conform to naming conventions and use file extensions, the file-screening technique used by AudioPreview will work for the majority of platforms. However, operating systems such as OS/2 and MacOS are not dependent on file extensions. Therefore, it is possible that multimedia content in these environments does not have to conform to naming standards and extension usage. In such circumstances, AudioPreview's file screener may erroneously reject the files as nonmultimedia content. Since Java offers no mechanism to access these extended file attributes or resource forks, there is no way to correctly screen such content.

Fortunately, the underlying JMF subsystem is not dependent on file extensions to identify files. As we discovered in Chapter 5, **DataSources** *are given the responsibility of analyzing a file. Part of these responsibilities includes returning the* **MIME** *type that represents a file.*

The **MIME** *type lets you know the category that a file belongs to (i.e., audio/wav indicates that the file is a .WAV file). Consequently, you could use the* **MIME** *type to screen out nonaudio files. Unfortunately, to obtain this information, we would have to load each file into a* **DataSource** *and the performance hit incurred would render our dialog extremely sluggish.*

Customizing the View

Besides filtering out files, AudioPreview attaches a special icon to the audio files it recognizes. A **MultimediaFileView()** object is attached to the dialog (see Figure 8-2) via the **JFileChooser's setFileView()** method.

```
filechooser.setFileView(new MultimediaFileView());
```

MultimediaFileView relies on the parent file **FileView** to implement the majority of its methods. However, it is responsible for controlling what icon is associated with a file, so it overrides the **getIcon(File f)** method. If the extension is a known audio file extension (such as .WAV, .au, .MID, or .RMF), it loads an audio icon and returns that icon to the caller. If the extension is unknown, it returns **false** and the default icon is displayed instead.

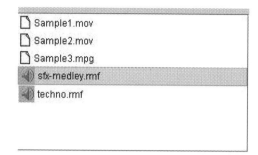

Figure 8-2   View of multimedia icons attached to an audio file.

Audio Sampler

After initializing the file filter and file viewer, the **JMFFileChooser** creates a **MultimediaPreview** object and attaches it to the dialog as an accessory (see Listing 8.2). Since accessories are notified when files become highlighted, it will be used to preview audio content as files become selected.

Listing 8.2 Illustration of attaching a multimedia accessory object.

```
MultimediaPreview mmpreview = new MultimediaPreview(fi-
lechooser);
mmpreview.setLayout( new BorderLayout());
filechooser.setAccessory(mmpreview);
```

Unlike the **MultimediaFileView** and **MultimediaFilter** classes, we specifically store the **MultimediaPreview** object in a local variable, **mmpreview**. This is necessary for two reasons: clean layout of the multimedia components and **Player** cleanup.

We specifically force the accessory to use **BorderLayout** because we may need to add multiple components (i.e., progress Players, Player controls, and visual components) to the accessory. Without the **BorderLayout**, positioning these controls will be difficult. In fact, if you don't use **BorderLayout** with your accessory objects, you may find that JMF components will not behave correctly when added to lightweight components like our dialog (see "Gravity Always Wins" later in this chapter for a discussion of why this occurs).

In addition, a local variable is needed to inform the **MultimediaPreview** object when it should clean up. Since the Java language has no explicit destructor, each object is at the mercy of the garbage collector to deallocate any resources it may have consumed.

For instance, if the user makes a selection and dismisses the **FileDialog**, the **MultimediaPreview** is not notified of this action until the garbage collector decides to destroy it. This becomes problematic if an audio file is being previewed when the dialog is dismissed. Since it is unaware of the dialog's dismissal, the audio file will continue to play and to consume resources on the device.

To avert the potential waste of resources, the **JMFFileChooser** calls the **MultimediaPreview** object's **cleanup()** method to notify it that all resources should be released as the dialog is being dismissed. This **cleanup()** method is not part of the **Jcomponent** interface; rather, it is designed to specifically address multimedia needs.

Core Tip

It is vital that applications that repeatedly open and play files ensure that they close the associated Player object between files. Some JMF runtimes permit multiple audio Players, but eventually, all runtimes exhaust resources and your program will disintegrate.

Do not assume that a Player closes synchronously. New JMF programmers often write a close routine similar to Listing 8.3. Unfortunately, this code is a time bomb waiting to explode.

The Player's **deallocate()** method will throw an exception if it is called when the Player is in **Started** state. Since the **stop** call is asynchronous, you cannot be assured that the Player has left **Started** state until the corresponding **StopEvent** is received. The code in this listing does not wait for this event, and risks calling **deallocate()** before the Player is stopped.

Listing 8.3 JMF code that assumes synchronous operation of stop, close, or deallocate may result in exceptions.

```
if ( player != null )
{
                    player.stop();
                    player.deallocate();
                    player.close();
                    player = null;
                    removeAll();
}
```

Listing 8.4 illustrates the proper procedure for shutting down a device. Note that the **stop()**, **deallocate()**, and **close()** methods wait for their terminating events before proceeding.

Listing 8.4 Properly written shutdown code waits for **StopEvent**, **DeallocateEvent**, and **ControllerClosedEvent** before proceeding.

```
bclosing = true;
bprcoessedevent = false;
beforeTime = System.currentTimeMillis();
player.stop();


synchronized (this )
{
    try
    {
        if ( bprcoessedevent != true )
        {
            wait();
        }
    }
    catch( InterruptedException e)
    {
    }
}

afterTime = System.currentTimeMillis();
System.out.println( "Stop took " + (afterTime - before-
Time) + " ms");


beforeTime = System.currentTimeMillis();
bprcoessedevent = false;
player.deallocate();

synchronized (this )
{
   try
    {
        if ( bprcoessedevent != true )
        {
            wait();
        }
    }
```

Listing 8.4 Properly written shutdown code waits for **StopEvent**, **DeallocateEvent**, and **ControllerClosedEvent** before proceeding.   (continued)

```
        catch( InterruptedException e)
        {
        }
    }
    afterTime = System.currentTimeMillis();
    System.out.println( "Deallocate took " + (afterTime - be-
    foreTime) + " ms");

    beforeTime = System.currentTimeMillis();
    bprcoessedevent = false;
    player.close();

    synchronized (this )
    {
        try
        {
                if ( bprcoessedevent != true )
            {
                wait();
            }
        }
        catch( InterruptedException e)
        {
        }
    }
    afterTime = System.currentTimeMillis();
    System.out.println( "Close took " + (afterTime - before-
    Time) + " ms");

    bclosing = false;
    player = null;

    public void controllerUpdate(ControllerEvent event)
                {
    if (event instanceof ControllerClosedEvent)
    {
        synchronized (this )
        {
            if ( bclosing == true )
            {
                bprcoessedevent = true;
                notify();
            }
```

> **Listing 8.4** Properly written shutdown code waits for **StopEvent**, **DeallocateEvent**, and **ControllerClosedEvent** before proceeding.   (continued)

```
        }


    }
    else if (event instanceof DeallocateEvent)
    {
        synchronized (this )
        {
            if ( bclosing == true )
            {
                bprcoessedevent = true;
                notify();
            }
        }
    }
    else if (event instanceof StopEvent)
    {
        synchronized (this )
        {
            if ( bclosing == true )
            {
                bprcoessedevent = true;
                notify();
            }
        }
    }


}
```

As we discovered in the analysis of AlohaJMF, objects that use JMF should minimize the usage of multimedia functions in their constructor. Consequently, the **MultimediaPreview** objects constructor only sets its preferred display size and attaches a **PropertyChangeListener** to its container.

When it receives a **JFileChooser.SELECTED_FILE_CHANGED_ PROPERTY** event, the object realizes that the user wishes to preview an audio file. Before it can play the file, it calls **ClosePlayer()** to check to see if it is currently previewing another multimedia file. If it is playing another file, it stops playback, releases all resources, and closes the device.

The first time a file is previewed, it can take a while for JMF to load and initialize the corresponding Player. To prevent the user from thinking that the dialog is hung and to keep the user from panicking, we display an empty progress bar before attempting to create the Player. This progress bar will gradually be filled in as we set up and initialize the Player.

Core Tip

It's tricky to construct a URL object from **PropertyChangeEvent***'s* **getNewValue()**. *Unlike an applet, we can't use* **getDocument-Base()** *to supply the necessary protocol for the file. However, we know that we'll always be using the "file:" protocol, since this is a file dialog. As a result, we'll prefix the actual file path with the "file:" protocol and construct the URL with the combined path and protocol.*

After cleaning up stray Players, **MultimediaPreview** retrieves the name of a file via the **PropertyChangeEvent getNewValue()** method. A URL object is constructed from the filename and we request that the Manager create a Player from that URL. If no exceptions are thrown, it is safe to attach a **ControllerListener** (via **addControllerListener()**) to the Player.

Unlike our first applet, we won't issue a **start()** and rely on the Player to implicitly transition itself through **Realized**, **Prefetched**, and **Started** states. Rather, we request that the Player **Realize** (via **realize()**), and manually transition between states by monitoring events in **controllerUpdate()**. Although this is more work, it enables our application to determine when playback starts and offers improved control over **MediaCaching**.

Core Tip

Many JMF programs construct their Players in a try block, but then they attempt to attach a listener to the Player outside the try block. If an exception occurs on Player creation, attaching a listener outside this block generates another exception and no mechanism will catch this error. To avert this situation, never assume that Player creation will succeed; always program defensively.

The **MultimediaPreview** object must retrieve events from two different listeners: **ControllerListener** and **PropertyChangeListener**. Although this situation will occur frequently in moderate to advanced JMF programs, few examples illustrate the syntax for constructing such an object.

Fortunately, the process is not arduous: Simply enumerate each interface you implement, separating each by a comma (see Listing 8.5 for an example).

Listing 8.5 Example of how to implement multiple listeners.

```
implements  PropertyChangeListener, ControllerListener
```

The first event we'll monitor is **RealizeCompleteEvent**. Although we could theoretically add Player controls here, we will delay doing so until the **PrefetchedComplete** event is received. When you're previewing local files, there is no significant difference between the two states. However, if you are playing files off a network or NFS drive, then the Player may take a little while to fill its internal buffers and transition from **Realized** into **Prefetched** state.

If you display Player controls during this intermediate stage, then users may have to wait an indeterminate amount of time before playback commences when they press the Play button. By contrast, once the Player is **prefetched**, we are guaranteed that there is some data to play if the user hits the Play button. Therefore, we will wait until the **Prefetched** state before displaying playback controls to ensure a responsive user interface.

Since the **RealizeCompleteEvent** has been liberated from attaching controls, its only responsibility is to advance the Player into the next state (via **player.prefetch()**). When the **PrefetchComplete** event is received, it is safe to display the controls associated with the Player. So, we retrieve the **ControlPanelComponent** associated with the Player and add it to the **MultimediaPreview** component.

Since we are responsible for state management, we'll advance the Player to **Started** state by calling **player.start()**. Automatically starting playback is not typical for JMF applications with playback controls. These controls imply that the user should dictate when playback should commence. Since **AudioPreview** is an audio previewer, we assume that the user always wants to hear the file when it is selected and automatically play it.

When we encounter the **EndOfMediaEvent** in **controllerUpdate()**, we know that we've successfully finished previewing the file. However, it is possible that the user will want to preview the file again. Therefore, we rewind the file to the beginning (via **setMediaTime(new Time(0))**) when the **EndOfMediaEvent** is received. This prevents the user from manually having to drag back the position slider to the beginning of the file.

Gravity Always Wins

So far, we've arbitrarily restricted **AudioPreview** to previewing audio files. This limitation is contradictory to one of the goals of JMF: seamless support for both audio and video media types.

AudioPreview was originally designed to preview both audio and visual content, and you can easily modify it to support video file formats such as MPEG. However, you'll discover that this video support is extremely unstable and results in odd painting bugs. If you're like most programmers, you'll spend untold hours trying to debug these oddities before you relent and look through the documentation for help. Fortunately, the known issues section of the JMF 1.0.x readme contains the following ominous warning that is paraphrased below:

> *The visual component and the control component struggle with Swing (JFC) because JMF components are heavy and Swing components are light.*

Unfortunately, Sun has understated the magnitude of this problem. Sun's JMFs visual components and Swing not only *do not interact very well*, they are inherently incompatible. For example, visual components paint over Swing buttons and components (see Figures 8.3 and 8.3a).

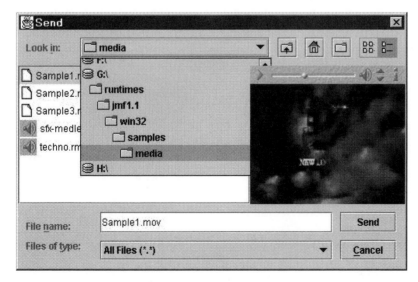

Figure 8-3 A Visual component painting over Swing component. In this illustration, the heavy video windows paints over the lightweight drop-down menu.

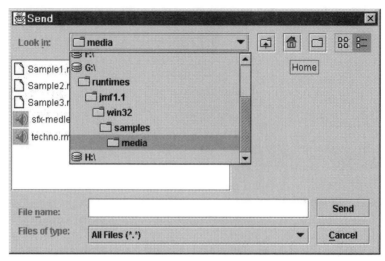

Figure 8–3a Lightweight drop-down menu that is not obstructed by heavy video window.

Although many Players' visual components react violently with Swing, some are relatively stable. For example, Sun's MPEG Player on Win32 resizes and paints correctly inside **AudioPreview** (see Figure 8-4). As a result, if you intend to use JMF and Swing in your projects, be sure to experiment very early in the process to verify the Player's compatibility with Swing.

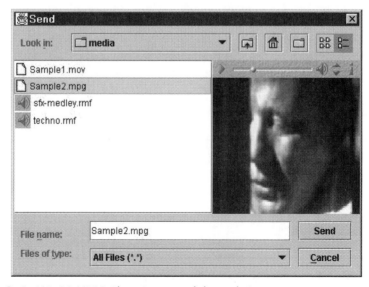

Figure 8–4 Win32 MPEG Player's compatibility with Swing.

These painting and interaction problems arise because JMF's visual components are heavy and Swing's are light. Heavy components have direct access to the native screen resources on the current platform. Since multimedia programs are performance-centric, it is important to have immediate access to these heavy resources.

By contrast, light components own no screen resources and are dependent on their parent for access to screen resources. As a result, light components are smaller and can be written in pure Java. This increases portability at the expense of performance.

Core Tip

The Intel JMF runtimes appear to be more Swing-friendly than Sun's JMF runtimes! All the video Players size and decode correctly and do not cause the artifacts illustrated in Figure 8-4. However, this apparent compatibility is cosmetic. The underlying heavy/light issues still exist with the Intel runtimes.

The conflicting goals for lightweight and heavyweight components have a number of ramifications, the most egregious of which is z-order inversion. Z-order inversion occurs when a heavy component is overlapped by a lightweight component (see Figure 8-5). Painting rules dictate that light components be drawn over heavy components. Unfortunately, since the heavy component draws into its own native window, it obliterates the previously rendered light component and gives the appearance that it is on top of the lightweight component (see Figures 8-5a and 8-5b).

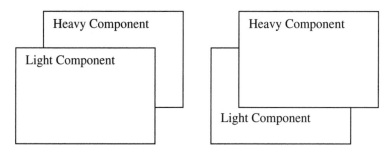

Figure 8–5   Illustration of Z-order problem with heavyweight components. Even though the Light Component (i.e., the details help tip) is conceptually on top of the Heavy Component (playback controls), the Heavy Component paints over the Light Component.

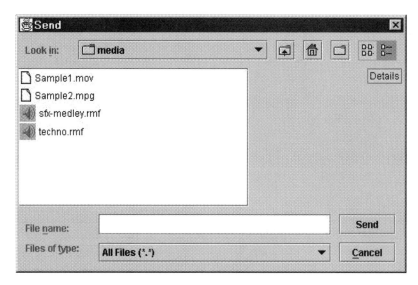

Figure 8–5a   The details help tip in the right corner is visible when no heavy component is present.

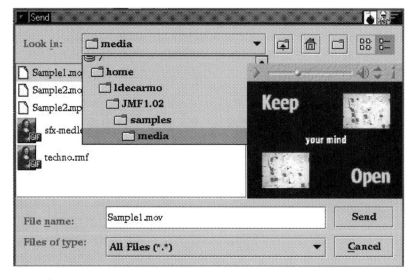

Figure 8–5b   Z inversion.

Sun has a number of recommendations and workarounds when you need to work with a mixture of lightweight and heavyweight components. Unfortunately, most of these workarounds essentially encourage you to minimize the interaction between these two models, and if you ever need to overlap heavy and light controls, there is no solution.

Sun freely admits that they are in a transitional phase between the world of heavy, AWT-based components and light, Swing components. Until they release a runtime that completes this transition, JMF programmers who wish to use Swing will have tremendous difficulty getting these environments to coexist.

Core Tip

Besides carefully positioning your light and heavy components so no overlap occurs, there is no way to overcome this problem. For additional details or workarounds on potential conflicts with heavy and light components, drop by http://java.sun.com/products/jfc/swingdoc-archive/mixing.html.

Monitoring Progress

So far, we've examined **AudioPreview**'s previewing capabilities on fast, local storage. This enables the Player to rapidly retrieve buffers and enter the **Prefetch** state. By contrast, **prefetch** buffers on remote devices must be downloaded over a considerably slower link before a device can enter **prefetch** state. While the device is **Prefetching**, we display a **JprogressBar** to inform the user of the time remaining before download completion.

AudioPreview uses a **JprogressBar** rather than the Player's **ProgressBarComponent** to minimize potential conflicts between the heavy **ProgressBarComponent** and Swing. Fortunately, the **ProgressBarComponent** has utility methods that enable us to synchronize it with the **JprogressBar**. For instance, Listing 8.6 illustrates how you can determine the percentage of content downloaded.

> **Listing 8.6** Sample formula to calculate the percentage of content downloaded. This formula divides the amount downloaded by one percent of the total download amount to determine the percentage of content retrieved.

```
// divide the amount downloaded, by one percent of the to-
tal
// to obtain the total percentage downloaded

long progress = ( cc.getContentProgress() / (cc.getCon-
tentLength()/100));
jmfProgress.setValue((int) progress);
```

The **CachingControl** is an optional interface for a Player, and unfortunately, Sun's Win32 1.0.1 JMF components do not support the **CachingControl** or report **CachingControlEvents**. Even more tragic is the fact that Sun failed to document this limitation in the "known problems" section of the readme document.

This omission is particularly vexing because there is no way to query the Player to see if the **CachingControl** is supported. You simply write the code and pray that the Player reports the **CachingControlEvent** to your **controllerUpdate()** method.

Core Tip

Because Sun's 1.0.1 Win32 JMF runtimes have no support for **CachingControl**s, *you need to use the Intel JMF runtime to develop and test your* **CachingControl** *code. Intel's* **CachingControlEvent** *processing is robust and works for both audio and video Players.*

Since the existence of a **CachingControl** for a given runtime is uncertain, you should not make the **CachingControl** an essential part of your application. Likewise, you should not avoid it entirely out of fear that it will prevent your application from being portable. Rather, you should use the **AudioPreview** programming model for **CachingControlEvent**s: The application can function if no **CachingControlEvent**s are reported, but the user's experience is dramatically enhanced when these events are received.

Souping Up AudioPreview

If you're adventurous, you can change **AudioPreview** from an audio-only viewer to an audio-visual viewer by uncommenting the following line in the **controllerUpdate()** method:

```
// add(AudioPreviewVisual, BorderLayout.CENTER);
```

You will also need to update the **MultimediaFilter** class so that it accepts video file extensions in addition to audio extensions. Adding this line is like opening Pandora's box of heavyweight versus lightweight interaction woes. If you add some intelligence to the **MultimediaFilter** and screen out problematic video files, you can restabilize **AudioPreview**.

Furthermore, if you don't like the fact that playback begins immediately, you can modify the **PrefetchCompleteEvent** to only display the visual components and not issue **player.start()**. This will enable the user to dictate when playback will start.

Summary

Mixing JMF with Swing is like being a scientist during the early phases of nuclear development at Los Alamos. Everyone knows there's a lot of potential, but the risks are great and when things go wrong, a catastrophe may result. These problems are due to the conflicts between light and heavy components.

JMF is a heavy component, and consequently, it has access to native screen resources. By contrast, Swing components are lightweight and dependent on their parent for access to native resources. This conflicting usage of native resources can create painting and other usability issues.

If you carefully control where and how your JMF components interact with Swing controls, you can create useful multimedia-enabled dialogs. However, these workarounds do not alleviate Sun's responsibility to provide subsystems that are stable and compatible. Until Sun delivers these resources, use Swing and JMF with extreme caution.

THE NEXT GENERATION: JAVABEANS AND JMF

To what can I compare this generation? They are like children sitting in the marketplaces and calling out to others: 'We played the flute for you, and you did not dance; we sang a dirge, and you did not mourn.'
Matthew 1:16-17 (NIV)

You know how to interpret the appearance of the sky, but you cannot interpret the signs of the times. A wicked and adulterous generation looks for a miraculous sign, but none will be given it except the sign of Jonah.
Matthew 16:3,4 (NIV)

Generations come and generations go, but the earth remains forever.
Ecclesiastes 1:4 (NIV)

Chapter 9

Object-oriented programs can be divided into two generations: manual and automated. First-generation, or manual, objects require that the programmer read a header file, understand the objects interface, and statically attach the objects to their programs. **AudioPreview** is a typical first-generation application, as you must read its documentation before you can reuse its objects in your program.

By contrast, second-generation objects are wrapped in object models that enable these objects to be dynamically linked to running programs. An object model provides a standardized, language-independent mechanism to interrogate an object and determine its feature set. Therefore, you no longer need to pore over documentation and header files to use an object.

Battle for World Dominance

Two object models dominate the programming landscape: the Component Object Model (COM) and JavaBeans. COM was designed by Microsoft to provide a language-independent mechanism to access and control objects. It provides APIs to query and set object attributes and methods and can be used by C++, Pascal, or BASIC.

Manually creating a COM object is an arduous process. It requires specific linking and naming conventions. If you forget one minor detail, your object is likely to cause an exception deep in the bowels of the COM subsystem when it is constructed. Fortunately, tools such as Visual C++ and Visual Basic provide wizards to create COM objects so you rarely have to create COM objects from scratch.

Although COM initially ran on Win32 platforms, it is not Windows-specific. In fact, Microsoft has partnered with several companies to provide COM support for UNIX platforms. Unfortunately, while COM provides language-independence, its executables are tied to a particular platform. As a result, a Solaris COM object must be recompiled before it can run on AIX or OS/2.

Unlike COM, JavaBeans are platform-neutral. These objects (called beans) can run on any platform supported by a Java VM. Furthermore, Sun used a simple nomenclature for bean creation so you can create them without needing a rapid development tool such as Visual Cafe.

JavaBeans do have one disadvantage: they are not language-neutral. They must be written in Java. However, if you have a pressing need to use another language, you could create a Java shell and call native methods to perform the actual work.

Core Tip

Sun's JavaBeans Bridge for ActiveX enables your JavaBeans to interface with ActiveX objects and applications. This bridge lets Visual Basic and Visual C++ programmers use your JMF-based JavaBeans.

Although object models make programming easier, they add an extra layer of fat that will affect your program. Multimedia applications are particularly sensitive to slowdowns since an extra millisecond of delay may cause audio breakup or video frames to be dropped. Fortunately, both COM and Java-Beans are lean and contain minimal overhead, so their impact is negligible.

COM originated as the object model for Microsoft's Object Linking and Embedding (OLE) API. Since the original incarnations of OLE were slow, COM garnered an undeserved reputation for sluggishness. In reality, COM provides a thin supervisory umbrella to control garbage collection, virtual methods, etc.

JavaBeans provide even less impact on performance since Java already contains garbage collection, abstract methods, and other basic elements.

Therefore, the basic beans class' only responsibility is to inform external applications about the capabilities of the bean.

To illustrate the difference between the programming model for first-generation and second-generation objects, we will create JumpingBean: a JavaBeans-enhanced version of **AudioPreview**.

Trespassing onto a Bean's Property

The first step in creating a Java bean is to determine how external applications will be able to manipulate it. A bean offers three types of external interfaces: properties, methods, and events. Properties are variables that influence the operation of a bean. For instance, a bean that played JMF content could have a **PlaybackDirection** property. If an application modified the **PlaybackDirection** property, the bean might play the content backward.

Applications use specially named methods to change bean properties. To retrieve a property, you call the *getter* method. Similarly, to change a property, you call the *setter* method. Both *getter* and *setter* methods have strict nomenclature. The *getter* method must be named *getPropertyName* or *isPropertyName* for Booleans, and the *setter* method must be called *setPropertyName,* where *PropertyName* is the name of the property the method should change.

Properties can have one of three attributes: read-only, write-only, and read write. Read-only properties have a *getter* method, but no *setter* method so their values can be queried but not changed. By contrast, write-only properties have a *setter* method, but no *getter* method, so you can change their values, but can't request their current value. Finally, read-write properties have both *getter* and *setter* methods.

JumpingBean contains three properties: **IconScreener**, **AutoPreview**, and **VisualDisplayOn** (see Table 9.1). **IconScreener** lets applications control the extensions that will be used as a file mask. If **AutoPreview** is true, playback will begin immediately. If it is false, the user will have to press the *Play* button to initiate playback.

As we discovered in the previous chapter, JMF visual components may react violently with Swing components. Therefore, by default, JumpingBean will not display these visual components. If your JMF runtime cooperates with Swing, the **VisualDisplayOn** property can be used to override this default setting. When it is TRUE, JumpingBean will display the visual component associated with the Player. When it is FALSE, JumpingBean will ignore any visual components it detects.

Table 9.1 JumpingBean's Properties			
Property	*Attribute*	*Type*	*Purpose*
IconScreener	Read-write	String	Specify extensions that should be previewed.
AutoPreview	Read-write	Boolean	Start playback (i.e., preview) without **Play** button.
VisualDisplayOn	Read-write	Boolean	Display visual component when previewing.

Like JMF, beans use events to inform applications when a property changes values. In fact, beans reuse the same **PropertyChangeSupport** object that Swing components use to notify listeners of changes. As a result, you need only implement a single **PropertyChangeListener** interface to monitor Swing and bean events (see Listing 9.1).

Listing 9.1 Illustration of parsing out Swing events and JumpingBean events. You can distinguish between Swing events by examining the **PropertyChangeEvent**'s name.

```
public void propertyChange(PropertyChangeEvent e)
{

   String prop = e.getPropertyName();

   if (prop == JFileChooser.SELECTED_FILE_CHANGED_PROPERTY)
   {
   }
   else if (prop == Jumping-
Bean.AUTO_PREVIEW_CHANGED_PROPERTY)
   {
   }
}
```

The major difference between the Swing and bean event models is that Swing has static functions (i.e., defined in a header file) to add and remove listeners. By contrast, there is no predefined naming convention to attach a listener to a bean. Therefore, you must interrogate the bean to determine the name of the methods used to attach and remove listeners.

Beans enable applications to determine methods, properties, and listeners by exposing a **BeanInfo** class. You can use **getPropertyDescriptors()** to retrieve the bean's properties and **getBeanDescriptor()** to retrieve the parameters and parameter types for the *getter, setter,* and *listener* methods.

Core Tip

We're only going to discuss the basics of bean creation so that we can create a multimedia-enabled bean. If you need more insights into bean development, I suggest that you examine JavaBeans By Example *by Henri Jubin.*

Conflict Between Theory and Reality

Theoretically, you should be able to transform any Java class into a Java bean by renaming the methods that retrieve and modify data to conform to the *getter* and *setter* conventions. However, we're going to make more extensive changes when we morph **AudioPreview** into JumpingBean. These modifications are necessary because **AudioPreview** has a cumbersome external interface, and it doesn't exploit the bean interface.

AudioPreview shows you how to fold multimedia classes into existing applications and was not meant to be reused by external applications. It forces all output into a **Jframe**, routes all output into a text area, and requires that the user press a button to display the enhanced **JfileChooser** dialog.

While these limitations are acceptable for a dedicated application, multimedia beans should be usable with any program and should not enforce a specific look and feel on the client application. Therefore, to ensure flexibility, JumpingBean directly subclasses the **JfileChooser** and jettisons the frame, text area, and button baggage encumbering **AudioPreview**.

The second reason for modifying **AudioPreview** is to add *getter* and *setter* methods to manipulate the three JumpingBean properties: **IconScreener**, **AutoPreview**, and **VisualDisplayOn**. Furthermore, we must integrate these properties into the core functions of all objects so that any changes to a given property instantly affect the operation of JumpingBean.

Flexibility Is Key

The majority of the code changes reside in the **JumpingBean** class. This class is based on the **JMFFileChooser** class used by **AudioPreview**. However, it subclasses **JfileChooser** rather than **Jframe**. Since Jumping-Bean provides the same interfaces as **JfileChooser**, anyone familiar with **JfileChooser** can drop this bean into their program and be productive.

Because it not a frame, we no longer need a **JtextArea**, **Jbutton**, or **ActionListener** for the button. Furthermore, since we are subclassing **JfileChooser**, we'll eliminate the **JfileChooser** member variable as well.

AudioPreview enforced the rule that when the *Send* button was pressed, a **JfileChooser** was displayed. However, beans cannot make assumptions like this. Rather, they must be able to control when a dialog will appear. As a result, we override the **showDialog()** method.

When the application calls **showDialog()**, we call the parent **JfileChooser** dialog. When the parent completes, our class regains control and we can clean up the multimedia resources we allocated. This technique is cleaner than the approach used by **AudioPreview**, since the bean controls when resources are released. By contrast, **AudioPreview** burdens the application with the responsibility of detecting when the dialog is finished and cleaning up as appropriate.

Three new variables have been added to JumpingBean to enable the new properties: **AutoPreview**, **VisualDisplayOn**, and **IconScreener**. **AutoPreview** and **VisualDisplayOn** are Booleans which control if playback will begin immediately or if a visual component will be used, respectively (see Table 9.1 for additional details on these variables). **IconScreener** uses a more complex data structure—an array of strings. Each index in the array is a file extension that JumpingBean should use in the file-screening process.

The *getter* and *setter* methods for these variables are oriented toward bean users. However, member classes, such as the **MultimediaFilter** and **MultimediaPreview** classes, will call these methods to determine the status of each property.

Core Tip

JumpingBean lets member classes query getter methods to determine the value of properties. An alternative solution would be to have these subclasses add a property change listener to JumpingBean so they can be notified when properties change. The listener alternative has the best performance since it prevents the subclass from having to poll for property changes.

JumpingBean customizes **JfileChooser** just like **AudioPreview**. The **MultimediaFilter** class is used as a file mask. The **Multimedia-FileView** class is responsible for associating icons with known multimedia content, and **MultimediaPreview** gives the user a preview of the file.

No changes to **MultimediaFileView** are necessary since its duties are the same for both **AudioPreview** and JumpingBean: display multimedia icons. By contrast, **MultimediaFilter** contains significant changes. First, the constructor must be modified to pass in a handle to the parent bean. We'll use this handle to access the bean's **IconScreener** property.

Second, rather than using constant extension strings such as 'wav' or 'au', this class retrieves an array of file extensions from the parent bean (each extension is stored in a string). It then attempts to match the current file extension with one of the bean's extensions (see Listing 9.2). If there's a match, we let the dialog display the file by returning TRUE; otherwise, we return FALSE and prevent the extension from being displayed.

Listing 9.2 Using parent properties to determine acceptable file extensions.

```
String[] extensions = bean.getIconScreener();

for ( int loop = 0; loop < extensions.length; loop++ )
{

    if (extensions[loop].equals(extension) )
    {
            bFound = true;
    }

}
```

Core Tip

Although we made no changes to the **MultimediaFileView** *class, some applications may want to control the icons associated with a file extension. To experiment with adding properties to a bean, you can add a new property to JumpingBean that enables programmers to control file extension icons. Once you've made these changes, drop by ftp://ftp.prenhall.com/pub/ptr/ unix_and_enabling_technologies.w-0481deCarmo and compare your modifications with a version of JumpingBean that has this additional property.*

Outpatient Surgery for MultimediaPreview

Very few changes are necessary to bean-enable **MultimediaPreview**. First, we must modify the constructor to accept a **JumpingBean** rather than a **JfileChooser**. Since **JumpingBean** is a superclass of **JfileChooser**, any code dependent on **JfileChooser** will continue to work.

Second, the handling of the **prefetch** event in **ControllerListener** (a.k.a., **controllerUpdate()**) must be altered. When this event is received, the listener queries the *getter* method for the parent bean's **AutoPreview** property. If **AutoPreview** is true, the user wants us to preview the file immediately, so we call the Player's **start()** method (see Listing 9.3). If **AutoPreview** is false, we leave the Player in **prefetch** state.

> **Listing 9.3** How **MultimediaPreview** modifies its behavior based on a bean's AutoPreview property.

```
if ( jumpingbean.isAutoPreview() )
{
    player.start();
}
```

Similarly, if the **VisualDisplayOn** property is true, we add the visual component to the chooser dialog (see Listing 9.4).

> **Listing 9.4** The **VisualDisplayOn** property dictates whether **MultimediaPreview** will show a visual component in the file dialog.

```
if ( alohaGUI != null && jumpingbean.isVisualDisplayOn() )
{
        add(alohaGUI, BorderLayout.CENTER);
}
```

Information Booth

Each bean must surface a **SimpleBeanInfo** class, and we use the **JumpingBeanBeanInfo** class to fulfill this requirement. **JumpingBeanBean-**

Info surfaces three properties in the **getPropertyDescriptors()**
method: **iconScreener**, **autoPreview**, and **visualDisplayOn** (see
Listing 9.5).

Each **PropertyDescriptor** object alerts the caller to the name of the
property and the corresponding *getter* and *setter* methods. If a particular
property does not support a *getter* or *setter* method, you can substitute
NULL for the method.

PropertyDescriptor.setBound() lets the caller know that when a
property is modified, the property change listener will be called with the new
value.

Listing 9.5 How **JumpingBeanBeanInfo** implements the
getPropertyDescriptors() method.

```
public PropertyDescriptor[] getPropertyDescriptors()
{
        try
        {
                PropertyDescriptor iconScreener = new Property-
Descriptor("iconScreener",beanClass, "getIconScreen-
er","setIconScreener");
                PropertyDescriptor autoPreview = new Property-
Descriptor("autoPreview",beanClass, "isAutoPreview","setAu-
toPreview");
                autoPreview.setBound(true);
                PropertyDescriptor visualDisplayOn = new Prop-
ertyDescriptor("visualDisplayOn",beanClass, "isVisualDis-
playOn","setVisualDisplayOn");
                visualDisplayOn.setBound(true);
                PropertyDescriptor[] rv = {
                        iconScreener
                        ,autoPreview
                        ,visualDisplayOn
                };
                return rv;
        }
        catch (IntrospectionException e)
        {
                throw new Error(e.toString());
        }
}
```

The last step in the bean development process is to package all of the class
files into a JAR file. A visual development environment such as Visual Café
will package the JAR file for you automatically. If you are a command line
junkie, JAR files can be constructed by hand.

First, you'll need to create a manifest file similar to the one below (it is called **jumpingbean.mf** in our illustration):

```
Manifest-Version: 1.0


Name: mmbean/JumpingBean.class
Java-Bean: True
```

Second, you'll need to run **jar.exe** (or **jar** on UNIX) to bundle the files into a logical bundle. Be sure that your manifest file indicates that **JumpingBean.class** is a bean, or other applications will not be able to find it inside the jar.

```
jar cfm jumpingbean.jar jumpingbean.mf mmbean
```

The *c* option causes the jar utility to create the file, *f* lets you give the jar file a name (i.e., **jumpingbean.jar**), *m* specifices that there will be a manifest file used to describe the contents of the **jumpingbean.jar** file, and *mmbean* is the directory that contains our classes.

The Joys of Testing

After you've completed bean development, you can use the BeanBox to test it (see Figure 9-1). The BeanBox is the core tool provided by the Bean Development Kit. It stresses every interface surfaced by your bean. For example, it queries all **BeanInfo** classes to determine properties, methods, and events supported by the bean. It then displays the default or customized **PropertyEditor** associated with each property. These editors can be used to modify bean settings as the bean is running.

To test JumpingBean with the BeanBox, you'll need to load the **JumpingBean.jar** file. If you place **JumpingBean.jar** in the **jars** subdirectory of wherever you installed your Bean Development Kit, BeanBox will load it automatically. You can also choose the *Load Jar* option under BeanBox *File* menu to load **JumpingBean.jar** manually.

Core Tip

*While developing your bean, you should load it manually rather than placing it in the **jars** subdirectory of the Bean Development Kit. Because your bean is in its formative stages, it probably has* *bugs that generate exceptions. These exceptions will be thrown each time the BeanBox is started, since it automatically loads every JAR file in the* **jars** *directory. Although BeanBox gracefully catches exceptions, the debug output and error dialogs are annoying.*

If you load the JAR file manually, the error messages will still be displayed, but at least they won't be shown if you use the BeanBox for other development or testing purposes.

Once the JAR file is processed, click on it with the mouse. BeanBox instantiates it and displays our multimedia-enhanced file dialog. In addition, it shows all modifiable properties for the dialog in a separate window. Although we surfaced only three properties, the BeanBox fills this window with over a dozen properties. This inconsistency is "the fault" of JumpingBean's parent class: the **JfileChooser**.

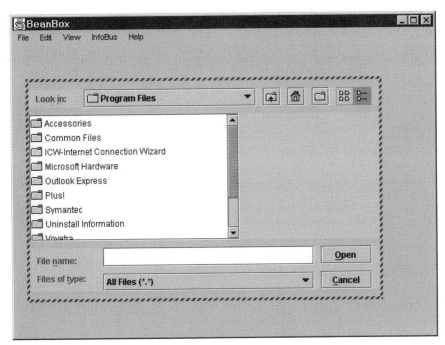

Figure 9–1 BeanBox displaying JumpingBean properties.

Since many of the **JFileChooser** methods follow the bean naming convention for *getter* and *setter* methods, the BeanBox correctly assumes that it can manipulate dialog features (or properties) via these methods. As a result, many of the features you can change programmatically can also be modified via a **PropertyEditor**.

Core Tip

*If a property is a primitive type (i.e., and **int**, **bool**, **float** etc.), the BeanBox provides a default **PropertyEditor**, so the user can change the property with a GUI element. If a property is not a primitive type, the bean should surface a custom **PropertyEditor** if it wishes external applications to modify the properties value.*

Core Tip

*The BeanBox application is not JMF-enabled. Consequently, you will need to add the JMF **.JAR** file to the **CLASSPATH** used to start it. If you fail to modify the batch file (or UNIX equivalent), it will spew out the following incomprehensible error message when you try to load JumpingBean:*

```
WARNING: Could not instantiate bean "mmbean.Jumping-
Bean" from JAR "jumpingbeans.jar"

But were unable to load the class "mmbean.Jumping-
Bean" because of

java.lang.NoClassDefFoundError

java.lang.NoClassDefFoundError
```

*This error is Java's attempt to inform you that it is unable to locate the JMF libraries, and it will happen even if you have correctly set up the **CLASSPATH** environment variable for JMF support. It occurs because the batch file overwrites the **classpath** with its own settings.*

*See Chapter 2 for detailed instructions on setting up the **CLASSPATH** environment variable and the **classpath** command line option.*

Summary

Object models provide the infrastructure so programs can dynamically discover and use objects. Sun's JavaBean is a Java-flavored object model that allows applications to inspect any object (bean). Each bean has three attributes: properties, methods, and events.

Properties modify the behavior of a bean. You can change a property by calling a special bean method called a *setter*. Similarly, the current value of a property can be retrieved by calling a *getter* method. Beans can also notify you when a property changes values by sending an event to listeners.

One significant advantage of this object model is that virtually any Java class can become a bean if it uses the correct naming convention for property controls. In fact, JavaBeans imposes so few rules, we were able to turn the **AudioPreview** application into a bean with minimal hassle.

Now that we've created a powerful bean, it's time to figure out how you can use it in non-Java applications.

GOING NATIVE

The savage and the civilised man differ so much
in the bottom of their hearts and in their inclinations, that what constitutes the supreme happi-
ness of one would reduce the other to despair.
The former breathes only peace and liberty; he
desires only to live and be free from labour;
even the ataraxia of the Stoic falls far short of
his profound indifference to every other object.
Civilised man, on the other hand, is always
moving, sweating, toiling and racking his
brains to find still more laborious occupations:
he goes on in drudgery to his last moment, and
even seeks death to put himself in a position to
live, or renounces life to acquire immortality.

**Jean Jacques Rousseau, _A Discourse on the
Origin of Inequality_, 1754**

'And it is I, Raksha [The Demon], who answers.
The man's cub is mine, Lungri–mine to me! He
shall not be killed. He shall live to run with the
Pack and to hunt with the Pack; and in the end,
look you, hunter of little naked cubs–frog-eater–
fish-killer–he shall hunt thee!'

Rudyard Kipling, _The Jungle Book_

Chapter 10

T he Java Native Interface (JNI) lets you exploit platform-specific features that are not available inside the Java Virtual Machine. Only the most experienced programmers should use JNI because of its lack of portability. [Sun JNI Web site, http://java.sun.com/docs/books/tutorial/native.1/index.html]

If Sun's goal in posting this warning about the JNI on its Web site was to scare away casual Java programmers from accessing their Java classes from external languages such as C, they were successful. Despite this forbidding statement, you do not need to be a C guru to access Java from non-Java programs. In fact, anyone with rudimentary C experience can quickly add Java support with just a few lines of code.

Although Java and the JMF are the best solutions for cross-platform development, there are a number of situations where you will need to access JMF objects from legacy C code. For example, if you previously wrote a monstrous Win32 or UNIX application and you don't want to rewrite it in Java. However, you need to add JumpingBean-type functionality to the program (i.e., previewing multimedia files). Since we've already written JumpingBean, it is ludicrous to recreate a native version of this object. Rather, it would be easier to create a bridge between your application and JumpingBean.

Core Tip

The original JDK 1.0 Native Method Interface had serious limitations. Its major advantage was that it permitted you to attach native methods to a class to access functionality that Java didn't provide. Unfortunately, the interfaces it used were not portable between VMs and it offered minimal control over a VM by external application. As a result, Sun was forced to create JNI.

Additional technical details on the comparison between JNI and the JDK 1.0 Native Method Interface can be found in the Essential Java Native Interface or on Sun's Web site:

http://java.sun.com/products/jdk/1.2/docs/guide/jni/ spec/intro.doc.html#16230

Fortunately, this bridge is easy to create with the JNI. JNI not only enables you to write native methods for Java classes, but you can actually launch the JVM and create Java threads from within your native program (see Figure 10-1). Furthermore, the same JNI program or utilities can work with any JNI-compliant VM.

We will exploit JNI to create BeanBridge: a C++ program that uses JumpingBean to display a dialog and retrieves the selected file from JumpingBean.

Core Tip

The syntax used in BeanBridge is specific to C++. If you need to port this code to C, you'll need to replace **env->** with **(*env)->** and add "**env**" as the first parameter with functions that begin with **env->**.

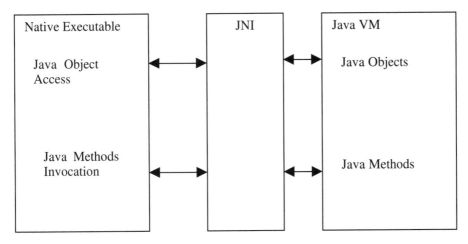

Figure 10-1 Diagram of how native programs interact with the JNI subsystem. All access to Java methods and objects must be done through JNI.

Preparing the Natives

To use the JNI in your C programs, you need to include **<jni.h>** in your programs and add the Java **include** directory to your compiler's include path. After you've compiled it, Win32 users should link with **javai.lib** to access the JVM libraries. UNIX users should link with **libjava.so**. Since the JNI API is identical for all operating systems with a C compiler, Bean-Bridge should recompile and run anywhere Java does.

The first thing BeanBridge does is call **JNI_GetDefaultJava-VMInitArgs()**. This causes the VM to fill a structure (**JDK1_1Init-Args**) with default values that will later be used to initialize the VM. This data structure includes a plethora of features such as the stack size the VM will use and whether the VM should enable debugging. However, the only field that we care about is **JDK1_1InitArgs.classpath**.

The VM will use the directories specified in the **classpath** field as the locations to search when it needs to load a .class file. Since different revisions of the 1.x VM will return widely ranging values in the **class-**

path field, the safest technique is to concatenate only the libraries you specifically need (or the paths necessary to load your current class) to the **JDK1_1InitArgs.classpath** field (see Listing 10.1).

Listing 10.1 Illustration of tacking on the necessary JMF and Swing paths to the VM's **classpath**.

```
strcat(vm_args.classpath,  ";f:\\books\\JMF\\jumping-
beans\\jumpingbeans.jar;e:\\runtimes\\swing-1.1beta2\\SWIN-
GALL.JAR;e:\\win32app\\JMF1.0\\lib\\jmf.jar;");


        res = JNI_CreateJavaVM(&jvm,&env,&vm_args);
```

Once you've initialized the **JDK1_1InitArgs.classpath** field, it is safe to create a VM with the **JNI_CreateJavaVM()** call. If this call succeeds, the next step is to load the JavaBeans class with **FindClass()**. **FindClass()** expects a fully-qualified classname, so you must prefix the JumpingBean class with its containing package, **mmbean**.

```
loadercls = env->FindClass("mmbean/JumpingBean");
```

Core Tip

*When you load a class in the Java interpreter from the command line, the '.' and the '/' characters are interchangeable (i.e., **mmbean/JumpingBean** is equivalent to **mmbean.JumpingBean**). Unfortunately, this is not true with **FindClass()**. It expects package elements to be separated with '/'. If you use the '.', the call will fail, and you will not be informed about the true cause of the failure.*

*Should **FindClass()** fail, ensure that you are using '/' and that the class can be found in the **classpath** specified by **JDK1_1InitArgs.classpath** variable. These are the two primary mistakes that cause problems with **FindClass()**.*

Before we can use the **JumpingBean** class, we must construct a new instance of the class. Therefore, we search for the **<init>** method via **Get-**

MethodID and, once we find it, we construct it with the **NewObject()** call (see Listing 10.2).

Listing 10.2 Calling the **JumpingBean** constructor.

```
mid = env->GetMethodID(loadercls, "<init>", "()V");
if (mid == 0)
{
            fprintf(stderr, "Can't find JumpingBean con-
structor\n");
            exit(1);

cls = (jclass) env->NewObject( loadercls, mid);
```

Core Tip

When you obtain an object from the VM, that object is valid only for the requesting thread. If your application uses multiple threads, you need to call **NewGlobalRef()** *to give other C++ threads access to that resource. If you fail to use* **NewGlobalRef()**, *the garbage collector may eliminate the object in question while a C++ thread is trying to use it.*

```
Static jobject crossThreadReference;


cls = (jclass) env->NewObject( loadercls, mid);

crossThreadReference = env->NewGlobalRef( obj );
```

To detect if **JumpingBean** successfully selected a file, we must compare its return value with **JFileChooser.APPROVE_OPTION**, a constant **int** from the **JfileChooser** class. The Java compiler can resolve this static variable at compile time, so it is easy and efficient to use it (see Listing 10.3). By contrast, the C++ compiler is oblivious of the **JfileChooser** and any constants it might contain. Therefore, we have to load this class at runtime and dynamically retrieve the **APPROVE_OPTION** variable (see Listing 10.4).

Listing 10.3 Java code to detect the return value.

```
if (returnVal == JFileChooser.APPROVE_OPTION)
{
        File file = filechooser.getSelectedFile();
        log.append("Sending file: " + file.getName() + "."
+ newline);
}
else
{
        log.append("Send command cancelled by user." + new-
line);
}
```

Unfortunately, the process to retrieve a static variable is tedious. First, you need to retrieve the Java-based **fieldID** object associated with the static **APPROVE_OPTION** variable via **GetStaticFieldID()**. Then you translate this Java object into a C++ integer by using **GetStaticIntField()**. This value can be compared to the return code of **JumpingBean**'s **show-dialog()** method to determine if a file was selected.

Listing 10.4 C++ code to retrieve constant field from **JfileChooser** class.

```
    jclass filechooser = env->FindClass("com/sun/java/
swing/JFileChooser");

    if (filechooser == 0)
    {
        fprintf(stderr, "Can't find base filechooser
class\n");
        exit(1);
    }

    jfieldID approvefield = env->GetStaticFieldID( fi-
lechooser, "APPROVE_OPTION", "I");


    jint success = env->GetStaticIntField( filechooser,
approvefield );

    env->DeleteLocalRef( filechooser );
```

Core Tip

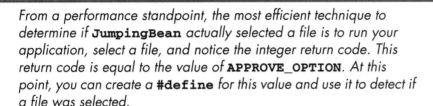

From a performance standpoint, the most efficient technique to determine if **JumpingBean** *actually selected a file is to run your application, select a file, and notice the integer return code. This return code is equal to the value of* **APPROVE_OPTION**. *At this point, you can create a* **#define** *for this value and use it to detect if a file was selected.*

The only drawback to this approach is that your program will break should Sun ever redefine the value associated with **JFileChooser.APPROVE_OPTION**. *However, this scenario is unlikely, as changing* **JFileChooser.APPROVE_OPTION** *would break shipping Java applications.*

If your only concern is performance, you may want to use this approach. If you need to create a robust program, dynamically loading the class and querying the value of the variable in question is preferable, since it is portable and always guaranteed to work.

Although the **JumpingBean** constructor creates file filter and previewer objects, you must call the **showOpenDialog()** method to display the dialog (see Listing 10.5). It is essential that you store the return code returned by **JumpingBean**, since it is the only mechanism you have to establish if it successfully detected a file.

Core Tip

In general, if you mix Java and C code, you should be sure not to access native multimedia resources from the native code (i.e., don't access a native API such as DirectShow and JMF simultaneously). On a few operating systems, you can safely interweave JMF calls with native multimedia calls. However, on the majority of platforms, it is not safe to intermix JMF and native multimedia calls and the results will vary from harmless error messages generated to exceptions being thrown.

Listing 10.5 Showing the `JumpingBean` dialog.

```
mid = env->GetMethodID(loadercls, "showOpenDialog", "(Lja-
va/awt/Component;)I");

if (mid == 0)
{
    fprintf(stderr, "Can't find showOpenDialog method\n");
    exit(1);
}

jint result = ( jint) env->CallObjectMethod( cls, mid,
cls);
```

`JumpingBean` indicates that the user has selected a file, we must pull this name from the `Jfilechooser` object. The Java code to do this is trivial, just use the **File** object from `JfileChooser.getSelectedFile()` and convert it to a string via **File.getName()** (see Listing 10.6).

Listing 10.6 Java code to retrieve selected filename from a `JfileChooser` object.

```
File file = filechooser.getSelectedFile();
          String filename =  file.getName() ;
```

Unfortunately, this task is more arduous in C++. First, you must get the file object from **JfileChooser**. Then you need to convert this object into a class via **GetObjectClass()**. You can then get a Java string via the class' **getName()** method. Finally, this string must be converted into a conventional null-terminated C string by the **GetStringUTFChars()** call (see Listing 10.7). At this point, we can finally print out the filename that the user selected.

Listing 10.7 C++ routine to convert `JfileChooser` file object into a C++ string.

```
jobject fileobj = (jobject) env->CallObjectMethod( cls,
mid );

if ( fileobj == 0 )
{
```

> **Listing 10.7** C++ routine to convert **JfileChooser** file object into a
> C++ string. (continued)

```cpp
    fprintf(stderr, "Can't get filename\n");
    exit(1);
}

jclass fileobjClass = env-> GetObjectClass( fileobj);

if ( fileobjClass == 0 )
{
    fprintf(stderr, "Can't get filename\n");
    exit(1);
}

mid = env->GetMethodID(fileobjClass, "getName", "()Ljava/
lang/String;");

if (mid == 0)
{
  fprintf(stderr, "Can't get filename\n");
  exit(1);
}

jstring jfilename = (jstring) env->CallObjectMethod( file-
obj, mid );


jboolean iscopy;

const char *javastr = env->GetStringUTFChars(jfilename,
&iscopy);

fprintf(stdout, "Selected file %s", javastr );
```

Core Tip

*There is a hidden danger when you call Java methods from C++:
poor performance. It is considerably slower to use Java methods in
C++ than if you call the same method from native Java code.
Furthermore, allocating Java objects inside C++ is very expensive.
Therefore, it is essential that you optimize your code to minimize
accessing routines in the Java VM.*

*One technique you can use to improve performance is to unroll
object allocation outside a loop. The two listings below perform the*

*same function, but since the **jstring** object is created outside the loop, the second version is almost twice as fast on Win32 platforms.*

Listing 10.8 Illustration of poor coding, since **String** object is allocated each time inside a loop.

```
for ( int loop = 0; loop < 1000; loop++ )
{
        jstring jfilename = (jstring) env->CallObject-
Method( fileobj, mid, env->NewStringUTF("data string")
);
}
```

Listing 10.9 Illustration of efficient coding. **String** object is allocated outside of the loop, resulting in superior performance.

```
jstring datastring = env->NewStringUTF("data string")
for ( int loop = 0; loop < 1000; loop++ )
{
        jstring jfilename = (jstring) env->CallObject-
Method( fileobj, mid, datastring);
}
```

Before our application terminates, we must release the resources we have acquired. Unlike Java programs that rely on a built-in garbage collector to free resources, there is no one to clean up after any mess we create in the C++ world. If we fail to release these resources, we will create a memory leak, and ultimately, if the leak is large enough, we will cause the VM and/or the host machine to run out of virtual memory.

Core Tip

*To give you some control over the operation of Java's garbage collector and prevent rampant memory leaks, you can define a native **finalize()** method in any Java class. **finalize()** offers us the opportunity to clean up any leaks before an object* *terminates. Unfortunately, you can't use* **finalize()** *to fix any leaks in BeanBridge, since BeanBridge exists outside the scope of a C++ class.*

Summary

Although virtually anyone can use JNI to launch a Java VM, it is nontrivial to manipulate Java objects and there is a performance penalty for accessing Java resources. Still, there are circumstances where you must interface Java and C or C++ code.

If you add JMF functionality to your C programs, be sure you don't mix JMF and native multimedia calls. Furthermore, you should carefully scrub your native source to ensure that you aren't utilizing Java resources in performance-sensitive areas of the code. If you access JMF calls judiciously inside your C or C++ source, it is possible to marry modern JMF functionality into legacy native code.

Now that we've put the final touches on accessing Java from native code, we will return to a pure Java topic: synchronization.

THE ART OF SYNCHRONIZATION

Amid the turmoil and tumult of battle, there may be seeming disorder and yet no real disorder at all; amid confusion and chaos, your array may be without head or tail, yet it will be proof against defeat

Sun Tzu, *The Art of War*

Hiding order beneath the cloak of disorder is simply a question of subdivision...

Sun Tzu, *The Art of War*

Chapter 11

S   ynchronization is the process of ensuring that two or more media
     streams are presented at the exact time specified by the author of the
     content. Humans expect audio-visual actions to happen simultaneously,
     and the human eye is not tolerant of content that is presented out of
sync. For example, many people become disconcerted during Kung Fu movies
when the actors' mouths move, but no audio is heard for several seconds.

Robust synchronization is the factor that differentiates serious multimedia
environments from multimedia toys, and it should include both intrafile and
cross-stream synchronization. Intrastream refers to the ability to ensure that
all streams within a given multimedia file are synchronized. Typical intrastream responsibilities include ensuring that the audio and video content in a
movie file are played in sync.

Cross-Stream

In the analog realm, synchronization entails displaying a signal as it is received.
However, synchronizing digital content on a computer is considerably more
complex. Digital media must be retrieved from an external source and decompressed. In addition, unless you're running on a real-time operating system,
you can never be sure when your thread will run or how many time slices it
will have when it does run.

These factors prevent decoders from operating at full speed, and eventually, the audio and/or video decoders fall behind (or get out of sync). Thus, the actual synchronization process involves algorithms to detect when a given stream falls behind and techniques to restore it to the proper presentation time if it gets out of sync.

Typically, one stream is chosen as the master stream, and all other streams are slaves. The slave streams synchronize their clocks to the master's clock. As a result, the master stream should be reliable and never drift. Typically, audio is chosen as the master stream because it is driven by an external hardware clock and because synchronizing audio to another clock involves a complicated process called interpolation (see tip below).

Core Tip

Audio synchronization is far more complex than video synchronization. Video compression algorithms normally have reference points in the stream where the decoder can safely jump to and begin decoding. The same technique is not possible with audio because jumping over arbitrary sections of audio will result in audible pops.

To avert these pops, a technique called interpolation is used to smoothly transition from one point in an audio file to another (see Figure 11-1).

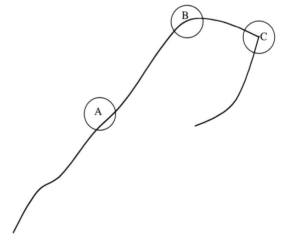

Figure 11-1   Illustration of interpolation. In this example, at time A, the algorithm is told that it should be at time B in the wave file. Rather than jumping to point B and causing a pop, the algorithm gradually transitions from point A to point C.

Crude synchronization techniques cause a video decoder to immediately jump to a future point in time when the system detects that it has fallen behind the master clock. In fact, if the delta (or difference) between the two clocks is minimal, the user will not notice if a frame or two is dropped. However, if there is a substantial difference between the clocks, advancing over a large number of frames will cause a video to appear choppy. As a result, sophisticated video synchronization algorithms smoothly transition to the master clock's time by gradually skipping frames.

Clearing Up Time

JMF accomplishes synchronization by leveraging the capabilities of the Player's **Clock** interface. As we previously discovered, a clock's **MediaTime** starts and stops with the presentation. By contrast, its **TimeBase** is an uninterruptible flow of time from a specific starting point and it enables the clock to map a media-specific time to a media-independent time source. As a result, if two or more clocks use the same **TimeBase**, they have a common denominator of time which can be used for synchronization purposes (see Figure 11-2).

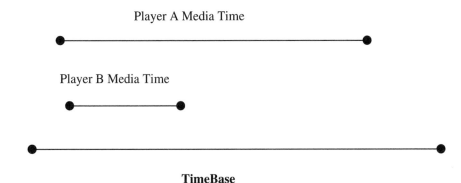

Figure 11-2 Synchronization of multiple Players with one **TimeBase**.

JMF lets you create a common time base between players via the **Clock**'s **setTimeBase()** method. Before you can use this API, you must determine which Player will contain the master clock for synchronization purposes. Once you have a master device, **setTimeBase()** informs slave Players of the **TimeBase** with which they should synchronize.

Just as a clock can reject rate requests other than 1.0, a clock can refuse to modify its **TimeBase** by throwing an **IncompatibleTimeBase** exception. For example, if a Player is attached to a **Push** data source, its clock must be the master and it cannot use a different **TimeBase**. This rule is enforced since **Push** data sources continuously transmit content and this data transmission is intimately tied to the **TimeBase**. Listing 11.1 illustrates how you can gracefully deal with clocks that reject requests to change their **TimeBase**.

Listing 11.1 Ensuring two **Controllers** use the same **TimeBase**.

```
try
{
    controllerA.setTimeBase( controllerB.getTimeBase() );
    System.out.println("Controller A supports B's time-
base...");
}
catch (IncompatibleTimeBaseException e   )
{
    try
    {
        System.out.println("Controller A refused B's Time-
Base");
        controllerB.setTimeBase( controllerA.getTimeBase()
);
        System.out.println("but Controller B supports A's
timebase...");

    }
    catch(IncompatibleTimeBaseException e)
    {
        throw new IncompatibleTimeBaseException("We give
up! Neither clock will cooperate!");
    }

}
```

Delving into Synchronization Details

Once you've created a common **TimeBase**, you may become overwhelmed at the complexity of controlling a synchronized Player. Synchronized Players require you to monitor multiple **ControllerListeners**, synchronize Player states, track Player latencies, and dole out API calls to subordinate Players.

The first requirement to enable synchronization is to implement the **ControllerListener** interface for each Player. Previously, this interface was used to monitor the state transitions for a single Player. Not only must you monitor the state transition events for each synchronized Player, but you'll also need to write some supervisory code to determine the overall states for all the Players.

This supervisory code is responsible for examining the transition events for each Player and deciding when an actual state transition occurs. Even though an individual Player sends an event, the synchronized Player does not enter that state until all subordinate Players have sent that event (see Figure 11-3). For instance, if one Player sends the **Realized** event, the synchronized Player remains in **Realizing** state until all players have sent the **Realized** event.

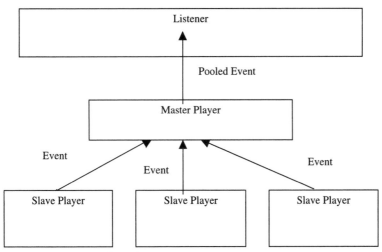

Figure 11-3 Overview of pooling events.

Synchronized Players also must have identical media times and rates. If all the Players are in **Stopped** state, you should issue the **setMediaTime()** call on each Player and then **prefetch()** each Player.

Once a synchronized Player is started, things become more complex. As we discovered, Players relax the **Controller**'s restrictions on the APIs that can be used in **Started** state. Unfortunately, these restrictions return when you use a synchronized Player. As a result, not only must you stop each Player, but you must issue the appropriate command (**setRate()** or **set-MediaTime()**) to each Player.

Synchronized Players also require meticulous control over latency or a Player will be rendered nonfunctional. Before starting a Player, you should call **getStartLatency()** to determine the maximum latency for each Player. **syncstart()** should then be issued on each Player with the maximum latency of the slowest Player plus a small time buffer to account for unforeseen circumstances or variations in execution speed. If you fail to account for this worst-case latency, individual Players will start at different times. This will make synchronization impossible, since synchronization requires a common starting time for all players.

Listing 11.2 Illustration of calculating maximum delay of slowest Player before starting.

```
private void startManagedControllers()
    {
        Vector notify = null;

        // grab a copy of the controller list...
        synchronized ( handler )
        {
            notify = (Vector) handler.controllers.clone();
            handler.numstarted = 0;
        }


        int numevents = notify.size();
        if ( numevents > 0 )
        {
            // we will keep track of the total latency
time for all
slave
controllers
            // we'll start each controller with the max la-
tency to
ensure they all
start at the
            // same time.....
            Time maxLatency = new Time ( 0 );


            for ( int loop = 0; loop < numevents; loop++ )
            {
                // get the controller
                Controller tempController = (Controller)
notify.elementAt( loop
);

                // get the start up latency time for
the controller
                Time slaveLatency = tempController.get-
StartLatency();

                // check to see if this controller knows
its latency AND
```

Listing 11.2 Illustration of calculating maximum delay of slowest
Player before starting. (continued)

```
that
                    // this controller's latency is greater
than previously
know max
latency
                    if ( slaveLatency != Control-
ler.LATENCY_UNKNOWN &&
                         slaveLatency.getNanoseconds() >
maxLatency.getNanoseconds() )
                    {
                        // if this is the biggest latency
we've seen, keep
track of it
                        maxLatency = slaveLatency;
                    }
                }

            // add a 5 millisecond buffer to account for
any startup
delays
            maxLatency = new Time( maxLatency.getNanosec-
onds() + 5 );

            // we must go through and start each control-
ler...
            for ( int loop = 0; loop < numevents; loop++ )
            {
                Controller temp = (Controller) notify.ele-
mentAt( loop );

                // start each controller with the max laten-
cy time in
order
                // to ensure each starts at the same
time....
                temp.syncStart( maxLatency );

            }
        }

    }
```

Once you issue **start()**, the clock's media time is in a state of suspended
animation until the **TimeBase** time arrives at the time specified by **sync-
Start()**. To determine how close the clock is to starting, use the **getSync-**

Start() method. This interface returns the amount of time before the **TimeBase** reaches the desired starting time. Once the clock reaches the starting time, this method behaves identically to **getMediaTime()**.

Excedrin for Synchronization Woes

Unless you are creating an exotic device and have specialized needs, there is no reason to deal with this synchronization minutia. JMF offers an abstraction layer for synchronized Players, which is as easy to use as a conventional Player. This technique allows your programs to view the synchronized group of Players as a single entity. You only need one **ControllerListener** and there is only one Player state to track. Furthermore, when you issue commands, the abstraction layer parcels out these commands to the subordinate Players on your behalf, so you no longer need to route commands to each Player.

You enable this abstraction layer by calling the controlling (or master) Player's **addController()** method for every subordinate Player you wish to control (see Listing 11.3). **addController()** permits the controlling Player to synchronize Player states, pool events and present a unified interface. This API must be used while the Player is in **Stopped** state, or it will throw a **ClockStartedError**.

Listing 11.3 Illustration of the use of **addController()**.

```
if (event instanceof RealizeCompleteEvent)
{
try
{
    cdplayer.addController( captionplayer );
}
catch(ClockStartedError e)
{
    System.out.println("Already started");
}
catch(NotRealizedError e)
{
    System.out.println("Not realized");
}
catch(IncompatibleTimeBaseException e)
{
    System.out.println("Can't change time base");
}

}
```

Adding a subordinate **Controller** is a traumatic experience to a managing Player. First, it tries to force the subordinate **Controller** to use its **TimeBase** via **setTimeBase()**. If the subordinate **Controller** cannot accept the new **TimeBase**, an **IncompatibleTimeBase** exception is thrown and the **addController()** process stops.

If the **TimeBase** is compatible, the managing Player then synchronizes the **Controller** with its media time (via **setMediaTime()**). The managing Player also calculates the greater of its latency time and the **Controller**'s startup latency and reports this value when **getStartLatency()** is called. As a result, **getStartLatency()** will always report the maximum startup latency for a synchronized group of players.

When you synchronize disparate media types, it is likely that each stream will have a different duration (see Figure 11-4). The managed Player will always report the length of the longest media stream amongst the group of Players, or **DURATION_UNKNOWN** if any Player's duration is unknown when **getDuration()** is called.

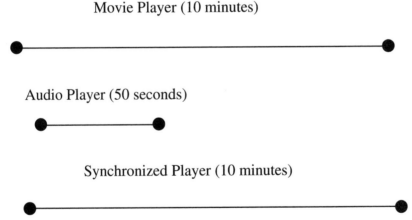

Movie Player (10 minutes)

Audio Player (50 seconds)

Synchronized Player (10 minutes)

Figure 11-4 Duration of synchronized Player with disparate media types.

Besides different media lengths, synchronized Players must grapple with varying presentation rates. For example, a video Player may be able to play at speeds five times faster than the default, while an audio Player may only be capable of the default rate of 1.0. Thus, one of the responsibilities of the managing Player is to synchronize playback rates.

The Manager first attempts to set the **Controller** to its presentation rate. If this fails, the Manager attempts to find a common rate that both objects support. If it cannot find a common rate, the managing Player will set itself and the **Controller** to 1.0, a rate that is guaranteed to work with all Players.

Even though the Player shields you from the complexities of multi-Player state management, your application needs to be aware of some specific synchronized Player state issues. For instance, if the managing Player (and associated **Controllers**) are in **Prefetched** state, and you add a **Controller** that is in **Realized** state, the Player will attempt to synchronize states (see Table 11.1).

First, the managing Player drops back into the **Prefetching** intermediate state. Then it calls **prefetch()** on the **Realized Controller**. When the new **Controller** enters **Prefetched** state, the managing Player transitions itself and any other associated **Controllers** into **Prefetched** state. This process illustrates why your application must carefully track states after issuing **addController()**, since this call may force the Player to gyrate states.

Table 11.1 State Transitions of Synchronized Players

Managed Player State	*Slave State*	*Current Synchronized Player State*	*Target Synchronized Player State or Result*
Realized	Unrealized	Realized	NotRealizedError
Prefetching	Unrealized	Prefetching	NotRealizedError
Prefetched	Unrealized	Prefetched	NotRealizedError
Starting	Unrealized	Starting	NotRealizedError
Started	Unrealized	Started	NotRealizedError
Realized	Realized	Realized	Realized
Prefetching	Realized	Realized	Prefetching
Prefetched	Realized	Realized	Prefetched
Starting	Realized	Realized	Starting
Started	Realized	Started	ClockStartedError

Table 11.1 State Transitions of Synchronized Players (continued)

Managed Player State	Slave State	Current Synchronized Player State	Target Synchronized Player State or Result
Realized	Realizing	Realizing	Realized
Prefetching	Realizing	Realizing	Prefetching
Prefetched	Realizing	Realizing	Prefetched
Starting	Realizing	Realizing	Starting
Started	Realizing	Started	ClockStartedError
Realized	Prefetching	Realized	Realized
Prefetching	Prefetching	Prefetching	Prefetching
Prefetched	Prefetching	Prefetching	Prefetched
Starting	Prefetching	Prefetching	Starting
Started	Prefetching	Prefetching	ClockStartedError
Realized	Prefetched	Realized	Realized
Prefetching	Prefetched	Prefetched	Prefetching
Prefetched	Prefetched	Prefetched	Prefetched
Starting	Prefetched	Starting	Starting
Started	Prefetched	Started	ClockStartedError
Realized	Started	Realized	Started
Prefetching	Started	Prefetching	Started
Prefetched	Started	Prefetched	Started
Starting	Started	Starting	Started
Started	Started	Started	ClockStartedError

Although **addController()** simplifies synchronization, there are some restrictions on its usage: Recursive management loops are illegal, and certain methods on a subordinate **Controller** should no longer be called.

Once you have a Player manage another **Controller**, JMF expects you not to add the managing Player's **Controller** to one of its subordinates. This is strictly an honor policy and the only enforcement is the likelihood that an exception will be thrown if you try it (see Figure 11-5).

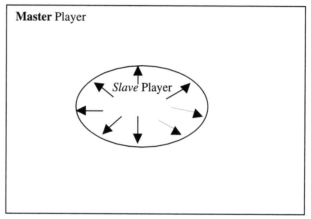

Figure 11-5   In this illustration, the *slave* Player is controlled by the **Master** Player. You should not try to make the **Master** a slave of the *slave* Player via **addController()**. If you try this, you will likely create an infinite loop between the Players.

After a **Controller** is added to a Player, you lose access to that **Controller**'s methods. While it is still syntactically possible to access these methods, the JMF specification states that their behavior is undefined and most likely will result in an exception.

Table 11.2 Comparison of Rules for Managed and Unmanaged Players

Action	Managed	Unmanaged Player
Access to methods	Use the master for most methods	All methods are accessible
Use of **addController()**	Restricted	Unlimited

Table 11.2 Comparison of Rules for Managed and Unmanaged Players (continued)		
Action	*Managed*	*Unmanaged Player*
Duration	Duration of longest Player	Duration of Player
Events	Pooled	Single Player only
Rate	Lowest common denominator for all Players	Player-specific
`ControllerEvents`	Sometimes fatal; normally can proceed with reduced functionality	Fatal

SMOOTH EVENT HANDLING

Although it is illegal to invoke methods on a managed **Controller**, it is permissible to retain any listeners you have attached to the **Controller**. However, these listeners should be used with caution. These events are a fraction of the synchronized Player's status and should not be relied upon solely for event management. The true condition of the synchronized Player is reported by the managing Player.

The managing Player's **Controller** is able to create the appearance of a single object by attaching a listener to every Player that it controls. Since it is listening to each Player's events, it knows their current states and target states. When all managed Players report a transition event, the managing Player reports the transition event (see Figure 11-3). This event consolidation prevents the application from having to create and monitor multiple listeners.

The managed **Controller** will report two categories of events: group events and **Controller**-specific events. Group events apply to all **Controllers** in the synchronized Player, and they include **Transition-Events**, **RateChangeEvents**, and **DurationUpdateEvents**. **Controller**-specific events are meaningful only in the context of the originating **Controller**. For example, **Subclassed ControllerEvents** or custom **ControllerErrorEvents** are useless if you don't know who generated them. You can distinguish between the two types of events by examining the **ControllerEvent**'s **getSource()** method. **get-Source()** will return the managing **Controller** if it is a group event, and a managed **Controller** if it is **Controller**-specific (see Listing 11.4).

> **Listing 11.4** Example of how to determine the `Controller`
> that generated an event. Either **getSource()** or
> **getSourceController()** methods can be used to
> detect the `Controller` that generated an event.

```
if ( player == event.getSource())
{
        if ( player == event.getSourceController() )
          System.out.println("Our player sent this
event...");
}
```

Normally, **ControllerErrorEvent** is the computer equivalent of the grim reaper. Once it arrives, your Player will soon die (or be closed). However, the **ControllerErrorEvent** has a different meaning when it is received by synchronized Players. Rather than terminating the entire Player, the **ControllerErrorEvent** causes the Player to ignore all events and methods of the offending **Controller** that reported the event. Thus, this process is similar to an amputation in that the managing **Controller** and all remaining managed **Controllers** will continue to function, but without the failing **Controller**.

If the managing Player is responsible for the error, then it is not possible to amputate its **Controller** and proceed, since this **Controller** is responsible for coalescing events and errors among subordinate **Controllers**. While Sun could have created a sophisticated algorithm to promote one of the subordinate **Controllers** to the managing **Controller**, applications would have to perform a host of activities (such as add listeners to the new **Controller**) to continue playback. Since this process would be overly complex and be of questionable stability, JMF closes the managing **Controller** and all managed **Controllers** when the manager is responsible for the **ControllerErrorEvent**.

Summary

Synchronizing Players is a complex process. You must manage states, events, and methods for multiple Players. JMF provides the **addController()** method to shield you from these intricacies and enables you to treat a synchronized Player similar to a conventional Player. By following a few programming guidelines, it is possible to add synchronization support to your existing JMF applications.

The subsequent chapters will supply you with the background necessary to create a robust text and music synchronization example. However, before we can build this example, we'll need to create custom Players to process text captions and digital audio data from an audio CD.

JOURNEY TO THE CENTER OF THE PLAYER

"I do not believe in the dangers and difficulties which you, Henry, seem to multiply; and the only way to learn, is like Arne Saknus-semm, to go and see." "Well," cried I, overcome at last, "let us go and see. Though how we can do that in the dark is another mystery."

"Fear nothing. We shall overcome these, and many other difficulties. Besides, as we approach the center, I expect to find it luminous—" "Nothing is impossible."

"So," he said, between his set teeth, "fatality will play me these terrible tricks. The elements themselves conspire to overwhelm me with mortification. Air, fire, and water combine their united efforts to oppose my passage. Well, they shall see what the earnest will of a determined man can do. I will not yield, I will not retreat even one inch; and we shall see who shall triumph in this great contest–man or nature"

Now that I think of the matter calmly, and that I reflect upon it dispassionately; now that months, years, have passed since this strange and unnatural adventure befell us–what am I to think, what am I to believe? No, it is utterly impossible! Our ears must have deceived us, and our eyes have cheated us! we have not seen what we believed we had seen. No human being could by any possibility have existed in that subterranean world! No generation of men could inhabit the lower caverns of the globe without taking note of those who peopled the surface, without communication with them. It was folly, folly, folly! nothing else!
Jules Verne, *Journey to the Center of the Earth*, 1864

Chapter 12

J MF is a flexible, object-oriented multimedia platform that enables your application to play a variety of multimedia content. It is also flexible enough to incorporate additional Players as new multimedia technologies arise.

Because creating new Players often requires intimate familiarity with the technical details of the file format and native hardware, Sun labels people who create Players as *Technology Providers*. By contrast, developers who use Players and other high-level JMF objects are referred to as *Client Programmers*, as they use existing services to create their applications.

Core Tip

Normally, Technology Providers are Original Equipment Manufacturers (OEMs) such as Intel, Sun, or IBM, who provide Players for popular hardware devices and file formats. However, don't be intimidated by Sun's naming convention. Anyone can be a Technology Provider, and it's possible to write these Players in 100% pure Java.

Unfortunately, while JMF oozes with the promise of extensibility, Sun has concentrated on documenting Client Programmer interfaces and has provided spartan documentation for Technology Providers. For example, early releases of the JMF documentation omitted instructions on how to create a new Player. While subsequent releases of the JMF documentation at least paid token attention to creating Players, this section of the documentation is too high level, and is inadequate for Player development. Therefore, in this chapter, I'll provide you with the missing details, so you can support any media format or data protocol.

Sticking Your Nose into a Player's Business

In Chapter 5, you learned that multimedia content is transported from its point of origin by a **DataSource** object and is delivered to the **MediaHandler** interface implemented by the Player. This separates the Player from file format details and enables you to plug in new **DataSource** objects when you need to support additional file formats or protocols. For example, to play a file over a new protocol (i.e., **mynewprotocol:**) rather than an existing protocol (i.e., **ftp:** or **http:**), you would write and install a new **DataSource** to support **mynewprotocol:**. If you were transporting a known multimedia file format over this protocol (e.g., a WAV file), the Manager would automatically match your new **DataSource** with an appropriate **MediaHandler**.

JMF defines two objects that extend the **MediaHandler** interface: **Player** and **MediaProxy**. **Player**s implement this interface to decode multimedia data. By contrast, **MediaProxie**s implement this interface to spoof **Player**s. **MediaProxie**s are intermediate objects that instruct the Manager how to find the true **DataSource** associated with a media stream or manipulate content before it is retrieved by a **Player**.

Video servers are the prototypical use for a **MediaProxy**. If thousands of users attempted to connect to a single video server, performance would dramatically degenerate. Instead, multiple video servers are used in combination with a **MediaProxy** to create the illusion of a single server. In this situation, the Manager instantiates the **MediaProxy** object, which analyzes network traffic and determines which video server has the most bandwidth. The **MediaProxy** points the Manager to the **DataSource** associated with that server and the manager connects the Player's **MediaHandler** to the server-specific **DataSource** (see Figure 12-1).

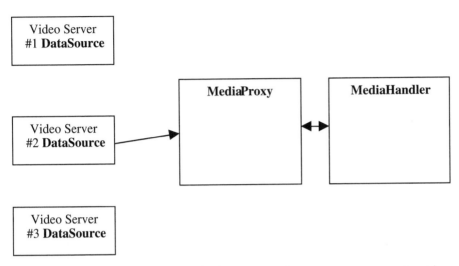

Figure 12-1   The `MediaProxy` in this figure routes the `MediaHandler` to the video server `DataSource` with the most bandwidth.

If you're going to be transporting a new file format over **mynewproto-col:** or any existing protocol, then you'll need to create a new **MediaHandler** to parse it. A new **MediaHandler** is necessary because **DataSource**s only deliver data; the **MediaHandler** must be created to parse the previously unknown file format (see Figures 12-2 and 12-3).

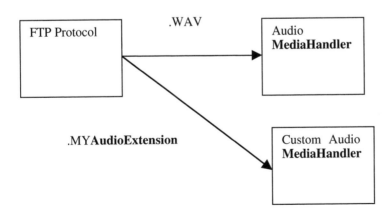

Figure 12-2   In this illustration, a custom **MediaHandler** must be written to decode the new audio format. However, the existing FTP **DataSource** can be reused.

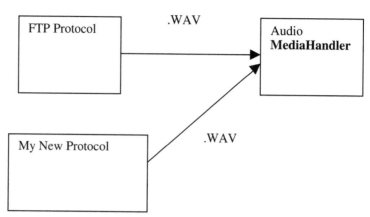

Figure 12-3   In this illustration, a custom **DataSource** must be written to transport the existing audio format. Both **DataSource**s can be connected to the same **MediaHandler**.

Since the CD audio and caption text Players in our synchronization example use new file formats and protocols, we must create two **DataSource**s and two **MediaHandler**s. We'll develop these **DataSource**s first since they are the first objects to touch the content.

Core Tip

*When you design JMF **MediaHandler** and **DataSource** objects to support a new file format and a new protocol respectively, you will encounter a chicken and egg dilemma. If you design the new **MediaHandler** first, there will be no mechanism to test the **DataSource**. Similarly, creating a **DataSource** without an associated **MediaHandler** is pointless. Therefore, the approach we'll use in this book is to create the **DataSource** first, and then a bootstrap **MediaHandler** shell that will let us debug our **DataSource**.*

Mysterious Lists

The first requirement in creating a **DataSource** is to understand how it is located by the Manager. As you learned in Chapter 5, the Manager assembles a list of **DataSource**s that potentially may support the protocol used to transfer the file. The information in this list is retrieved from a black box known as the JMF package prefix list.

A package prefix list, in Java multimedia terminology, is a series of strings that are the prefixes for a given class package. For instance, our caption **DataSource**'s package name is **interactivejava.media.protocol.caption.DataSource**, and the corresponding prefix is **interactivejava.media.protocol**.

JMF uses two of these prefix lists: the protocol prefix list and the content prefix list. The protocol prefix list maintains a list of **DataSource**s installed in the system, while the content prefix list tracks the **MediaHandler**s or **MediaProxie**s available to process media types transmitted over these protocols.

The first time you create a protocol, you may be tempted to give the package a custom name, like **my.new.protocol.is.cool**. However, you'll quickly discover that JMF enforces a strict naming convention for both **DataSource**s and **MediaHandler**s and any nonconforming packing is ignored. Without this policy, the Manager would have to walk through each package and try the classes within to see if they were **DataSource**s or **MediaHandler**s. The rigid naming convention permits rapid traversal of JMF objects and ensures that packages contain the desired classes.

DataSources must be named in the following manner:

```
package-prefix.media.protocol.protocol.DataSource
```

where **package-prefix** is the name of your package and **protocol** is the title of your protocol. In our case, we will create an **interactivejava** package using a text protocol so its identifier would be **interactivejava.media.protocol.caption.DataSource**.

Similarly, **MediaHandler**s use the following descriptor:

```
package-prefix.media.content.content-type
```

where **package-prefix** is the name of your package and **content-type** is the media type processed by this **MediaHandler**. Our text-based **MediaHandler** called **CaptionMediaHandler** will process files in the **text.mcml** format. Therefore, its name will be **interactivejava.media.protocol.caption**.

Installation Black Magic

If you follow Sun's instructions, installing a new prefix for your **DataSource** or **MediaHandler** may be the most frustrating JMF development task you will ever undertake. The official documents contain no sample code, nor do they show you the interfaces necessary to accomplish the task. Rather, you are given cryptic instructions and left to fend for yourself.

The first thing you must do is find out where JMF stores these strings. However, a cursory glance at your Java documentation will reveal that this information is intentionally vague (usually it is stored in the **jmf.properties** file, but Sun could change this in the future).

Fortunately, JMF includes a Package Manager that is platform-independent and automates the entire prefix installation process. To install a new prefix, you request the existing list from the Package Manager, add your new prefix to the list, and inform the Package Manager of the changes (see Listing 12.1).

Listing 12.1 How you can utilize the Package Manager to install a prefix. This code must be run each time your program executes since the changes to the prefix list are temporary and are discarded when your application terminates.

```
Vector packagePrefix = PackageManager.getContentPrefix-
List();
      String myPackagePrefix = new String("interactive-
java");

// has this package been installed before?
if ( packagePrefix.indexOf(myPackagePrefix) == -1 )
{
    packagePrefix.addElement(myPackagePrefix);
    PackageManager.setContentPrefixList(packagePrefix);

    // write to permanent storage
    PackageManager.commitContentPrefixList();

}
else
{
    System.out.println("Package already installed....");
}


Vector v = PackageManager.getProtocolPrefixList();
String interactivejavaPrefix = new String("interactiveja-
va");
// has this package been installed before?
if ( interactivejavaPrefix.indexOf(myPackagePrefix) == -1 )
{
    v.addElement(interactivejavaPrefix);
```

Listing 12.1 How you can utilize the Package Manager to install a prefix. This code must be run each time your program executes since the changes to the prefix list are temporary and are discarded when your application terminates. (continued)

```
    PackageManager.setProtocolPrefixList(v);

    // write to permanent storage
    PackageManager.commitProtocolPrefixList();
}
else
{
    System.out.println("Package already installed....");
}
```

Before you install a package, be sure to verify that the package has not been previously installed on the machine. The easiest way to perform this test is to use the **indexOf()** method of the vector returned by **getProtocolPrefixList()** or **getContentPrefixList()** for your package name (see Listing 12.1). Since the Package Manager does not check for duplicate entries, if you don't check for previous installations, you will replicate your package in the **jmf.properties** file (see Figure 12-4).

```
content.prefixes=javax|com.sun|com.intel|com.real|inter-
activejava|interactivejava|interactivejava
protocol.prefixes=javax|com.sun|com.intel|com.real|inter-
activejava|interactivejava|interactivejava
```

Figure 12-4 The **interactivejava** package name was replicated in the **jmf.properties** file because an application neglected to check for previous installations.

If your new **DataSource** or **MediaHandler** will be used only in your application, the approach illustrated in Listing 12.1 is tolerable. However, if you want a general-purpose multimedia object that is reusable by other JMF executables, you'll need to save the prefix list to permanent storage (i.e., disk, flash memory, etc.).

Other developers' JMF applications require permanent changes to the prefix list because it would be impossible for them to guess the names of your packages to install them themselves. Fortunately, if you permanently install your prefixes, the Manager can find and use your packages for any application. You commit your prefix changes by issuing **commitProtocolPrefixList()** or **commitContentPrefixList()** for protocols or content types, respectively.

Core Tip

Because Java is a secure system, it prevents rogue applets from changing vital system resources. Since Java considers the prefix list a protected resource, applets cannot make permanent changes to the list. Fortunately, this restriction does not apply to applications, so any permanent installation changes must be performed by an application.

Applets can request permission to save prefixes on the client machine's local file system (see Listing 12.2). The JMFSecurity package provides a quick fix. And, since applets usually don't install packages on the client machine, this approach is not recommended.

> **Listing 12.2** Illustration of applet request to install prefixes on local storage.

```
import com.sun.media.util.JMFSecurity;

// Create an instance of a player for this media
try {
    // ask the VM for permission to read/write to local
storage......
    JMFSecurity.enablePrivilege.invoke(JMFSecurity.privi-
legeManager,
    JMFSecurity.writePropArgs);
    JMFSecurity.enablePrivilege.invoke(JMFSecurity.privi-
legeManager,
    JMFSecurity.readPropArgs);
} catch (Exception e) {}


Vector packagePrefix = PackageManager.getContentPrefix-
List();
String myPackagePrefix = new String("interactivejava");
packagePrefix.addElement(myPackagePrefix);
PackageManager.setContentPrefixList(packagePrefix);


Vector v = PackageManager.getProtocolPrefixList();
```

> **Listing 12.2** Illustration of applet request to install prefixes on local storage.   (continued)

```
String interactivejavaPrefix = new String("interactiveja-
va");
v.addElement(interactivejavaPrefix);
PackageManager.setProtocolPrefixList(v);

PackageManager.commitContentPrefixList();
PackageManager.commitProtocolPrefixList();
```

Looking Under the Covers of a DataSource

In Chapter 5, we briefly examined the technique used to attach a **Data-Source** to a compatible **MediaHandler**. Although all JMF programmers should have a basic understanding of how these objects interoperate, it is impossible to develop a **DataSource** or **MediaHandler** without intimate knowledge of how these objects communicate. As a result, we are going to explore the algorithms used to connect these objects.

The Manager is the supervisory object responsible for assembling Players. For each **DataSource** on the protocol prefix list, the Manager instantiates the corresponding **DataSource** object. It then calls the **DataSource**'s **connect()** method. The **connect()** method ties the source to the object specified by the **MediaLocator**. For example, if it is a file, the file is opened and it is verified for usage. If the **DataSource** experiences a problem during **connect()**, it may throw a **java.io.IOException**.

The Manager calls the **DataSource**'s **getContentType()** to retrieve the Multipurpose Internet Mail Extensions (MIME) content type that describes the media content emitted by the **DataSource**. Although MIME types were originally intended for Internet mail applications, other Internet applications (such as browsers) have reused them to describe the type of media they are transporting. Examples of content types include digital audio wrapped in a WAV file (**audio.x-wav**) and video packaged in the AVI file format (**video.x-msvideo**). After obtaining the content type, the Manager constructs a list of **MediaHandler**s that are compatible with that content type.

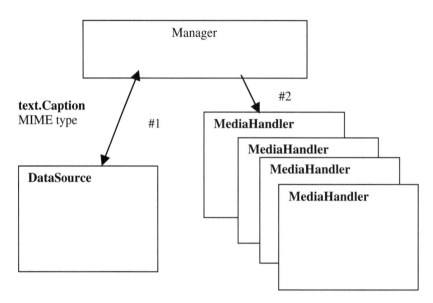

Figure 12–5 Based on a **DataSource**'s content type, the Manager assembles a list of potentially compatible **MediaHandlers**.

The Manager instantiates each **MediaHandler** in the list and attaches it to the **DataSource** by calling the **MediaHandler**'s **setSource()** method. If no exceptions or errors occur, the Manager examines the **MediaHandler** to see if it is also a Player. If it is a Player, then it returns a reference to the **Player** object to your application.

Players can also be constructed from a **DataSource**. In this scenario, the Manager is given a **DataSource** object, and is responsible for finding a compatible **MediaHandler**. It calls the **DataSource**'s **getContent-Type()** method to determine its file format.

The Manager uses the MIME type to assemble a list of compatible Players. It then instantiates each of these Players and attaches the source to them via the **SetSource()** method. If it finds a compatible Player, the process is halted and the current Player is returned to the caller as requested.

If no compatible Player is found, it creates a list of Players that will connect to the *unknown* content type (unknown is JMF's equivalent of a generic **MediaHandler**). The Manager attempts to attach the **DataSource** to each of these Players. If no compatible Player is found, the Manager gives up and throws a **NoPlayerException**.

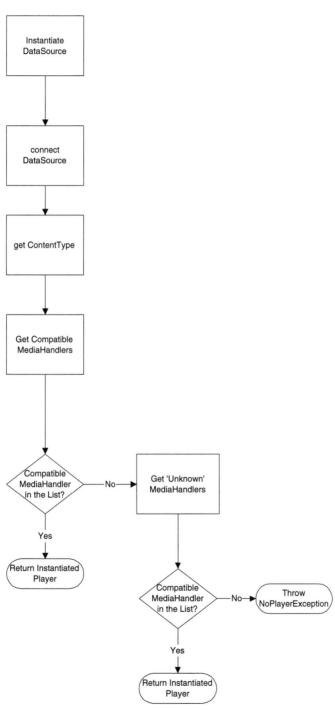

Figure 12–6 Flowchart for Player assembly.

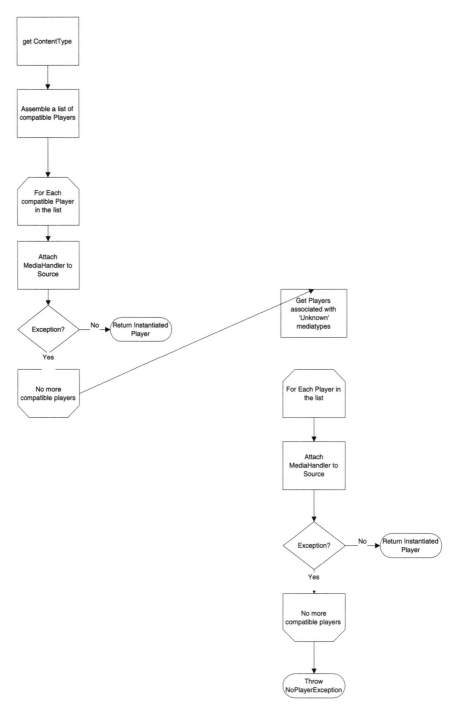

Figure 12–7 Flowchart for Player assembly with a **DataSource**.

Speaking with a Forked Tongue

In our previous examples, we described **DataSource**s that delivered a single media stream (or **SourceStream**) with one type of content (such as digital audio). However, many multimedia file formats can contain several media types. For instance, DVD content contains separate audio, video, and subpicture (or caption) streams. For these complex data types, JMF permits the **DataSource** two output options: interleaving and separation.

A **DataSource** may interleave (or mix) multiple streams and generate a single output stream (see Figure 12-8). It may also separate each stream into a unique output stream (see Figure 12-9). This option is similar to a fork in the road; each stream flows to a different destination and must be processed separately. Neither alternative is superior, so the rationale for selection may range from file format dependencies to programming ease. In Chapter 13, you'll learn how to create a **DataSource** with multiple output streams, and Chapter 15 will show you how to create a single-stream **DataSource**.

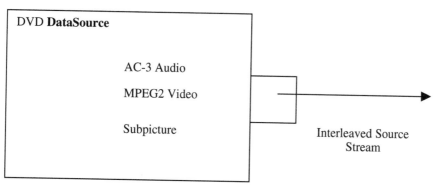

Figure 12–8   A DVD **DataSource** with interleaved streams. In this illustration, the **DataSource** combines the audio, video, and subpicture streams and delivers them to the **MediaHandler** in a single stream.

You can detect the type of source stream(s) a **DataSource** uses by examining the number of streams in the array returned by the **getStreams()** method (see Listing 12.3). If the array contains only one source stream, the stream is either an interleaved format or it contains heterogeneous media format. By contrast, if the array consists of multiple elements, then there are multiple source streams emanating from the **DataSource**.

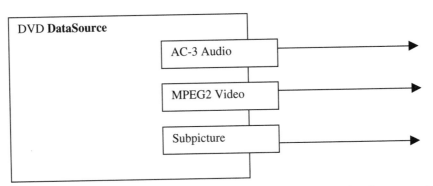

Figure 12-9 A DVD `DataSource` with multiple source streams. In this illustration, the `DataSource` utilizes three separate output streams. The `MediaHandler` is responsible for rendering each stream separately.

Listing 12.3 Retrieving multiple streams from a `DataSource`. This illustration is taken from the multistream `Text DataSource` in Chapter 13.

```
try
{
        handler.pullstreams = ( (MCMLTextDataSource) han-
dler.dataSrc).getStreams();
                }
catch (java.io.IOException ex)
{
        //
        // The DataSource threw an IOException.
        //
        throw ex;
}


//
// we assume that the pullstreams array
// contains only 1 PullSourceStream.
//
handler.timestream = handler.pullstreams[0];
handler.textstream = handler.pullstreams[1];
```

Sibling Rivalry

There are two types of **DataSource**s: Push and Pull. Push **DataSources** transmit content without intervention by the **MediaHandler**. By contrast, a **MediaHandler** directs a Pull **DataSource** when to process data.

Since both types of **DataSource**s inherit from the same parent object, they share many of the same interfaces. However, there is one significant difference between the two categories: the mechanism used to access content in the source stream.

You can obtain content from a Pull **DataSource** by calling its **read()** method. If there isn't enough data to satisfy the request, a Pull **DataSource** will block until it can fulfill your request.

Although **read()** can be used on a Push **DataSource**, it is not the preferred mechanism to retrieve content. A Push **DataSource read()** call will return immediately regardless of whether it has fulfilled the caller's request (see Figure 12.10). Exclusive use of this method has significant performance ramifications. Because you are unsure when data is available, you would have to constantly poll the **DataSource** to see if something has changed (polling is the process of repeatedly calling a function in the hopes that something has changed). This approach wastes processing power, though, since the time the CPU spends guessing if something changed could be used elsewhere.

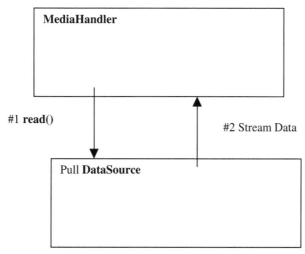

Figure 12-10   How the data is transferred from a Pull **MediaHandler**. In this example, the **MediaHandler** controls the flow of data.

Because the Pull **DataSource** will block if it can't satisfy your request, use the **read()** method with caution. Poorly written **MediaHandler**s may unexpectedly block and be unresponsive to user commands. As a result, most **MediaHandler**s use multiple threads to ensure that they can simultaneously process user requests and read from the **DataSource**.

Core Tip

It is theoretically possible (although not recommended) to write a single-threaded **MediaHandler** *that doesn't block, and therefore, is responsive to user commands. The* **willReadBlock()** *method of* **PullSourceStream** *alerts you if the* **read()** *will block. As a result, you can avoid calling* **read()** *until you are assured that it won't block.*

Unfortunately, this approach is not robust and has problems. First, it could result in choppy playback, since you aren't retrieving data as soon as the decoding algorithm is ready. Second, if the **MediaHandler** *encounters a single-threaded* **DataSource** *that must block to fulfill the request, it will never begin playback.*

Since only the Push **DataSource** knows when content is available, the most efficient means of delivering data to the **MediaHandler** would be an interrupt (or callback) mechanism. Interrupts alert interested parties that the **DataSource**'s status has changed. As a result, when the interrupt is received, the **MediaHandler** knows the **DataSource** has content to transfer. If a **MediaHandler** wishes to receive these interrupts, it implements the **SourceTransferHandler** interface.

Core Tip

Do not confuse the notion of a generic interrupt with a hardware interrupt. Hardware interrupts stop all application-level software processing until they complete. By contrast, the notion of **DataSource** *interrupt indicates that a thread not owned by a* **MediaHandler** *calls into the* **MediaHandler** *to inform it that data is available.*

Since multiple threads are involved, the **MediaHandler** *can decode content and simultaneously be notified that additional data is available for decoding. This architecture ensures the smooth flow of multimedia content throughout the system when processing pushed content.*

The **SourceTransferHandler** is a spartan interface with only one method: **transferData()**. The Push **DataSource** calls this method to inform the **MediaHandler** that data has become available and can be read via the **read()** method. This technique is the most efficient since it eliminates the need to poll (see Figure 12-11).

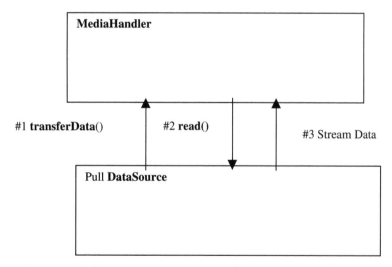

Figure 12-11 How the Push **DataSource** transfers content. In this figure, the **MediaHandler** is passive and reacts to data supplied by the **DataSource**.

To receive a callback, the **MediaHandler** must attach its **SourceTransferHandler** to every stream flowing from the **DataSource**. It first calls **DataSource.getStreams()** to calculate the total number of streams to attach to, then it informs each stream to notify it of data availability via **PushSourceStream.setTransferHandler()**.

Trouble in Paradise?

The current JMF architecture requires a new **MediaHandler** for each protocol or file format it encounters. Each of these **MediaHandlers** contains the decompression routines necessary to play the file. However, if the same compression algorithm is used in a different file format or protocol, there is no way to reuse the decompression routines locked inside a **MediaHandler**. Consequently, you may have to duplicate the decompression routine in each **MediaHandler** you write.

This duplication of source leads to maintenance problems and bugs. Fortunately, a reusable CODEC interface is one of the important new features that will be provided by JMF 2.0 (see Chapter 21 for more information on JMF 2.0).

Core Tip

Most major operating systems such as QuickTime, Win32, and OS/2 contain CODEC interfaces that enable file format access to compression and decompression routines. Until JMF provides equivalent CODEC support, it will struggle to match the functionality provided by native environments.

Summary

To create multimedia applications that access custom file formats, you will need a **MediaHandler** and/or a **DataSource**. A **MediaHandler** enables your programs to support new compression types, and a **DataSource** facilitates new protocols and file formats.

JMF has stringent rules for installing both **MediaHandler**s and **DataSource**s. Failure to follow these guidelines will have dire consequences, including a nonfunctional program. Once they are properly installed, the

Manager contains routines that can instantly connect your new **MediaHandler** or **DataSource** to existing **MediaHandler**s and/or a **DataSource**. Furthermore, if they are installed permanently, all JMF applications will automatically support your new functionality.

Now that we've armed you with the information necessary to create Players and **DataSource**s, in the next chapter we'll focus on the pure Java portion of our synchronization architecture: the Caption Player.

THE MULTIMEDIA CAPTION DATASOURCE

But words are things, and a small drop of ink, falling like dew, upon a thought, produces that which makes thousands, perhaps millions, think.

Lord Byron, *Don Juan*

An average English word is four letters and a half. By hard, honest labor I've dug all the large words out of my vocabulary and shaved it down till the average is three and a half... I never write "metropolis" for seven cents, because I can get the same money for "city." I never write "policeman," because I can get the same price for "cop."... I never write "valetudinarian" at all, for not even hunger and wretchedness can humble me to the point where I will do a word like that for seven cents; I wouldn't do it for fifteen.

Mark Twain,
Spelling and Pictures, 1906

Chapter 13

T he first task in our synchronization project is the Caption Player. This Player displays textual data in a visual control at specific points in time. Although you could use it as a standalone player, it was designed to augment audio or video players. Potential uses for the Caption Player would be to add Closed Caption text or subtitles to foreign movies, or to display the words to a song on a CD (this is especially helpful for "singers" like James Brown).

To play captions, you'll need a Caption **DataSource** and a Caption **MediaHandler**. The Caption **DataSource** retrieves data from a specially formatted file and routes the textual data in the file to the Caption **Media-Handler**. Because it never touches any hardware resources and is not per-formance-sensitive, we can write it in 100% pure Java (see Figure13-1).

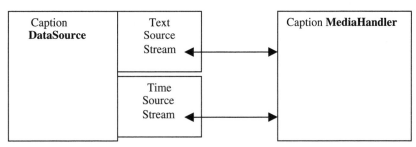

Figure 13-1 Components used to play back captions.

Yet Another Markup Language?

The Caption **DataSource** process files are stored in the Multimedia Caption Markup Language (MCML). MCML is a simple, tag-based markup language. Like HTML, each tag begins with a <, is followed by a tag identifier, and is terminated by a >. Most tags are used in pairs, with the terminating tag prefaced by '/' (i.e., <tag> and </tag>).

Parameters may be attached to a tag by listing them after the tag identifier, but before the terminating >. Parameters start with an *identifier*, then a =, and finally a *parameter* value.

MCML currently supports four tags: **header**, **time**, **displaytext**, and **paragraph**. The header tag, **<mcml>**, indicates that a file is formatted in MCML. This must be the first tag encountered in the file, as all other tags will are ignored until it is encountered. Properly formatted files should be terminated with the corresponding **</mcml>**, although this is not a requirement (see Listing 13.1 for MCML syntax rules).

Listing 13.1 Syntax for **time** tag, where *x* and *y* represent time values in milliseconds.

```
<mcml>
<time length=#>
            <displaytext>
 <p>text data
</displaytext >
</time>
</mcml>
```

The **time** tag informs the Player that all enclosed tags should be interpreted for a specific quantity of time. The tag relies on the **length=#** parameter to control how many milliseconds the **time** tag will be active. If **length=#** parameter is not specified, the tag's length is assumed to be infinite.

The **displaytext** tag must be enclosed by starting and ending **time** tags (**<time>** and **</time>**, respectively). All text elements within the **displaytext** tags will be shown during the time specified by the **time** tag (see Listing 13.2).

> **Listing 13.2** In this illustration, **Sample** will be active during the first 100 milliseconds, **Second try** will be active for the next 100 milliseconds, and **Goodbye** will be remain active until the MCML parser is stopped.

```
<mcml>
<time length=100>
<displaytext> Sample</displaytext >
</time>
<time length=100>
<displaytext> Second try</displaytext >
</time>
<time>
<displaytext> Goodbye</displaytext >
</time>
</mcml>
```

The paragraph style is identical to HTML's **<p>** paragraph style. You can use it to separate paragraphs or insert blank lines into a display.

If an unknown tag is encountered, all information and embedded tags will be ignored until the corresponding terminating tag is encountered.

The beauty of using a tag-oriented language is that it can be expanded to accommodate new media formats in the future by simply adding new tags. Furthermore, since older parsers ignore the new tags, they can safely process the new file format (see Listing 13.3).

> **Listing 13.3** Example input file for text-based Player.

```
<mcml>
<time length=10>
< displaytext >Hello World!!!!!</displaytext >
</time>
<time length=20>
< displaytext >Goodbye World!!!!! </displaytext >
</time>
<mcml>
```

Multipurpose Tool

Since MCML is a general-purpose language that may be used by programs besides our Caption Player, we're going to design the MCML parser so that it can be plugged into any Java program. Therefore, the **mcml** class will not depend on the internal workings of our Caption **DataSource**.

To construct the **mcml** object, you pass it the name of the mcml file it should parse. In keeping with our minimalist tradition, the **mcml** constructor verifies that the file exists and returns to the caller. When you want to analyze the file, you call the **parse()** method.

We don't parse the mcml content in the constructor for two reasons: robustness and performance. If an error occurs while parsing the file, the constructor will abort, leaving the user without an **mcml** object. By contrast, using a separate parsing function enables us to load a different file into the same object and try again. Furthermore, the use of a separate method for parsing gives the caller the option of parsing the file on a separate thread if the file is complex.

The **mcml** class relies on Java's **StreamTokenizer** to separate tags and text. Before any content is parsed, we ask the **StreamTokenizer** to treat '<' and '/' as special characters and unique tokens. This ensures that we can detect the beginnings of tags and tag terminations cleanly. Failure to add these items might cause them to be embedded with a tag, and thereby, more difficult to detect.

The class uses two helper functions: **gettag()** and **gettexttag()**. **gettag()** retrieves a tag from the tokenizer. If the tag has parameters (such as the **time** tag), it will retrieve these parameters from the tag.

This method also permits the caller to look for a specific tag and be notified if another tag is encountered first. This feature prevents hangs in poorly written MCML code. For instance, if the writer forgets to place a terminating **</time>** tag in the file, and the parser encounters the terminating **</mcml>** tag first, this feature enables the parser to exit without waiting infinitely for the missing **</time>** tag.

The other utility function, **gettexttag()**, detects the end of textual data in the **<displaytext>** tag. Although this sounds trivial, **gettexttag()** should be able to skip over unknown tags and must be able to detect tags (such as **<p>**), which legitimately belong in the stream (see Listing 13.4).

Listing 13.4 How the MCML parser skips over unknown tags.

```
private void skipunknowntag( String unknowntag )
{

        while ( true )
        {
          if ( gettag( unknowntag, false ) && bTerminating-
Tag)
          {
              break;
          }
        }

}
```

MCML's **parse()** method uses a layered algorithm to analyze tags. This layered approach ties methods to specific tags. When an embedded tag is encountered, the method (i.e., outer layer method) calls another method (i.e., inner layer method) to process these embedded tags. The inner layer method will not return until the termination tag for the outer method is parsed (see Figure 13.2).

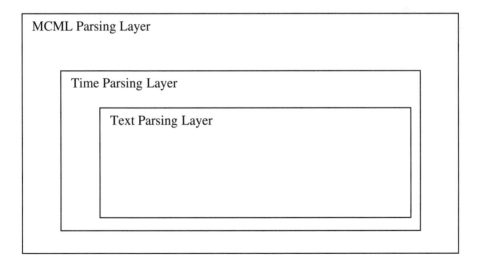

Figure 13-2 Explanation of layered parsing architecture. Tag processing methods rely on other methods to handle inner (or layered tags).

The **getbasetag()** method illustrates how the layered process works. This method looks for the **<mcml>** tag. Once it finds this tag, it calls the inner layer method, **gettimetag()**, to process all embedded tags. When **gettimetag()** finds the terminating **</mcml>** tag, it returns to its caller, **getbasetag()**.

As the parser progresses in the file, it encounters text enclosed in **<time>** tags. We store three representations of this text: raw text, raw timing information, and a Vector. The first alternative simply adds all raw text we parse into a linear String called **totalText**. Since this is a linear String, it is impossible to detect where the text associated with one **<text>** tag ends and the other begins.

The second representation of textual content saves all timing information into a separate String called **timingInfo**. For every **<text>** tag, we store the total time the String should be displayed and the length of the String. Rather than storing this information in binary form, the class converts it to text and appends it to the String. You can use **timinginfo** to inform you when to display the text stored in the **totalText** String and the number of characters in **totalText** (see Listing 13.5).

Listing 13.5 Technique used to add timing information to a String. The display time and String length for every **<time>** tag are converted into text and stored in a String.

```
timingInfo += Long.toString( currenttextinfo.length, 10 )
+ " ";
timingInfo += Long.toString( currenttextinfo.text.
length(), 10 ) + " ";
```

Core Tip

Vectors are typeless arrays that can dynamically grow as needed. Background material on Vectors and other core Java types can be found in Bruce Eckel's Thinking in Java.

The most convenient representation of text data is stored in a Vector. Each Vector element is a **TextDescriptor** class that represents the key elements of the **<time>** tag: the display text and the length of time it should be displayed. This alternative combines all of the functionality of the **totalText** and **timingInfo** Strings into a single class (see Listing 13.6). Furthermore, random access to any **<text>** information can be accomplished by using Vector's **elementAt()** method.

Listing 13.6 Adding time elements to a Vector.

```
TextDescriptor temptextinfo = new TextDescriptor();

temptextinfo.text     = currenttextinfo.text;
temptextinfo.length = currenttextinfo.length;
temptextinfo.totallength = totalText.length();
totalText += currenttextinfo.text;

// timing info begins with time to display
// this information will be used in the timing stream
String temptime;

temptime = Long.toString( currenttextinfo.length, 10 )
+ " ";
temptime += Long.toString( currenttextinfo.text.length(),
10 ) + " ";


temptextinfo.timinglength = temptime.length();
timeinfo.addElement( temptextinfo );
```

The Vector alternative is the preferable solution for native Java classes. However, it does not fit into the JMF model of sending linear streams of bytes to a destination. As a result, our Caption **DataSource** streams the **totalText** and **timingInfo** Strings to the Caption **MediaHandler**.

Putting MCML to Use

The core class of our Caption **DataSource** is called **MCMLTextData-Source**. It extends the **PullDataSource** class.

The **MCMLTextDataSource**'s **getContentType()** method lets the Manager or other JMF objects query the MIME type associated with the file loaded by the **DataSource**. If the file contains valid MCML tags, **getContentType()** will return "**text.mcml**".

If the Manager is able to find a compatible **MediaHandler** for our Caption **DataSource**, it will call **connect()** to link the two objects together. Since all the risky methods were called in the constructor, it is unlikely that **connect()** will fail.

Applications often need to determine the length of the file they are playing before playback commences. These types of requests are serviced by the **DataSource**'s **getDuration()** method. Our implementation of this method queries the **mcml** object for the total time in milliseconds. It converts the millisecond value to nanoseconds, constructs a **Time** object with the result and returns the **Time** object to the caller.

Listing 13.7 getDuration() processing.

```
// the MCML parser knows the length in time of the file--
return
// this in getDuration()
public Time getDuration()
{
Time fileTime;
fileTime = new Time( (double) istream.totallength() /
1000);

return fileTime;
}
```

The Origination of Streams

Once we are connected, the system uses **getStreams()** to determine the number of streams that emanate from our **DataSource**. Unlike most **DataSource**s, the **MCMLTextDataSource** has multiple output streams (see Figure 13-3). One stream outputs text characters, and the other streams send out timing information to control how these characters are displayed.

The **MediaHandler** is responsible for parsing the timing information stream to determine how much information to display and when it should be shown. If this information were combined in a single stream, it would simplify parsing, since you would only have to keep one set of parsing variables rather than two.

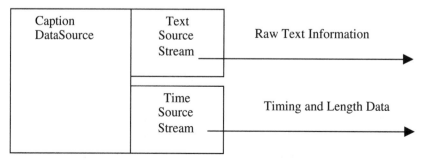

Figure 13-3 Architectural diagram of streams flowing from the Caption **DataSource**.

Unfortunately, a single stream would dramatically reduce flexibility. The multiple stream approach permits new multimedia types to be added and controlled by the timing stream without changing the **MediaHandler**. For instance, if we added multiple language caption support to MCML, each language could be sent in a separate stream. Since the timing stream is architected to control multiple streams, the **MediaHandler** could choose the caption language (and associated stream) for the locale it cares about and ignore the rest (see Figure 13-4).

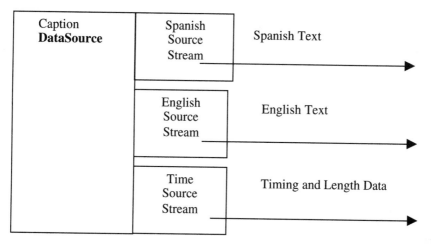

Figure 13–4 Using the multiple stream approach to transport several languages, each in a unique stream.

To supply the caller with the **PullSourceStream** array, the **get-Streams()** method creates and initializes the **PullSourceStream**(s) that it will be using. **MCMLTextDataSource** creates two **Source Streams**: a **TextSourceStream** and a **TimeTextSourceStream**.

Both the **TextSourceStream** and **TimeTextSourceStream** are like Sun's **ByteArraySourceStream** example, since they stream content into an array of bytes. The primary difference between these classes is that **TextSourceStream** streams textual data, while **TimeTextSourceStream** streams timing control information.

When it is constructed, **TextSourceStream** sets the **textContent** String to the entire text stream from the MCML file via **mcml.getFileText()**. **textContent** is used as a reservoir of data which the **TextSourceStream**'s **read()** method uses to stream data from.

TextSourceStream's constructor initializes two additional variables to monitor data transport: **length** and **index**. **length** indicates the length of all the text in the MCML file, while **index** tracks our current location in the text stream. As data is transferred from **textContent**, we increment **index**.

getContentLength() uses these variables to report the total amount remaining to read. Similarly, **endOfStream()** alerts the caller when we've run out of data if **index** has exceeded the text length.

The **MediaHandler** pulls data from the **DataSource** by calling the **TextSourceStream**'s **read()** method. **read()** attempts to fill the caller's buffer with text. If it is low on text, **read()** partially fills the buffer and alerts the caller that only a portion of their request was filled.

Once **read()** determines the amount it wishes to copy, it calls **System.arraycopy()** to copy bytes from **textContent** to the caller's buffer array. Then it advances the **index** variable by the amount we've streamed into the caller's buffer. Failure to advance the **index** correctly will result in duplicate information being copied in future calls to **read()**.

Core Tip

In an ideal world, we could use **System.arraycopy()** *to copy directly from our* **String** *object (***textContent***) into the caller's byte array (***buffer***). Although the syntax is legal, it will cause a runtime exception; the String object isn't an array of bytes, like a C String would be.*

```
System.arraycopy((Object) textContent, (int) index,
                 (Object) buffer, offset,
                 (int) bytesAvailable);
```

Therefore, we must convert our String array to an array of bytes, then call **System.arraycopy**. *This is not as efficient as directly using the* **String** *object, but it gets us around this roadblock.*

```
byte [] temp = textContent.getBytes();
System.arraycopy((Object) temp, (int) index,
                 (Object) buffer, offset,
                 (int) bytesAvailable);
```

Finally, **read()** returns the total number of bytes that it copied into the caller's buffer. If the **MediaHandler** notices that this amount is less than the total amount requested, it assumes that the **TextSourceStream** has run out of content and takes the appropriate action.

TextSourceStream also has limited support for the **Seekable** interface. This interface enables external objects to control the position where the **PullSourceStream** will begin streaming data. Our implementation of **PullSourceStream** cannot move to any location other than 0. Therefore, we cause **TextSourceStream**'s **isRandomAccess()** to return FALSE. This alerts interested parties that we can't jump to any location in the stream and that we offer minimal positioning support.

Core Tip

*The **CaptionMediaHandler** will not be using the **Seekable** interface, so this code is for illustration purposes only. The actual seek code is entirely contained in the Caption **MediaHandler**.*

To change the **TextSourceStream**'s position, call **seek()**. The **seek()** method's *where* parameter informs us of the location in the stream where we should change **index**. If the *where* value is legitimate, we set our **index** variable to be equal to it. Once the **index** is changed, the next **read()** request starts transferring data from that point.

Core Tip

*The Sun documentation is vague about the meaning of the where parameter used by **seek()**. If this value represented time, it would make seeking very difficult, since we don't know the time associated with each text character. Yet, if this value indicated the position in bytes, we could set the **index** variable to the where value. Fortunately, since related routines such as **read()** and **available()** use bytes, Sun is clearly implying that where specifies a byte location in the stream.*

Navigating the Streams

After **TextSourceStream** and **TimeTextSourceStream** streams are created in **MCMLTextDataSource's getSource()**, the **Positionable** interface can be used to control the position where **MCMLTextDataSource** starts streaming. Unlike the **Seekable** interface, the **Positionable** interface operates on time values rather than on bytes. The *rounding* parameter informs us how to react if we're unable to seek to the desired position. For example, the caller may request that we seek to time 10, and the only valid alternatives are 5 and 17. **Roundup** causes us to seek to 17, and **RoundDown** forces us to seek to 5. Similarly, **RoundNearest** will chooses 5, because it's closer to 10 than to 17.

setPosition(), the worker method for the **Positionable** interface, is responsible for converting the time request from the caller into the byte positions that **TextSourceStream** and **TimeTextSourceStream** expect (see Listing 13.8). If you're lazy, you can force all seek requests to seek to time position 0. This alternative minimizes your workload, since time position 0 always equates to byte position 0 in the corresponding source streams.

Unfortunately, this implementation prevents users from seeking inside an MCML file and limits usefulness when being synchronized with an audio or video stream. Therefore, **setPosition()** contains the algorithm below to determine the correct position to update the streams.

Listing 13.8 DataSource algorithm to search within an MCML file.

```
int loop;
int timinglength = 0;
int textlength = 0;

for ( loop = 0; loop < istream.getNumTextElements();
loop++ )
{
  textinfo = istream.getTimingInfo(loop);
  if ( textinfo.length >= ( where.getSeconds() * 1000 ) )
  {
    fFound = true;

  }
  else
  {
    timinglength += textinfo.timinglength;
    textlength += textinfo.totallength;
  }
}

if ( fFound )
{

    textdata.seek(textlength);
    timedata.seek(timinglength);
}
```

This algorithm examines the time associated with every tag. If the tag's time is greater than the time we're trying to seek to, we know that this tag is passed the point we're trying to search to, and abort the search. If the tag's time is before our seek point, then we must update the **timinglength** and **textlength** variables.

timinglength represents the offset in the bytes in the time data stream that corresponds to the requested seek time. Likewise, **textlength** stores the offset in the bytes in the text data stream that corresponds to the requested seek time. Because each tag stores the number of bytes it consumes in both the time and text streams, we increment each variable with the information in the **tag** object.

Summary

The Multimedia Caption Markup Language (MCML) uses an HTML-like syntax to display text Strings at specific points in time. **MCMLTextData-Source** is responsible for parsing these files and streaming them to a **MediaHandler**. It uses an **mcml** object to parse a file, and **Text-SourceStream** and **TimeTextSourceStream** objects to stream data to the **MediaHandler**.

We will use these foundational elements to transmit data to the **Media-Handler** that will be described in the next chapter.

MEDIAHANDLER PRIMER

Men use thought only as authority for their injustice, and employ speech only to conceal their thoughts.
Voltaire, *Dialogue xiv, Le Chapon et la Poularde*, 1763

Chapter 14

Although the MCML **DataSource** we created in the previous chapter is a powerful tool, it is worthless without a companion **Media-Handler** (or Player). We need a **MediaHandler** to pull data from our **DataSource**, decode it, and present it to the user. Therefore, we are going to create **CaptionMediaHandler**, a Player that decodes and displays MCML content.

What's the Big Secret Anyway?

Sun has done an admirable job of documenting the **Player** interface and creating sample programs to show you how to use it. Furthermore, they provide an FTP sample for programmers who need to understand **Data-Source**s. However, Sun briefly mentions in *The JMF Player Guide* that Player development is possible, but gives few details on how to create one. They do provide sample **Controller** source code, but a Player is a super-set of the **Controller**, and many Player-specific issues are not addressed in the sample.

Core Tip

Although Microsoft's 16-bit version of MCI was a primitive multimedia environment, it became popular because it offered developers a well-documented mechanism to add devices (or Players, in JMF terminology). Until JMF offers equivalent robust documentation for Player creation, its market penetration will be stunted.

The dearth of information on how to create a Player may be due to the turmoil in the underlying Player interfaces. Although Sun has never officially cited uncertainty as the reason it hasn't written Player creation guidelines, the "Future Releases" section of *The JMF 1.0 Player Guide* contains a suspicious statement summarized below:

Incomplete Players–A JMF Player expose interfaces to manipulate internal media streams. These interfaces are in progress and should be published in a future release.

Core Tip

As we will discover in Chapter 21, Sun has announced dramatic enhancements to the Player interface in the next major release of JMF. Although these changes are substantial, Sun has pledged that the release will be backwards-compatible with JMF 1.0.

Since Sun is implying that the **Player** interface will be enhanced by a follow-on JMF release, you may wonder if it is prudent to develop a JMF Player. In reality, because Sun has thoroughly documented **Player** interfaces and associated states, they are unlikely to abandon this infrastructure and break applications dependent upon the JMF 1.0 **Player** interface. Rather, they are likely to add supplemental interfaces to the **Player** interface to enable new functionality.

Core Tip

Sun tries to maintain backwards-compatibility when it ships new products. However, the need for backwards-compatibility must be balanced by the need for progress. In situations where progress requires a new interface to replace an older one, Sun depreciates the old interface.

Depreciation alerts the programmers that the interface they are using has been superseded by a newer interface. This warning gives the programmers time to update their code, while ensuring that their programs continue to function.

In the unlikely event Sun decides to completely overhaul the **Player** *interface, and replace it with a next generation* **Player** *interface, the Player interface would become depreciated. Under this worst-case scenario, any Player you created would continue to function and you would have time to add the new interfaces.*

Bark Worse Than its Bite

Although it is shrouded in mystery, Player development is not as intimidating as Sun would have you believe. In fact, if you follow the guidelines below, you will soon be churning out high-performance Players:

- Create a basic Player before trying to add advanced features.
- Report events on threads.
- Perform asynchronous state transitions on threads.
- Divide the workload for the **prefetch** and **realize** threads according to JMF guidelines.

The first step in Player development is to fill in the empty shell that is provided on the CD that accompanies this book. This shell will enable you to concentrate on the core features of your Player (i.e., retrieving, manipulating, and displaying content) without being distracted by nonessential methods (see Table 14.1 for the breakdown of essential versus nonessential methods). Once these basic methods are functional, you can enhance the Player with the bonus methods listed in Table 14.1. Although these bonus methods provide important functions (such as getting and setting media time), the Player can limp along without them.

Table 14.1 Required vs. Enchancement Methods

Minimal Methods	Enhancement methods
setRate	setMediaTime
getRate	mapToTimeBase
setSource	getSyncTime
deallocate	getMediaNanoseconds
realize	getStopTime
prefetch	setStopTime
start	getMediaTime
stop	getDuration
getState	addControllerListener
getControl	removeControllerListener
getTimeBase	getStartLatency
setPreviousState	setTimeBase
setCurrentState	getVisualComponent
setTargetState	
getControls	
getTargetState	
getControlPanelComponent	
close	

After a Player is constructed, the Manager calls **setSource()** to attach your Player to a potential **DataSource**. If your Player uses a generic multimedia file format, such as a .WAV file, then you don't care what **DataSource** is used. However, if you have a Player that uses custom file or stream format, such as an MCML file, your Player must validate that **setSource()** is connecting you to the correct **DataSource**. If the **DataSource** is unacceptable, your Player should throw an **IncompatibleSourceException** exception.

Head of State

State transition processing is the most challenging part of Player development. Not only are you responsible for tracking the current state, but you must also determine when a state transition should be performed on a separate thread.

Core Tip

When a Player creates a thread, it should ensure that the thread is added to the Player's **ThreadGroup***.* **ThreadGroup***s enable you to change attributes on selected threads without affecting those attributes on threads outside the* **ThreadGroup***. Sun indicates that threads created by a Player should belong to a separate* **ThreadGroup** *from the application. Unfortunately, they neglect to mention the rationale behind this recommendation.*

One benefit of this approach is that you can boost the priority of all threads in a Player's **ThreadGroup** *without affecting the priority of the application's other threads. This ensures the Player's threads will be dispatched first. Without such a feature, Player threads with real-time requirements would compete with non-real-time application threads for precious processing resources. If the Player's threads can't get enough time slices, the presentation may become choppy.*

There are two types of state transitions: synchronous and asynchronous. Synchronous state transitions are virtually instantaneous and can be performed on the caller's thread. Asynchronous transitions are time-consuming and must be performed on a separate thread. Table 14.2 lists which state transitions are asynchronous and whether a transition requires a separate thread.

Table 14.2 State Transition Overview and Thread Requirements

State	Target State	Asynchronous?	Thread Required?
UnRealized	Realizing	No	No
Realizing	Realized	Yes	Yes
Realized	Prefetching	No	No
Prefetching	Prefetch	Yes	Yes
Prefetched	Started	Yes	Yes
Started		Yes	Yes

When a Player is constructed, it should default to **Unrealized** state. When the Player's **realize()** method is called, the Player should perform the following actions:

1. Set the Player's state to **Realizing**.
2. Set the target state to **Realized**.
3. Start a thread to transition between the current **Realizing** state and the new target state.
4. Return to the caller.

If a Player is in **Realized**, **Prefetched**, or **Started** state when **realize()** is invoked, an error should not be reported. Rather, you should send a **RealizeCompleteEvent** to interested **Listener**s; this event may be sent on the caller's thread.

The **Realizing** thread we created in Step 3 has a specific purpose. Resist the urge to overload it with additional functionality. JMF wants this thread to access only nonexclusive resources. This is an honor policy, since no one is policing your thread to ensure that it complies with the guideline. If you attempt to access an exclusive resource (such as a video decoder), you may break JMF applications that expect to be able to **realize()** multiple Players.

Besides avoiding exclusive resources, you should not attempt to prefetch all the buffers necessary for playback (i.e., read the entire file into memory).

Reading too much data on this thread creates unfriendly applications and reduces the **Prefetching** thread to a figurehead.

JMF applications cannot display playback controls until they receive the **RealizeCompleteEvent**. Therefore, if you read the entire file on the **Realize** thread, the application will not be able to render playback controls until you finish your I/O operations. If the file is large, users may become impatient without visual feedback during this extended waiting period.

Furthermore, if you process the entire file on the **Realize** thread, the **Prefetching** state (and associated thread) becomes a meaningless place-holder. One of the primary responsibilities of the **Prefetch** thread is to fill enough buffers to ensure smooth playback. If these buffers are already filled, then this thread's lone remaining responsibility is to acquire exclusive resources (if any exist). Since some Players, such as our **MCMLPlayer**, do not use exclusive resources, the **Prefetch** thread literally will do nothing if all the buffers have been filled during realization.

To ensure that the **Realize** thread cooperates with the **Prefetch** thread, the **Realize** thread should restrict itself to the following activities:

1. Perform basic handshaking with the source stream (i.e., get all initialization information).
2. If you support a **CachingControl**, it should be created.
3. Read the minimum amount of data from the stream necessary to advance to the next phase.
4. Send the **RealizeCompleteEvent** to alert the application that the state transition is complete.
5. Exit the thread.

When the application receives the **RealizeCompleteEvent**, it will call the Player's **prefetch()** method. This method has the following responsibilities:

1. Set the Player's state to **Prefetching**.
2. Set the target state to **Prefetched**.
3. Start a thread to transition between the current **Prefetching** state and the new target state.
4. Return to the caller.

The **Prefetch** thread we created in Step 3 above has two responsibilities: to fill the **Prefetch** buffers and to acquire exclusive resources.

The primary role of the **Prefetch** thread is to fill a pool of buffers with multimedia content so that the presentation engine can begin immediately when an application calls the **start()** method. Unfortunately, there is no predefined number of buffers that the **Prefetch** thread must fill; each Player must tailor the number of **Prefetch** buffers to suit the content they are trying to decode. The following guidelines will help you calculate the number of buffers:

1. Calculate the data consumption rate for the stream (i.e., 176,400 bytes per second for CD-quality audio).
2. Calculate the worst-case data throughput times for your **Data-Source** (i.e., access times for a hard drive or CD-ROM drive).
3. The **Prefetch** buffer should be able to store at least three times the consumption rate, plus an extra buffer to compensate for the worst-case **DataSource** performance.

Step 2 above is the most challenging to calculate since Sun offers no mechanism to query the performance characteristics of a **DataSource**. Therefore, you must experiment with each **DataSource** and guesstimate its throughput. Alas, this technique fails when your Player encounters an unknown **DataSource**. Until JMF can supply performance metrics, prefetching will be a haphazard process.

Core Tip

In an ideal world, you would use the same number of **Prefetch** buffers with all **DataSources**. Unfortunately, each **DataSource** will have unique performance characteristics. For instance, FTP and HTTP protocols are considerably slower than the file protocol, since they must transport remote content. Consequently, these protocols may require a larger number of buffers to insulate the Player from network jitter such as transmission errors, network delays, etc.

If your content has a high data consumption rate per second (i.e., digital audio or video), you should carefully monitor the type of **DataSource** you are connecting with in **setSource()**. If the **DataSource** is slow, you must compensate by increasing the amount of content you prefetch.

Besides prefetching buffers and acquiring resources, the **Prefetch** thread must deal with the shortcut prefetch processing. To simplify the life of application programmers, JMF permits **prefetch()** to be called from **Unrealized**, **Realizing**, or **Realized** states. In each case, the Player's target state is **Prefetched**, but the **Prefetch** thread must perform extra state transitions when it is called in **Unrealized** state (see Table 14.3).

First, it must transition its state to **Realizing**, then perform all of the actions necessary to realize the Player. Finally, it sends the **RealizeCompleteEvent** and proceeds with the conventional prefetching process. Rather than duplicating all of the **Realize** thread's code, your **Prefetch** thread can reuse the methods contained in the **Realize** thread.

For instance, if the Player's state is **Unrealized**, the **Prefetch** thread can call the Player's **realize()** method. This will create a **Realize** thread and eventually place the Player in **Realized** state. Since this method is asynchronous, you cannot assume that the realization process is complete when it returns. Instead, **join()** the **Realize** thread after calling **realize()**. This blocks the **Prefetch** thread until the Player transitions to **Realized** state.

By contrast, if the Player's state is **Realizing**, you can skip the **realize()** call and immediately **join()** the **Realize** thread. In either case, once the **Realize** thread is finished, proceed with the prefetching process.

Core Tip

You should never do shortcut prefetch processing on an application's thread. All the implicit state transitions must be handled on the **Prefetch** *thread since the JMF specification guarantees that these state transitions will be done asynchronously.*

If you perform this processing on the application thread, it will be blocked until realization completes and may result in an unresponsive application.

Should the Player already be in **Prefetched** or **Started** state when **realize()** is invoked, an error should not be reported. Rather, you should send a **PrefetchCompleteEvent** to interested **Listener**s.

Table 14.3 `prefetch()`'s Responsibilities Vary Depending on Player State

State	Actions Required
Unrealized	Realize Player
	Wait for **Realize** thread to complete
	Report **RealizeCompleteEvent**
	Create **Prefetch** thread
	Prefetch Player
	Report **PrefetchCompleteEvent**
Realizing	Wait for **Realize** thread to complete
	Report **RealizeCompleteEvent**
	Create **Prefetch** thread
	Prefetch Player
	Report **PrefetchCompleteEvent**
Realized	Create **Prefetch** thread
	Prefetch Player
	Report **PrefetchCompleteEvent**

The last state-related method is **start()**. It is responsible for beginning a presentation and is usually called by an application after the **Prefetch-CompleteEvent** is received. **start()** routines typically perform the following actions:

1. Handle shortcut processing.
2. Set current state and target state to **Started**.
3. Send **StartEvent** to all **Listeners**.
4. Acquire any visual components.
5. Decode and display content.
6. Report **EndOfMediaEvent** when out of data.
7. Set state to **Prefetch** state.

Like **prefetch()**, JMF allows programmers to call **start()** from virtually any state, and it is the Player's responsibility to safely navigate from the current state to **Started** state. Table 14.4 enumerates the task required to transition from **Unrealized**, **Realizing**, **Prefetching**, and **Prefetched** states to **Started** state.

Table 14.4 **start()**'s Responsibilities Vary Depending on Player State

State	Actions Required
Unrealized	Realize Player
	Wait for **Realize** thread to complete
	Report **RealizeCompleteEvent**
	Prefetch Player
	Wait for **Prefetch** thread to complete
	Report **PrefetchCompleteEvent**
	Create **Start** thread
	Report **StartEvent**
	Start Player (i.e., decode content)
	Report **EndOfMediaEvent**
	Set state to **prefetch** state
Realizing	Wait for **Realize** thread to complete
	Report **RealizeCompleteEvent**
	Prefetch Player
	Wait for **Prefetch** thread to complete
	Report **PrefetchCompleteEvent**
	Create **Start** thread
	Report **StartEvent**
	Start Player (i.e., decode content)
	Report **EndOfMediaEvent**
	Set state to **Prefetch** state
Realized	Prefetch Player
	Wait for **Prefetch** thread to complete
	Report **PrefetchCompleteEvent**
	Create **Start** thread
	Report **StartEvent**
	Start Player (i.e., decode content)
	Report **EndOfMediaEvent**
	Set state to **Prefetch** state

Table 14.4 `start()`'s Responsibilities Vary Depending on Player State (continued)	
`Prefetching`	Wait for **Prefetch** thread to complete
	Report **PrefetchCompleteEvent**
	Create **Start** thread
	Report **StartEvent**
	Start Player (i.e., decode content)
	Report **EndOfMediaEvent**
	Set state to **Prefetch** state
`Prefetched`	Create **Start** thread
	Report **StartEvent**
	Start Player (i.e., decode content)
	Report **EndOfMediaEvent**
	Set state to **Prefetch** state

`start()` reuses **realize** and **prefetch** methods and threads to smoothly transition into **Started** state. For example, if the Player's state is **Unrealized**, it calls the Player's **prefetch** method and waits for prefetching to complete before starting playback. Similarly, if the state is **Realizing**, `start()` waits for the **Realize** thread to finish, begins the prefetch process and blocks until the **Prefetch** thread concludes before starting playback.

If the Player is already **Realized**, `start()` calls `prefetch()` and halts until the **Prefetch** thread concludes before beginning playback. By contrast, if the Player is **Prefetching**, `start()` only needs to pause until the **Prefetch** thread concludes before starting playback.

Once the Player is started, it is responsible for detecting end of media events and reporting playback completion to the caller.

Hitting the Breaks

Applications can abort playback at any point by calling the `stop()` method. If the Player is **Realizing, Prefetching**, or **Started**, `stop()` interrupts the worker thread, then adjusts the Player's state (see Table 14.5).

Table 14.5 Current and Target States After **stop()** Processing is Completed

State Before Stop	State After Stop	Target State After Stop
UnRealized	UnRealized	Realizing
Realizing	UnRealized	Realizing
Realized	Realized	Prefetching
Prefetching	Realized	Prefetching
Prefetched	Prefetched	Started
Started	Prefetched	Started

Core Tip

Virtually all multimedia environments offer two stop APIs: pause and flush. Pause stops playback, but leaves decoded buffers in the renderer device. Since all of the buffers are intact, playback can be resumed at the exact point where it was stopped. Furthermore, pausing is rapid since it requires no buffer manipulation.

By contrast, flush not only stops playback, but it also releases all of the Player's **Prefetched** buffers. Elimination of these buffers makes a flush more time-consuming than a pause. Since buffers have been released on the renderer device, it is often not possible to resume playback at the exact point where it was flushed.

Players that stream content over the Internet are particularly sensitive to the difference between stop and flush. If buffers are flushed, they must be prefetched over a potentially slow connection. By contrast, pausing playback allows it to be rapidly resumed.

Unfortunately, JMF only defines one stop method, and it is the responsibility of the Player developer to determine if **stop()** acts like a pause or if it operates like a flush. If you absolutely must have both types of stops in your Player, you will need to add a custom method (this is the technique used by the Real G2 Player described in Chapter 19).

The Player's Achilles Heel

JMF applications rely on events to report error conditions, state transitions, and other asynchronous activities. Our sample Players use the **updateListeners()** method to report these events to listeners. Although it is legal to use the primary worker threads (**Realize**, **Prefetch**, or **Start**) to send these events, it is dangerous to do so.

Worker threads should not be used to send events because **updateListeners()** is synchronous. The worker thread is held captive until the application returns from **updateListeners()** (see Figure 14-1). As a result, poorly written applications can steal time slices away from the worker thread and can potentially cause the presentation to break up.

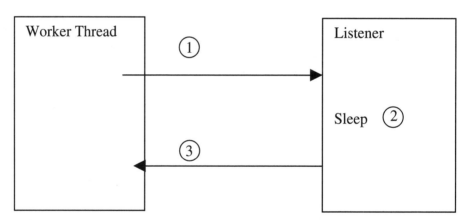

Figure 14–1 Synchronous event reporting model. In this illustration, while the listener sleeps, the worker thread (i.e., **Start**, **Prefetch**, or **Realize**) is blocked.

The preferred event reporting technique is to dedicate a thread to communicate with **ControllerListeners** (see Figure 14-2). Worker threads asynchronously add events to the event thread's queue. The event thread pulls them off of the queue and calls **updateListeners()** for each **ControllerListener**. Unlike the other worker threads, the event thread has no real-time requirements, so poorly written applications can no longer affect the Player's performance.

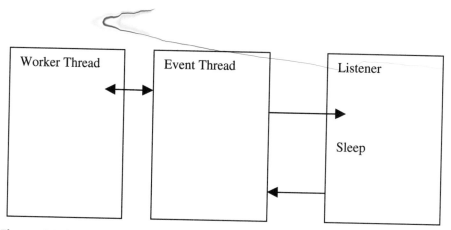

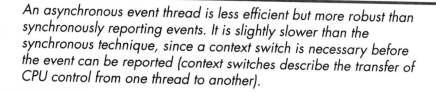

Figure 14-2 Asynchronous event reporting model. In this illustration, since events are being reported by a separate thread, the worker thread is unaffected if the listener blocks for an extended period of time.

Core Tip

An asynchronous event thread is less efficient but more robust than synchronously reporting events. It is slightly slower than the synchronous technique, since a context switch is necessary before the event can be reported (context switches describe the transfer of CPU control from one thread to another).

Cleaning Up the Mess

Attention to detail is the factor that differentiates a robust Player from a toy. One of these details is proper handling of the termination methods: **deallocate()** and **close()**. When applications call **deallocate()**, they expect your Player to release all exclusive resources and free all nonessential memory. To fulfill this request, the following steps will be necessary:

1. Verify that the current state is valid.
2. Stop worker threads.
3. Demote state to at least **Realized**.
4. Report the **DeallocateEvent** to **Listener**s.

The first thing your **deallocate()** routine should do is verify that the Player is not in **Started** state. Unfortunately, Sun neglected to mention why this restriction should be enforced. One likely explanation is that it simplifies Player programming, as you don't have to worry about stopping the **Start** thread.

You are responsible for stopping all worker threads, except the event reporting thread. Once these threads are stopped, the Player's current state must be adjusted (Table 14.6 lists the target states after deallocation). We don't stop the event thread, since it's used to send the **DeallocateEvent** and all future events.

Core Tip

Efficient Players do not destroy worker threads during **deallocate()** *processing, since the caller may subsequently call* **realize()**, **prefetch()**, *or* **start()**. *If the worker threads are destroyed during deallocation, they must be recreated, and this needlessly delays restarting the presentation.*

Table 14.6 State Transition Rules After **deallocate()** Call

Before State	*After State*
Prefetch	Realize
Prefetching	Realize
Realize	Realize
Realizing	Unrealized
Unrealized	Unrealized

Close() is a harsher version of **deallocate()**: It must destroy all threads and resources it has acquired. These activities include:

1. Killing worker threads.
2. Releasing **Prefetch** memory buffers.
3. Stopping and disconnecting from the attached **DataSource**.
4. Sending the terminal **ControllerClosedEvent**.

deallocate() and **close()** operate asynchronously since they must communicate and terminate other Player threads. In general, if a method communicates with a worker thread (i.e., **Prefetch** or **Start**) via semaphores, you should use a separate thread for this communication. When the worker is terminated, the completion event (i.e., **DeallocateEvent** and **ControllerClosedEvent**) should be sent on the separate thread. If you do this processing on the caller's thread, the caller is held captive if a worker thread takes a long time to shut down.

Summary

Although Sun gives minimal guidance for developing Players, basic principles can be inferred from the JMF application guides. These principles include using worker threads for state transitions, reporting events on a separate thread, and releasing resources when they are finished. These principles will also be the basis for our MCML handler.

THE CAPTION MEDIAHANDLER

And every tongue, through utter drought,
Was withered at the root;
We could not speak, no more than if
We had been choked with soot,
Ah! well-a-day! what evil looks
Had I from old and young!
Instead of the cross, the Albatross
About my neck was hung

**Samuel Taylor Coleridge, *The Rime of the
Ancient Mariner*, 1798**

Chapter 15

The **CaptionMediaHandler** processes MCML files and is composed of the following objects: a **ControlPanelComponent**, a **VisualComponent**, and a **ThreadGroup**.

The **ControlPanelComponent**, called **CaptionControlPanelComponent**, provides a default user interface to control the Player (see Figures 15-1 and 15-2). It is a subclass of the **SwingComponent** control and contains a *Start* button to initiate playback, and a *Stop* button to pause playback, and a *JSlider* to search within the content. The first two controls are straightforward: They invoke **Player.start()** and **Player.stop()**, respectively, when pressed.

Figure 15-1 Solaris version of **CaptionControlPanelComponent**.

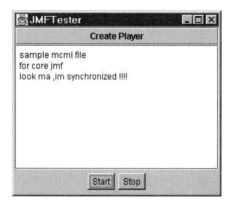

Figure 15–2 Win32 version of `CaptionControlPanelComponent`.

The slider control is more intriguing. The **CaptionControlPanelCom-ponent** registers a **ChangeListener** with the slider. When the user has finished moving the slider, the **stateChanged()** method retrieves the slider's current position and converts this position into a **Time** object. This **Time** object is used to change the Player's media time via **setMediaTime()**.

Listing 15.1 The slider's `ChangeListener`.

```
slider.addChangeListener(this);

public void stateChanged( com.sun.java.swing.event.Chan-
geEvent evt )
{
    JSlider source = (JSlider) evt.getSource();
    if ( source.getValueIsAdjusting() == false )
    {
        Time newtime = new Time( (double) source.getVal-
ue() );
handler.setMediaTime( newtime );

    }
}
```

The **CaptionControlPanelComponent** exposes a **setMaximum()** method that the **MediaHandler** can call to inform it of the total playing time of a file. Until this method is called, the slider does not have a valid range and is essentially unusable.

During the realization process, the **CaptionMediaHandler** connects to its **DataSource** and retrieves the file time. It immediately calls the **set-**

Maximum() method, and the slider is informed of its maximum potential value. Since it is not possible for an application to obtain a **ControlPanel-Component** before realization is complete, the user can never obtain a **CaptionControlPanelComponent** object whose slider has an uninitialized range.

Core Tip

Do not try to shove too much functionality into **ControlPanel-Component** *'s constructor. For instance, if you tried to set a valid range for the* **CaptionControlPanelComponent** *'s slider in the* **CaptionControlPanelComponent** *'s constructor, an exception would be thrown, since the Player is clueless about the length of the file.*

Instead, a **ControlPanelComponent** *should rely on the Player to supply it with initialization information, and this information must be retrieved from the Player before the realization process is complete. Once a Player becomes realized, JMF mandates that the* **ControlPanelComponent** *be fully functional.*

ControlPanelComponent Should Listen!

ControlPanelComponents are worthless if they don't attach a listener to a Player. Unless they are aware of a Player's state, invalid buttons are selectable and sliders can't be updated when media positions change. For instance, if a Player is in **Stopped** state, the *Stop* button is irrelevant and should be disabled. Likewise, once the Player enters **Started** state, the *Play* button should be disabled.

If you decide to make your **ControlPanelComponent** a listener, don't do it in the **ControlPanelComponent** constructor. While the compiler will not generate an error, it will generate an exception at runtime, since the Player is not fully constructed when it calls the **ControlPanelComponent**'s constructor. As a result, it is not prepared to add a listener.

To avoid this problem, the **CaptionControlPanelComponent** adds a listener when the **Realize** thread informs it of the media's length. At this point, the Player is constructed and capable of supporting multiple listeners.

Text Never Looked So Good

The **CaptionMediaHandler** also supplies a video component called **CaptionVisualComponent**, where it writes the text from the MCML file. The **CaptionVisualComponent** is a subclass of **JScrollPane** and contains only one component: a **JTextArea** object.

It surfaces two methods that the Player can use to access the **JTextArea** object: **append()** and **setText()**. Since the **JTextArea** object is inaccessible to external classes, these methods enable clients such as the Player to append or initialize the text in the **CaptionVisualComponent**.

Core Tip

*A common mistake many people make is forgetting to add a Player's **VisualComponent** to their application frame or window. You can immediately diagnose when this error is made with a video Player since you hear the audio track but see no video. By contrast, if you forget to add the **CaptionVisualComponent** to your application frame or window, nothing will be seen on the screen and you may spend many fruitless hours trying to debug why the Player isn't working.*

Listing 15.2 Be sure to add the **VisualComponent** to your application when using the **CaptionMediaHandler**.

```
if ( visualComponent == null )
{
  if (( visualComponent = player.getVisualComponent())
!= null)
  {

     contentPane.add(visualComponent, BorderLayout.CEN-
TER );

  }

}
```

*To avoid a headache, always remember to check if a Player has a **VisualComponent** and display it when appropriate (see Listing 15.2)!*

It's All in the Threads!

All the **CaptionMediaHandler**'s processor-intensive activities are performed on worker threads to follow JMF's asynchronous programming model. For instance, **realize()** does little besides spawning a **CaptionRealize** thread object. The **CaptionRealize** thread first sets the **CaptionMediaHandler**'s current state to **Realizing** and its target state to **Realized**.

After initializing states, it calls **getInitialTextInfo()**, the thread's worker method. This method establishes communication between the **MediaHandler** and the attached **DataSource**, and reads just enough information so that the **VisualComponent** can initialize.

The first step in this process is to retrieve **handler.pullstreams** (an array of **SourceStreams** streams) from the **DataSource** (see Listing 15.3). Most **DataSource**s only contain one stream. However, we specifically designed the **MCMLTextDataSource** to use two streams. Therefore, this array will contain two elements: a time-based stream and a text stream.

```
handler.pullstreams = ( (MCMLTextDataSource)
handler.dataSrc).getStreams();
handler.dataSrc.start();
```

Since MCML files are small, we can safely read both streams into memory. However, the actual transfer of content is delayed until the **Prefetching** phase, to speed up the realization process. We ask stream how many bytes it contains and allocate a byte array large enough to hold each stream.

```
handler.timebuffer = new byte[(int)
handler.timestream.getContentLength()];
      handler.textbuffer = new byte[(int)
handler.textstream.getContentLength()];
```

The **Realize** thread's final act is to determine the stream's duration. This information is then forwarded to the **CaptionControlPanelComponent** so it can set the valid range for its slider.

```
      handler.filetime = handler.dataSrc.getDuration();
controlcomponent.setMaximum( (int)
handler.filetime.getSeconds() );
```

Core Tip

The guidelines I've given for the **realize()** *thread are flexible and should be adjusted based on your specific requirements. For instance, some JMF Players download the entire file during realization, presumably to improve performance and also to determine file size.*

When **getInitialTextInfo()** completes, the **Realize** thread sets the state to **Realized**, sends the **RealizeCompleteEvent** to all listeners, and then terminates.

The next thread to be started is the **CaptionPrefetch** thread. Since we are manipulating and displaying text, the caption device can support an infinite number of users and therefore is nonexclusive. As a result, this thread has no exclusive resources to acquire and can concentrate on filling data buffers.

After setting the **CaptionMediaHandler**'s current and target states, the **Prefetch** thread calls a worker method: **fillPrefetchBuffers()**. This method reads the entire contents of both streams, and places them into the time and text byte arrays allocated during in the realization process.

Listing 15.3 Reading data from the Caption **DataSource SourceStreams**.

```
try
{
  int n = handler.timestream.read(handler.timebuffer, 0,
timestreamlen);
  if (n != -1 )
  {
    n = handler.textstream.read(handler.textbuffer, 0,
(int) handler.textstream.getContentLength());
  }
}
catch (java.io.IOException ex)
{
  throw ex;
}
```

After this, it pulls the timing and text length information for each **<displaytext>** tag out of the timing information array and textual part of the text array, respectively. Each tag is added to **textdescriptor** (a Vector of text information). This process repeats until we exhaust the arrays of data. Since the prefetch process has completed, the **CaptionMediaHandler**'s state is updated and a **PrefetchCompleteEvent** is sent to all callers.

When the user initiates playback, a **CaptionStart** thread is created to display the text we retrieved in the **Prefetch** thread. It immediately sets the state to **Started**, posts a **StartEvent** to the caller, and begins displaying the caption information in the **VisualComponent**.

Each text tag element in **textdescriptor** is processed sequentially. The **Start** thread examines the tag's time stamp, and if the Player's media time is less than the tag's time stamp (i.e., the tag expires in the future), we display the tag and wait for its scheduled completion time. If playback proceeds smoothly, the system will wake our thread when the tag's valid time period expires, and this process will continue until we run out of tags.

If an exception happens, our **wait()** exception handler will be invoked. Typically, when we catch an exception, we break out of our display tag loop, stop the media device, and terminate the thread (see Listing 15.4).

Listing 15.4 Exception processing in the **CaptionStart** thread.

```
catch ( InterruptedException e )
{

// caller is updating our media time
    if ( bStopFlag)
    {
       bAborted = true;
       break;
    }
    else
    {
       bInterrupted = true;
       loop = 0;
       totaltimeseen = 0;
       playbackstarttime = ((int) handler.starttime.
getSeconds() * 1000) + ( (int) timeBaseTime.getSeconds() *
1000) ;

    }
}
```

However, if the user calls **setMediaTime()** when the Player is playing, the Player should immediately begin playback at the new media position. In this scenario, we retrieve the new playback time requested by the user and resume playback.

Core Tip

setMediaTime() *can wreak havoc in your code if you're not careful. For instance, you must be able to handle scenarios such as the user seeking backward in time while you are playing. Failure to anticipate these circumstances will, at a minimum, result in an unstable Player, and could result in an unforeseen exception.*

Consequently, for safety purposes, the **CaptionStart** *thread always restarts its tag parsing at the first tag, to ensure that tags are not mistakenly skipped over.*

When the Player hits the stopping point requested by the user or runs out of data, we exit the tag decode and display loop, report the **EndOfMedia-Event**, and terminate.

Events Are the Spice of Life

When the **Realize**, **Prefetch**, and **Start** threads wish to send events to listeners, they pass the event to the **SendThread** class (this class blocks until an event needs to be sent). The **addEvent()** method is used to wake up the **SendThread** and request that it send the requested event to listeners (see Listing 15.5).

sendOutEvents() is responsible for notifying the listener of any events that have transpired since the last time **SendThread** was awake. It walks through a vector of events, posts each event with **handler.update-Listeners()**, and removes the event from the **eventVector** (see Listing 15.6).

Listing 15.5 The `addEvent()` method alerts the `SendThread` that an event must be posted to all listeners.

```
public void addEvent( javax.media.ControllerEvent e )
{
    synchronized ( this )
    {
        eventVector.addElement( e );
        this.notify();
    }

}
```

Listing 15.6 `sendOutEvents` processes events for `SendThread`.

```
public void sendOutEvents( )
{

    int numevents = eventVector.size();
    for ( int eventloop = 0; eventloop < numevents; event-
loop++ )
    {
        handler.updateListeners ( (ControllerEvent)
eventVector.elementAt( 0 ) );
        eventVector.removeElementAt( 0 );
    }

}
```

The **run()** method is an infinite loop of waiting for an event and servicing that event with the **sendOutEvents()** method. It contains one trick: Before it blocks, it checks to see if another thread added an event to the vector while **SendThread** didn't own the thread semaphore. If there is an event, it services the thread rather than blocking (see Listing 15.7).

If **run()** blocks instead of sending an event, the application and Player could end up in a state of suspended animation. For instance, if a **Realize-CompleteEvent** were in the **eventVector** and the thread ignored it and blocked, the application would wait forever for the **RealizeComple-teEvent** event before it issued a **prefetch**. Similarly, the Player would never send another event to wake up **SendThread** until the application received the **RealizeCompleteEvent**.

Listing 15.7 Event thread block routine. The event thread checks to see if an event is in the **eventVector** before blocking to prevent deadlock.

```
try
{
        if ( eventVector.size() == 0 )
        {
            wait();
        }

        if ( bStopFlag )
        {
            break;
        }
        else
        {
            sendOutEvents();
        }
        }
        catch (InterruptedException ex)
        {
        break;
}
```

A Whole New Class of Events

If your application contains a slider that represents the current media time, you have three options to synchronize the slider position with media progression: using a generic timer, polling the Player, and using a custom Player event. A generic timer that fires on a periodic basis doesn't represent the true media time; the media may advance slightly faster or slower than the system clock. In addition, the timer will continue to fire even when playback pauses, so custom code is required to synchronize media time to the timer event.

A second option is to spawn a separate thread a poll the Player's media time (via **getMediaTime()**) on a periodic basis. You must ensure that this thread is notified if playback is paused or if errors occur, otherwise it will needlessly bother the Player with **getMediaTime()** requests when nothing has changed.

The final option is to rely on the Player to periodically inform the application about the media time. Surprisingly, JMF does not build this functionality into each Player, so we need a custom event to track media progression. The beauty of JMF's object-oriented design is that you can customize Players to fit your particular needs. For instance, the **CaptionMediaHandler** uses a new class of event called **PositionAdviseEvent** to inform applications about the current Playback position.

```
public class PositionAdviseEvent extends
javax.media.ControllerEvent
```

PositionAdviseEvent is a superior solution, since the Player already has a unique thread to handle playback and no additional threads are created. This event is like a **StartEvent**, but it doesn't report state transition information because the Player's current and target states remain unchanged. Like **StartEvent**, you retrieve the current media time from the event by calling **getMediaTime()**.

Your application calls **setPosAdvise()** to inform it how frequently it should report **PositionAdviseEvents** to listeners. If **setPosAdvise()** is not called with a valid **Time** parameter, the Player will not report **PositionAdviseEvent** to listeners. This ensures that applications unaware of our custom event are not inundated with **PositionAdviseEvents**.

```
public void setPosAdvise(Time frequency)
{
   advisefrequency = (int) frequency.getSeconds() * 1000;
}
```

Core Tip

OS/2's MCI was the first multimedia environment to support periodic notifications of the current media time via the **MCI_SETPOSITIONADVISE** *call. Other multimedia platforms such as Win16 and Win32 MCI require polling the driver for media time; as a result, they're less efficient.*

Microsoft eliminated this restriction in DirectShow since clock objects can fire periodic notifications of media time. Hopefully, Sun will follow suit and provide similar functionality to our **PositionAdviseEvent** *in all Players in a future version of JMF.*

SendThread may seem as if it adds unnecessary overhead to your Player since a context switch is necessary for every event that it posts. In an ideal world, it would be unnecessary because listeners would respond instantly to events. Alas, listeners typically perform actions such as updating sliders and other GUI objects in response to events. These actions consume serious quantities of time and, as the call is synchronous, the Player's thread is unusable while it is stuck in the listener.

If we were to report the **PositionAdviseEvent** on the **Start** thread, playback would cease during the duration of event processing. However, our Players can shrug off sluggish listeners, since the **Start** thread never directly interfaces with the listener.

Compilation and Debugging Help

Since this **MediaHandler** directly references classes in the **interactivejava.media.protocol.caption** package, you need to ensure that the **interactivejava** JAR file can be located by both your Java compiler and Java run time.

Once you compile the Player and **DataSource**, you will encounter the intimidating task of testing combined objects. Under normal circumstances, you must rely on the Manager to find and connect your Player and **DataSource**. Unfortunately, early in the development process ,this often doesn't work, and the Manager gives few hints about why it rejects your requests.

You can, however, skip over the Manager and construct a Player yourself (see Listing 15.8). Although this technique is unacceptable for production code, it will minimize the work effort during the development phase.

Production-level **MediaHandler**s and **DataSource**s do not contain test classes. As a result, you must write a separate application to test them. However, during the development process, we can add a class specifically to test our Player (**TextTest.java**). This reduces development time since the test application and Player exist in the same project. When testing is complete, be sure to remove the test class from the JAR file so others don't have to be bothered by it.

Listing 15.8 Manually instantiating a Player without intervention by the Manager.

```
MediaLocator mcmlfile = new MediaLocator("mcmltext:" + tex-
tfile);
player = new CaptionMediaHandler();
textSource = new MCMLTextDataSource(   );
textSource.setLocator ( mcmlfile );
String contentType =  textSource.getContentType();

try
{
    textSource.connect();
    player.setSource( textSource );
}
catch ( IncompatibleSourceException e )
{

    System.out.println("Bad data source....");
}
catch ( IOException e )
{
    System.out.println("General I/O error....");

}

// Add ourselves as a listener for a player's events
player.addControllerListener(this);
```

Summary

The **CaptionMediaHandler** implements the guidelines suggested in Chapter 14, including asynchronous state transitions, event processing, and proper division of workload between the **Prefetch** and **Realize** threads. It also adds support for a custom event called the **PositionAdviseEvent** that enables you to monitor playback progress without having to spawn an additional thread.

Now that we've completed our MCML Player and associated **Data-Source**, it is time to write a CD Player.

GRAPPLING WITH THE CD

Music hath charms to soothe the savage breast.
William Congreve, *The Mourning Bride*

Music, the greatest good that mortals know, And all of heaven we have below.
Joseph Addison, *A Song for St. Cecilia's Day*, 1694

I really liked it [the opera Tosca], even the music was nice.
Yogi Berra

Chapter 16

Although we've had some challenges, the JMF architecture has been robust enough to support any multimedia feature we've tried to implement. Unfortunately, the JMF stream-based architecture is incompatible with the older, nonstreaming devices such as CDs or laserdiscs. Therefore, we will have to create a hack to enable a JMF-based CD Player called CDJolt.

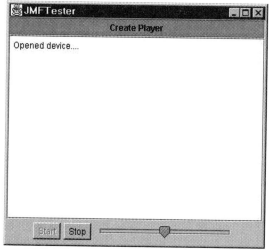

Figure 16–1 CDJolt in action.

To understand why JMF has difficulty with nonstreaming devices, let's revisit the assumptions of JMF. First, JMF assumes that every device will use a clock. Since all multimedia devices use clocks, this presumption is not problematic.

JMF also assumes that every device will transport content from a source location to a target location, where it will be decoded. Since this presupposition is valid for all digital multimedia devices, few developers question it. However, when you use a hybrid digital/analog device such as a CD-ROM drive, this assumption becomes invalid.

There are two techniques to play back audio from a CD-ROM drive. The first alternative is to read the digital audio data from the drive and stream it to an audio card or speakers that can decode digital audio (see Figure 16-1). The second option is to have the drive read the digital data from the disc and send analog audio to the speakers (or to the line-in jack of an audio card) (see Figure 16-2).

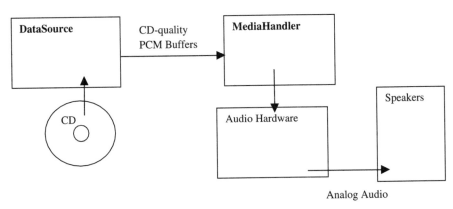

Figure 16–2   How digital streaming from a CD-ROM operates.

The first alternative drops into JMF cleanly. A **DataSource** can be used to stream content from the drive into a streaming CD **MediaHandler** that in turn feeds data to a sound device. By contrast, when the drive decodes audio data and outputs analog audio waveforms to an external device, it voids the need for a **DataSource** since content is not being transported. Furthermore, the **MediaHandler**'s duties are reduced to starting and stopping the device and reporting any errors that may occur during playback.

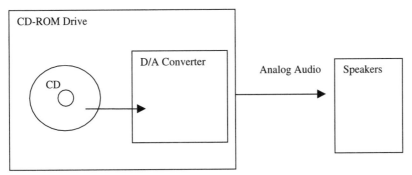

Figure 16–3 How a CD-ROM transforms digital content from a disc into analog output.

The Emperor Has No Clothes

Alas, although a **DataSource** is unnecessary for a nonstreaming device, JMF mandates that the Player be connected to a **DataSource** before playback may begin. Consequently, we must create a bogus **DataSource**, called **CDDataSource**, before we can play back analog CD audio content.

Core Tip

If it is any consolation, DirectShow has the same problem with non-streaming media as JMF: It needs a source filter to stream content before it can be decoded. Both platforms were designed to support streaming media and do not adjust well to nonstreaming devices. The only difference between the approaches is that it is easier to patch JMF to work around the streaming assumption. DirectShow requires more extensive surgery before it can deal with non-streaming content.

OS/2 is one of the few stream-based multimedia platforms that can seamlessly support nonstreaming media. OS/2's primary multimedia interface is the Media Control Interface (MCI). For streaming media, each MCI device uses the Stream Programming Interface (SPI) to transport content. By contrast, nonstreaming MCI devices can use the most efficient communication mechanism and do not have to use SPI.

CDDataSource will not transport any content to the **MediaHandler** since the CD-ROM drive is reading digital data from the drive and converting it to analog audio without intervention from the main computer. Therefore, it is only responsible for verifying that it is operating on the correct protocol and creating a **CDSourceStream** object.

This **DataSource** can only be used on CD-ROM drives and may only be accessed by a new protocol entitled "**cdaudio:**". If protocol is valid, the **getContentType()** method will report that the **DataSource**'s source stream uses the '**audio.nonstreamingcdaudio**' format (see Listing 16.1).

Listing 16.1 Verification that the correct protocol is being used with the CD **DataSource**.

```
String locatorString = getLocator().toExternalForm();

        String typeString = "unknown";

        if (locatorString.startsWith("cdaudio::"))
                typeString = "audio.nonstreamingcdau-
dio";

        return typeString;
```

Core Tip

*Since the CD **DataSource** contains so little functionality, if you remove a few lines of code, you will have an empty **DataSource** template which you can reuse when you develop new **DataSource**s.*

To be a legitimate Pull **DataSource**, we must also create a **PullSourceStream** class called **CDSourceStream**. This source stream will be a true shell, since the **MediaHandler** will ignore it and its containing **DataSource**.

The Natives Are Returning

The core of CDJolt is its Player (or **MediaHandler**). This Player is responsible for locating the CD-ROM drive, opening a handle to the drive, starting and stopping playback, and closing the device when the Player is closed. Since Java offers no interface to control the CD-ROM drive, we will have to resort to client-side JNI for this functionality.

There are two flavors of JNI: server-side and client-side. The C++ Bean-Bridge program we designed in Chapter 10 is illustrative of server-side JNI programming. This program starts the JVM and uses it as a client object. By contrast, client-side JNI programming describes a scenario where the JVM uses JNI code as a worker (or client).

Rather than calling low-level CD methods throughout the MediaHandler, we're going to create a single class, called **CDAudio**, that abstracts the features of a CD-ROM drive (see Listing 16.2). This class exposes native methods to open, play, pause, resume, stop, and close the CD device. It is intentionally thin on function; additional capabilities will be provided by the **MediaHandler** classes that use it.

The actual name of the native library that the **CDAudio** class will attempt to load is JMFCD. This book contains the Win32 implementation of this library (**JMFCD.DLL**). To run this sample on UNIX, you must port the Win32 source to create the shared library (i.e., **libJMFC.so**).

Listing 16.2 Overview of class used to access CD data.

```
class CDAudio
{
 public native void openCD();
 public native void playCD();
 public native void pauseCD();
 public native void resumeCD();
 public native void seekCD(int seekto );
 public int numtracks();
 public native void closeCD();
}
```

Core Tip

If you decide to change the package name for the **CDMedia-Handler***, you will need to recompile the associated JNI library or DLL. Recompilation is necessary because the package signature is embedded in the executable's entry points (see Listing 16.3). Consequently, once the package signature changes,*

*the Java class loader will refuse to load the library until the name
change is resolved.*

> **Listing 16.3** Since the package name is embedded in the JNI
> method, if you change the package name, you must regenerate
> the JNI header file and recompile the associated JNI code.

```
Java_interactivejava_media_content_cdaudio_CDAudio_JNI
play
    (JNIEnv *env, jobject CDAudio, jint deviceid)
```

The Joys of Win32 Multimedia Programming

As we discussed in Chapter 2, implementing a JMF Player on a modern multimedia environment such as QuickTime or DirectShow is relatively painless.
Unfortunately, Win32 uses the archaic MCI interface to control CD-ROM
drives. Although it runs on powerful, 32-bit platforms, MCI retains many irritating restrictions from its 16-bit Windows 3.1 heritage. One of these restrictions virtually cripples CDJolt: Only one thread can communicate with the
MCI subsystem.

This problem is vexing, because JMF mandates that **Realizing**, **Prefetching**, and **Start** state transitions be performed on separate threads
to ensure asynchronous operation. Since the Win32 Java VM creates a native
Win32 thread for each Java thread, we have three native threads that need to
access the MCI CD device.

Core Tip

*Do not assume that a JVM automatically spawns a native thread for
each Java thread object you create. The Java specification does not
guarantee that you will receive a native thread for every Java
thread, since Java must be able to run on operating systems without
threads. As a result, threads operate differently on each platform.
For example, all Win32 JVMs spawn a native thread for each Java
thread. Solaris JVMs before 1.1.6 did not spawn kernel threads for
each Java thread. Fortunately, most UNIX JVMs now equate Java
threads with native threads.*

Unfortunately, if multiple threads attempt to control the CD, Win32's version of MCI chokes and returns an error. Therefore, we have two options: perform realization and prefetch activities on the **Start** thread, or create a dedicated thread to process all communication with the CD.

Placing all resource-consuming activities on the **Start** thread is the last resort, since it isn't compliant with JMF guidelines and eliminates the need for worker threads. As we previously discovered, after Players have been **prefetched, start()** should begin playback immediately. By stuffing resource allocation and consumption into the **Start** thread, this thread no longer will have instantaneous response. Furthermore, this alternative renders the **realize()** and **prefetch()** threads worthless since they cannot communicate with the CD.

The preferred technique to handle this Win32 restriction is to create a thread whose sole responsibility is to communicate with the CD. This thread (known as the **MCIHack** thread) operates in an infinite loop of blocking, waking up when an action is requested, informing the CD of the request, and notifying the caller that the request completed (see Listing 16.5). When the Player is terminating, it sets the **bStopFlag** to true. This flag causes the thread to break out of the infinite loop and terminate. The entire source for this thread can be found in **MCIHack.java**.

Listing 16.4 The main processing loop in the dedicated MCI thread.

```
public void run()
    {

        while (true)
        {
            synchronized (this)
            {
                try
                {
                    wait();

                    if ( bStopFlag )
                    {
                        handler.cdaudio.close();
                        break;
                    }

                    switch (
handler.RequestedAction )
```

Listing 16.4 The main processing loop in the dedicated MCI thread.

```
                                          {
                                            case
CDMediaHandler.OPEN_CD:
handler.cdaudio.open();
handler.NotifyPrefecthThread();
                                                break;
                                            case
CDMediaHandler.PLAY_CD:
                                                handler.cdaudio.play();
handler.NotifyStartThread();
                                                break;
                                            case
CDMediaHandler.PAUSE_CD:
                                                handler.cdaudio.pause();
                                                break;
                                            case
CDMediaHandler.CLOSE_CD:
                                                handler.cdaudio.close();
                                                break;
                                            case
CDMediaHandler.RESUME_CD:
                                                handler.cdaudio.resume();
                                                break;


                                            }
                                          }
                                          catch (InterruptedException ex)
                                          {
                                              // ignore
                                          }
                                      }
                                  }

} // run
```

When the **Realize**, **Prefetch**, and **Start** threads wish to commu-
nicate with the **MCIHack** thread, they update the **MediaHandler**'s
RequestedAction variable, **notify()** the **MCIHack** thread of the
request, and block on the **MCIHack** thread's semaphore until the **MCI-
Hack** completes (see Listing 16.5). It is essential that you block until
MCIHack finishes, or you may notify listeners that they have completed

state transition (i.e., **realize**, **prefetch**, or **start**) while the state transition is still occurring.

Listing 16.5 How the **start** worker thread requests that the **MCIHack** thread start playback.

```
handler.RequestedAction = CDMediaHandler.PLAY_CD;
handler.NotifyHackThread();

// wait for thread to complete......
synchronized (this )
{
    try
    {
            wait();
    }
    catch (InterruptedException ex)
    {
    }
}
```

Core Tip

*If you implement CDJolt on UNIX or another operating system, the **MCIHack** thread will continue to work. However, you may wish to remove this thread and call **CDAudio** class directly from the **Realize**, **Prefetch**, and **Start** threads to improve performance.*

MCI Details

The actual native code for CDJolt is found in **cdcontrol.cpp**. It will compile on both OS/2 and Win32. The native **CDAudio.open** is the first method applications should call (see Listing 16.6). It opens the CD device, initializes the time format to milliseconds, and returns a device ID (or handle) to the **CDAudio** class. The class tucks this device ID into a private variable for use by all other native CD methods.

Listing 16.6 JNI code to open the CD-ROM device.

```
// first, open the device.

#ifdef OS2
    mopDuetPart.hwndCallback       = (HWND) 0;              /*
For MM_MCIPASSDEVICE */
    mopDuetPart.usDeviceID         = (USHORT)  0; /* this is
returned    */
    mopDuetPart.pszDeviceType      = (PSZ)
MCI_DEVTYPE_CD_AUDIO;
    mopDuetPart.pszElementName     = (PSZ)    NULL; /* doesn't
matter         */
#elif WIN32
    mopDuetPart.dwCallback         = 0;            /* For
MM_MCIPASSDEVICE */
    mopDuetPart.wDeviceID          = 0; /* this is returned    */
    mopDuetPart.lpstrDeviceType    = (LPSTR)
MCI_DEVTYPE_CD_AUDIO;
    mopDuetPart.lpstrElementName   = (LPSTR)    NULL; /*
doesn't matter         */
#endif


    ulError = SendCommand( 0,
                           MCI_OPEN,
#ifdef WIN32
                           MCI_OPEN_TYPE |
#endif

                           MCI_WAIT | MCI_OPEN_TYPE_ID |
MCI_OPEN_SHAREABLE,
                           (PVOID) &mopDuetPart );
```

Core Tip

*We pass this device handle to every native method except the open
routine for performance reasons. You could have the native code
query the JVM for the value of the class' device handle variable, but
as we discussed previously, there is a significant performance hit
when you communicate with the JVM from C or C++. Consequently,
we pass this device ID directly to the native code so it doesn't need
to call back into the JVM.*

The native code is very spartan. It is not threaded and has no minimum response time. In fact, buggy CD-ROM microcode has been known to hold threads captive for extended periods. Therefore, anyone using the **CDAudio** class is responsible for ensuring that calls are placed on a separate thread.

Once the device is opened, the **MCIHack** thread starts playback by calling **CDAudio.open()**. The MCI JNI code to start playback is shown in Listing 16.7.

Listing 16.7 Win32 JNI code to start playing the CD.

```
JNIEXPORT void JNICALL
Java_interactivejava_media_content_cdaudio_CDAudio_JNIplay
   (JNIEnv *env, jobject CDAudio, jint deviceid)

{
    MCI_PLAY_PARMS      mppGroup;                   /* play parms
for MCI_PLAY        */

        SendCommand( deviceid,
                              MCI_PLAY,
                              0,
                              (PVOID) &mppGroup );

}
```

When the CD **MediaHandler** is closed, it requests that the **MCIHack** thread close the CD object. The MCI JNI code to close the CD is shown in Listing 16.8.

Core Tip

Failure to close the CD will have different results depending on your operating system. The Java garbage collector cannot close the CD since it was allocated by JNI code. As a result, the native operating system garbage collection will be responsible for cleaning up the mess. For example, OS/2 stops the CD from playing when the application terminates. By contrast, Win 9x and NT let the CD play even though its owner died.

Listing 16.8 Win32 JNI code to close the CD.

```
JNIEXPORT void JNICALL
Java_interactivejava_media_content_cdaudio_CDAudio_JNIclose

   (JNIEnv *env, jobject CDAudio, jint deviceid)
{
     MCI_GENERIC_PARMS mciGenericParms;            /* generic
parms for MCI_CLOSE    */


                         SendCommand( deviceid,
                                       MCI_CLOSE,
                                       MCI_WAIT,
                                       (PVOID)
&mciGenericParms );
}
```

Core Tip

Additional details on interfacing Win32 MCI calls to Java can be found in my PC Magazine article, "Java and Digital Audio: An Excellent Brew,"

http://www.zdnet.com/pcmag/pctech/content/15/14/ir1514.001.html

This article shows you how to integrate Java to JDK 1.0.x-style native code. The first thing you'll notice is that JNI syntax is dramatically simpler than the previous code. We no longer need a translation layer to map Java structures to C structures; rather, we are passed C-style structures directly.

This brief, but ugly, venture into the world of Win32 multimedia programming should make you grateful for the consistency and portability provided by JMF. It also gives you insight into the aggravation JMF runtime developers experience on a daily basis as they try to port JMF to a specific operating system.

Decisions, Decisions...

Because we are writing a nonstreaming Player, many of the thread responsibility guidelines we mentioned in the previous chapter are moot. For instance, a nonstreaming device has no buffers to fill, so the **Prefetch** threads only need to acquire the exclusive resources associated with the device. Similarly, the **Realize** thread can't fill any buffers, so it is only responsible for acquiring nonexclusive resources.

Since there is only one resource associated with the **CDAudio** class (a handle to the device), you could acquire this resource in either the **Realize** or **Prefetch** thread. Since CD devices are nonexclusive (i.e., they permit multiple applications to access them), it is permissible to open the device on the **Realize** thread.

Furthermore, we can't determine the playing time of the CD until we open the device. JMF mandates that applications be able to access the **ControlPanelComponent** via **getControlPanelComponent()** after the **RealizeCompleteEvent** has been received. However, the position slider in our **ControlPanelComponent** needs the total playing time to set the bounds for the slider. If we waited until Prefetch completion to obtain this information, we could not set the upper bounds for the slider; this is unacceptable. Therefore, we must open the device on the **Realize** thread.

The remaining responsibilities of the **Realize** thread are to ensure that the class has been successfully created and to transition the Player from **Realizing** to **Realized** state.

When Is a Thread Truly Necessary?

Chapter 14 enumerated the **MediaHandler** methods that operate asynchronously and require threads to complete their operations (see Table 14.2). However, there are circumstances where additional methods may be forced to use threads to ensure asynchronous operation.

For example, the **CaptionMediaHandler** we created in the previous chapter doesn't control external hardware devices; it can stop instantly. Therefore, you don't have to create a separate thread to stop the handler. By contrast, when **stop()** is called, CDJolt must stop an external device before reporting the **StopByRequestEvent** to the caller. Since stopping the CD-ROM drive can take an indeterminate quantity of time, CDJolt must use a special **Stop** thread (called **CDStop**) to comply with JMF's asynchronous guidelines for a **MediaHandler**.

The current design of CDJolt and the Caption **MediaHandler** spawns a separate thread for each **start()**, **realize()**, or **prefetch()** call. While this is tolerable for a sample Player in a non-production environment, it has a significant performance penalty that is unacceptable for a production environment.

A well-tuned Player should only create a thread for these methods once. Subsequent calls to said methods should reuse the existing thread object rather than creating a new thread. Unfortunately, while reusing threads boosts performance, it dramatically complicates the code. Care must be taken to ensure that worker threads are idle before trying to wake them, or you will encounter race conditions and deadlocks.

It's All Downhill from Here

Our last action item is to fill out the **CDMediaHandler** class. This class is responsible for spawning threads for asynchronous commands (i.e., **prefetch**, **start** etc.), creating the control, and caching components and cleaning up resources.

When an asynchronous command is received, we examine the current state. If the desired state has already been processed (i.e., the user is calling **realize()** and we are already **Prefetched**), then we report the **RealizeCompleteEvent** to the user and return. Otherwise, we create the appropriate worker thread and allow it to report the event. We could have the thread send the event in all cases; however, it would be extremely inefficient to spawn a thread simply to report an event.

The **CDMediaHandler** also creates button-based controls that an external application can use to drive CDJolt. This control is primitive; it only supports starting, stopping, and repositioning the device. When the user hits the Start button, the control issues a **start()** call. When stop is requested, the Player is told to **stop()**.

If the **ControlPanelComponent** slider is moved, **setMediaTime()** is called to update the Player's position. If the CD is still playing when **setMediaTime()** is called, the **MediaHandler** is responsible for ensuring that playback continues after repositioning the device (see Listing 16.9).

Listing 16.9 setMediaTime() processing in CDMediaHandler.
When setMediaTime() is called, the MediaHandler seeks the CD
to the new time, then updates the Start thread (if necessary) with the
new media time.

```
synchronized (mcihackthread )
{

    RequestedAction = CDMediaHandler.SEEK_CD;
    threadtoNotify = HACK_THREAD;
    SeekPosition = (int) now.getSeconds();
    starttime = SeekPosition * 1000;
    NotifyHackThread();

    try
    {
        mcihackthread.wait();
    }
    catch (InterruptedException ex)
    {
      // ignore
    }

    System.out.println("End Setting media time.......");

}


// we are responsible for continuing playback IF
// we are already started....

if ( getState() == Controller.Started )
{

    // wait for thread to complete......
    synchronized (mcihackthread )
    {
        RequestedAction = CDMediaHandler.PLAY_CD;
        threadtoNotify = HACK_THREAD;
        NotifyHackThread();

        try
        {
```

Listing 16.9 `setMediaTime()` processing in `CDMediaHandler`. When `setMediaTime()` is called, the `MediaHandler` seeks the CD to the new time, then updates the `Start` thread (if necessary) with the new media time.   (continued)

```
            mcihackthread.wait();
      }
    catch (InterruptedException ex)
    {
          // ignore
    }

      }
}
```

Finally, the last task CDJolt must perform is to clean up the threads and objects it has allocated. **deallocate()** cleans stops and destroys any thread objects. For performance reasons, we don't close the **CDaudio** object, since the user can still **realize** or **prefetch** the device in the future. Although it is permissible to close hardware resources in this method, you'd have to reopen it when the device was subsequently **prefetch**ing, which will cause a big performance hit.

Unlike **deallocate()**, **close()** not only destroys all existing threads including the event thread, but it also closes hardware resources it has acquired. **close()** processing is trickier than **deallocate()** since you can call it while you are playing the CD. Consequently, it must be intelligent enough to stop the playback thread, then destroy it.

close() also must ensure that the releasing of a hardware device is a synchronous process. Under normal circumstances, a call to **cdaudio.close()** would be sufficient to eliminate hardware resources. Unfortunately, the Win32 MCI restrictions force us to use the **HackThread** to close the device (see Listing 16.10). Because the **HackThread** operates asynchronously, if we fail to wait for it to complete, we could destroy the **HackThread** before it successfully closes the device. Should this happen, resources will go unowned and the device may continue playing ad infinitum.

Listing 16.10 Overview of `close()` processing in the `CDMediaHandler`.

```
if (mcihackthread != null)
{
        mcihackthread.setStopFlag(true);
        threadtoNotify = MAIN_THREAD;
        RequestedAction = CLOSE_CD;

        NotifyHackThread();

        synchronized ( this )
        {
            try
          {
            wait();
                }
            catch (InterruptedException ex)
            {
              // ignore
            }

}
```

Summary

Nonstreaming devices do not fit smoothly into the JMF architecture. One primary problem is that JMF Players are required to support a **DataSource** even if they do not need one. Fortunately, it is possible to create fake **Data-Sources** and attach them to a nonstreaming **MediaHandler**. Because it is only required to connect with a **DataSource**, the **MediaHandler** can safely ignore the **DataSource** and proceed with its duties. These responsibilities include accessing native device resources, and spawning threads to respond to commands that clean up. We used client-side Java programming to open, stop, play, pause, and seek the CD-ROM drive. Due to limitations in the Win32 MCI interface, a separate thread was given the responsibility of communicating with the drive.

We finally have all of the pieces in place for our synchronization example, so the next chapter will illustrate how you can synchronize the Caption Player to CDJolt.

THE ULTIMATE SYNCHRONIZATION: THE MARRIAGE OF PLAYERS

Grief walks upon the heels of pleasure;
married in haste, we repent at leisure.

William Congreve, *The Mourning Bride*

Thou must be married to no man but me;
For I am he am born to tame you Kate,
And bring you from a wild Kate to a Kate.

William Shakespeare,
Taming of the Shrew

O ver the past four chapters, we've assembled all of the pieces (i.e., a Caption **DataSource** and **MediaHandler** and a CD **Data-Source** and **MediaHandler**) necessary to create a robust synchronization example. We'll call this application JMFMarriage since it joins two seemingly incompatible Players into one cohesive unit.

Figure 17-1 JMFMarriage combines the caption and CD **MediaHandlers**.

All of These Chapters for This Little Code?

As we discovered in Chapter 11, when you join multiple **Players**, the first thing you need to decide on is which **Player** will be the master and which **Player**(s) will be the slave. **CDJolt** must be the master **Player** for **JMFMarriage** for two reasons: it will throw an exception if you attempt to make it a slave, and the Caption **Player** has been specifically designed to be a slave.

CORE TIP

The easiest way to detect if a **Player** *supports being a slave is to try to set the Player's* **TimeBase***. Players like* **CDJolt** *will throw an* **IncompatibleTimeBaseException** *if they won't accept another Player's* **TimeBase***. Consequently, it is not possible to synchronize two* **CDJolt** *objects or* **CDJolt** *with any master-only* **Players***.*

JMFMarriage first creates the two Players and attaches itself as a **ControllerListener** to both Players (see Listing 17.1). Since the Players will report events to the same **controllerUpdate()** method, we use the event's **getSource()** method to determine the **Controller** responsible for sending the event.

Listing 17.1 Code to open the CD and Caption Players.

```
cdplayer = new CDMediaHandler();

// Add ourselves as a listener for a player's events
cdplayer.addControllerListener(this);

MediaLocator mcmlfile = new MediaLocator("take6.mcml");

captionplayer = new CaptionMediaHandler();


textSource = new MCMLTextDataSource(   );

textSource.setLocator ( mcmlfile );
```

Listing 17.1 Code to open the CD and Caption Players. (continued)

```
String contentType = textSource.getContentType();

try
{
    textSource.connect();
    captionplayer.setSource( textSource );
}
catch ( IncompatibleSourceException e )
{

    System.out.println("Bad data source....");
}
catch ( IOException e )
{
    System.out.println("General I/O error....");

}

// Add ourselves as a listener for a player's events
cdplayer.addControllerListener(this);
captionplayer.addControllerListener(this);
```

Sun's documentation warns that Players will throw a **NotRealized-Error** if you attempt to add an **Unrealized Controller** to them. Consequently, **JMFMarriage** does not try to synchronize the Players until both are **Realized**. When the user presses the **CreatePlayer** button, it calls **realize()** on both Players and waits for two **Realize-CompleteEvents** (see Listing 17.2).

Listing 17.2 **realize()** is called before attempting to synchronize the Players.

```
private class SendListener implements ActionListener
    {
        public void actionPerformed(ActionEvent e)
        {
                cdplayer.realize();
                captionplayer.realize();
        }
```

If you are synchronizing Players, wait until all Players realize before you attempt to add a given Player's **ControlPanelComponent** *to your application. If you decide to display a* **ControlPanel-Component** *too early, it will be unable to start the* **Unrealized** *or* **Realizing** *Players and may result in an exception being thrown.*

These restrictions do not apply to **VisualComponents** *and they may be added to your application any time after a Player realizes.*

When both **RealizeCompleteEvent**s are processed, JMFMarriage retrieves the **ControlPanelComponent** of the master Player (CDJolt) and the **VisualComponent** of the slave Player and adds them to the application frame (see Listing 17.3). Then it requests the Caption Player be added as a slave **Controller** to CDJolt. Once the Caption Player becomes a slave to CDJolt, CDJolt hides all of complexities of managing multiple Players from our application. We can safely treat it as a single device.

```
cdplayer.addController( captionplayer );
```

The application then relinquishes the user interface control to CDJolt's **ControlPanelComponent**. This **ControlPanelComponent** will start and stop the synchronized Players on our behalf.

Listing 17.3 Proper procedure for adding **ControlPanel-Components** to a synchronized Player.

```
if (controlComponent == null &&
             cdplayer.getState() == Controller.Realized &&
             captionplayer.getState() == Controller.Real-
ized )
{

    if (( controlComponent = cdplayer.getControlPanelCompo-
nent()) != null)
    {
        try
        {
```

Listing 17.3 Proper procedure for adding `ControlPanel-Component`s to a synchronized Player. (continued)

```
    cdplayer.addController( captionplayer );
    }
    catch(ClockStartedError e)
    {
      System.out.println("Already started");
    }
    catch(NotRealizedError e)
    {
      System.out.println("Not realized");
    }
    catch(IncompatibleTimeBaseException e)
    {
      System.out.println("Can't change time base");
    }

    contentPane.add(controlComponent, BorderLayout.
SOUTH );

  }
}
```

CORE TIP

If you add a **ControlPanelComponent** *or* **VisualComponent**
to a **Jframe***, the size of the* **Jframe** *may be altered. As a result,
you should query the* **Jframe** *for its preferred size and size the*
Jframe *accordingly (see Listing 17.4). If you don't resize the frame,
the user will be forced to manually resize the window.*

Listing 17.4 roper resizing of a **Jframe** after adding a
component.

```
    Dimension x = contentPane.getPreferredSize();

    setSize( x );

    validate();
```

A Player's Work Is More Complicated

JMF makes synchronization simple for applications: Decide on the master Player, realize the **ControlPanelComponent** at the appropriate time, and add the slave Players to the master after all Players have realized. By contrast, enabling synchronization is a daunting task for the Player developer. The master Player is responsible for adding and removing **Controllers**, marshalling methods, coalescing slave events, and starting slave devices in a synchronized fashion.

A master Player first becomes cognizant that it will be responsible for slave players when its **addController()** method is invoked. Since a Player must not be **Unrealized** or **Started** when **addController()** is called, the master does basic error checking and throws an exception if either of these rules are violated.

```
if ( state == Controller.Started)
        {
                throw new ClockStartedError("illegal method
call");

        }
        else if (state == Controller.Unrealized )
        {
                throw new NotRealizedError("not realized");
        }
```

The master then tries to force the slave player to use its **TimeBase** so that the two Players will play in sync. Theoretically, if the slave player refuses the new **TimeBase** and throws an exception, the master Player can use the slave's **TimeBase** as its own. However, in CDJolt, we give up and return an exception if any Player rejects our **TimeBase**.

Selecting a **TimeBase** can be treacherous. If you choose the system time clock as your **TimeBase**, you can never be sure that it will be granular enough, since the accuracy of the system time clock varies wildly between operating systems (see Table 2.1). Consequently, it is preferable to use an external hardware clock that will be reliable on all platforms.

Alas, most JMF Players do not have access to a hardware clock, so they are stuck with the system time clock. Fortunately, CDJolt has the option to use the CD-ROM drive's hardware clock. This clock calculates time based on the current CD location and the amount of digital audio data the drive's analog to digital audio decoders have consumed.

Thus, it would be preferable if CDJolt could use the drive's internal time as its **TimeBase** since this time is more accurate than the system clock. Unfortunately, the drive's clock is only active when data is being decoded and is paused when playback stops. Therefore, we must use the less accurate system time clock as our **TimeBase** (see Listing 17.5).

Listing 17.5 `addController()` processing in `CDMediaHandler`.

```
slavecontroller.setTimeBase( tb );
{
    controllers.addElement (slavecontroller);

    // deal with latency
    if (slavecontroller.getDuration().getNanoseconds() >
this.duration.getNanoseconds() )
    {
        this.duration = slavecontroller.getDuration();
    }

     slavecontroller.addControllerListener( this );

    if ( state != c.getState() )
    {
        //setState( c.getState() );

    }
}
```

CORE TIP

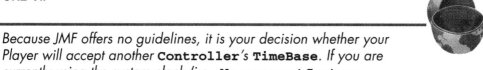

Because JMF offers no guidelines, it is your decision whether your Player will accept another **Controller**'s **TimeBase**. *If you are currently using the system clock (i.e.,* **Manager.getSystem-TimeBase()**), *then there is no legitimate reason why your Player shouldn't accept another* **TimeBase**. *However, if you're using a different* **TimeBase** *(such as a clock on a hardware device), then your Player probably should reject requests to use another* **TimeBase** *since the new* **TimeBase** *is likely to be less accurate.*

After setting the **TimeBase**, we add the **Controller** to our vector of slave controllers and ensure the master Player's state matches that of the slave Players. Then we register the master device as a listener of the slave's events. At this point, the slave controller has been successfully absorbed into our master Player so we can return to the caller.

Ordering the Slaves Around

All subsequent calls to the master Player not only modify the master's settings, but are also routed to the slave Player(s). For instance, if you **prefetch()** the master, it implicitly **prefetch**es not only itself, but the slaves. See Table 17.1 for a listing of the commands that a master device must route to slaves. Virtually all commands must be routed to slaves except calls that are applicable only to that Player (i.e., **addController()**, **removeController()**, and **setSource()**, etc.).

To inform the slave of the API request, we grab a copy of the vector of a **Controller** and call the method in question for each slave **Controller**. Listing 17.6 illustrates how the **Prefetch** thread farms our **prefetch** calls to slaves.

Listing 17.6 Master Player **prefetch()** processing.

```
Vector notify;
synchronized ( handler )
{
    notify = (Vector) handler.controllers.clone();
    handler.numprefetched = 0;
}


int numevents = notify.size();
if ( numevents > 0 )
{
    for ( int loop = 0; loop < numevents; loop++ )
    {
      Controller temp = (Controller) notify.elementAt(
loop );

      temp.prefetch( );

    }
}
```

CORE TIP

Be sure to relinquish any master Player semaphores before calling a slave **Controller** *method. Asynchronous slave methods will generate events that may call back into the master, and these events may not be able to be processed if the master semaphore is already locked.*

Figure 17.2 gives an illustration of deadlock when calling a slave **Controller**.

In this example, the master calls a slave method (#1), but the master retains a lock on a semaphore. Since the slave method is quick, it uses the master's thread to report the event (#2). The master's listener tries to obtain the semaphore, but blocks since it is already taken. The slave is blocked and can't return to the master resulting in a hang condition.

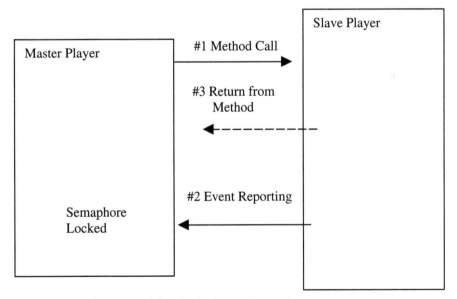

Figure 17-2   Illustration of deadlock when calling a slave **Controller**.

Table 17.1 Commands That Must Be Routed to Slaves

Command	Must be Routed to Slaves?
Realize()	Yes
Prefetch()	Yes
Start()	Yes
SetTimeBase()	Yes
GetTimeBase()	Yes
Close()	Yes
Deallocate()	Yes

Once the slave's methods are called by the master, they will generate events. JMF mandates that the application should only be notified of an event if all Players (master and slave) have reported that event. Consequently, we track the total number of Players that have posted a given event. When all slaves have reported the event, and if the master is ready to report the same event, we request that the **SendEvent** thread notify all listeners of the master Player of the synchronized event (see Listing 17.6).

Listing 17.7 Illustration of queuing events until all Players report the event. The application is notified once all slaves and the master are ready.

```
numstopped++;

if ( numstopped == controllers.size() )
{
        PrefetchCompleteEvent pce = new PrefetchComplete-
Event(this,

                                                Control-
ler.Realized,

                                                Control-
ler.Prefetching,

                                                Control-
ler.Prefetched);
        sender.addEvent( pce );

}
```

The Starting Block

The final responsibility of a master is to ensure that it and its slaves start play-back at the same time. This is accomplished by determining the Player with the maximum startup latency and calling each slave's **syncStart()** method with enough padding to ensure that every Player starts at the same time.

For instance, CDJolt has dramatically different startup latencies depend-ing on whether the CD-ROM head is already spinning (or playing). If it is spinning, the latency is virtually negligible. If the head is stationary, the delay could be several seconds as it prepares for playback.

Because of these variables, CDJolt does not use a hard-coded constant value for startup latency. Rather, the Player dynamically calculates the maxi-mum startup latency each time **start()** is called. Since the Caption Player has no startup latency, CDJolt's latency value is used to calculate the time for **syncStart()** for all Players.

CORE TIP

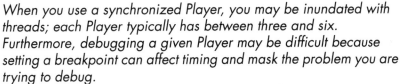

When you use a synchronized Player, you may be inundated with threads; each Player typically has between three and six. Furthermore, debugging a given Player may be difficult because setting a breakpoint can affect timing and mask the problem you are trying to debug.

You can work around these difficulties by either writing to standard output or to a file. Although these approaches are archaic, they are often your only alternative in these situations.

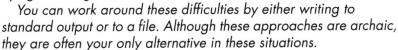

What Could Have Been?

Although JMF's synchronization architecture simplifies the life of the appli-cation programmer, the underlying Player implementation details are too complex. Despite the fact that none of these steps is difficult, the sheer vol-ume of work required almost ensures that you will have a bug or two in your initial Player development.

If you are careful and test thoroughly, you can minimize these bugs and catch them early in the development process. Table 17.2 provides an outline of the methods you should test first, as well as the common bugs you'll encounter.

Table 17.2 Synchronized Debugging Tips

Master Synchronized Player Method	Bugs to Watch Out For
`addController()`	1. Incorrect calculation of combined Players duration. 2. Forgetting to add a listener to the slave.
`removeController()`	1. Forgetting to remove the listener to the slave.
`prefetch()`	1. Failure to report **PrefetchCompleteEvent** for combined Player. 2. Failure to release the master Player's semaphore when calling asynchronous slave methods. 3. Failure to inform slave **Controller**s of **prefetch()** call.
`start()`	1. Incorrect calculation of combined startup latency 2. Incorrect implementation of **syncStart()**. 3. Failure to report **StartEvent** for combined Player. 4. Failure to call slave **Controller**'s **syncstart()** method.
`stop()`	1. Failure to report **StopEvent** for combined Player. 2. Failure to release master Player semaphore when calling asynchronous slave methods. 3. Failure to inform slave **Controller**s of **stop()** call.
`deallocate()`	1. Failure to report **DeallocateEvent** for combined Player. 2. Failure to release the master Player's semaphore when calling asynchronous slave methods. 3. Failure to inform slave **Controller**s of **deallocate()** call.
`close()`	1. Failure to close all slave Players. 2. Failure to report **ControllerClosedEvent** for combined Player. 3. Failure to release the master Player's semaphore when calling asynchronous slave methods. 4. Failure to inform slave **Controller**s of **close()** call.

CORE TIP

Most modern multimedia environments shield the Player developer from synchronization responsibilities. Both DirectShow and MCI provide synchronization managers that ensure that slave device objects remain in sync with the master device object. In these environments, individual devices (or Players) are only responsible for ensuring that they remain in sync with the synchronization manager's clock, and do not have to deal with the burden of managing slaves.

Hopefully, Sun will reexamine the functions required to implement synchronization in a Player in the next major JMF release. One potential solution would be to add a synchronization manager (or base class) to JMF. This would simultaneously be backwards-compatible with JMF 1.x, while reducing the complexity of Player development.

Summary

After building all of the components for our JMFMarriage application over several chapters, so little application development was required that it seems anticlimactic. You follow a few guidelines and emerge with the functional synchronized Player application.

By contrast, synchronized Player development is more intense, and there are numerous tasks you must complete before a Player can become a master Player. If you follow the guidelines suggested in this chapter, you will have a powerful tool.

MEDDLING IN A PLAYER'S BUSINESS WITH A MEDIAPROXY

*A perverse man stirs up dissension, and a
gossip separates close friends.*
Proverbs 16:28 (NIV)

*Without wood a fire goes out; without
gossip a quarrel dies down.*
Proverbs 26:20 (NIV)

Chapter 18

One of the goals of object-oriented programming is to create objects that can be reused by multiple projects. Consequently, once you write an object-oriented Player, it should be able to be reused to play related media types. For example, a properly written digital audio Player cannot only process standard audio formats (such as au, WAV or AIFF), but also seemingly incompatible formats such as MIDI.

The easiest way to write such a Player is to capture the output of a **DataSource**, convert this output to a common format that the Player understands, and stream this standardized format to the Player. This data conversion is not possible with the typical JMF Player because there is no way to modify the content once the media leaves the **DataSource**. Fortunately, the **MediaProxy** interface lets you tap into the output of a **DataSource** before content is streamed to a Player (see Figure 18.1).

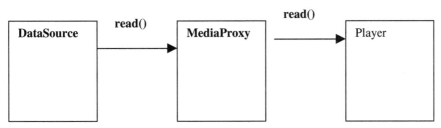

Figure 18-1 Overview of **MediaProxy** operation.

As you learned in Chapter 13, the Manager searches the content prefix list for **MediaHandler**s or **MediaProxy**s that can process the content type produced by **DataSource**. If the Manager finds a compatible **MediaHandler**, its search is terminated.

If the Manager discovers a compatible **MediaProxy**, it calls the **MediaProxy**'s **getDataSource()** method to obtain a new **DataSource**, retrieves the content type associated with the new **DataSource** via **getContentType()**, and begins a new search for a compatible **MediaHandler** or **MediaProxy** (see Figure 18-2).

Figure 18-2 Manager search process when **MediaProxy**s are involved.

MediaProxy Overview

MediaProxys are a cross between a **DataSource** and a Player. They are similar to Players, since they receive a stream of data from a **DataSource**. However, unlike a Player, they don't perform the final decoding of the data. Rather, they stream the modified content through a **DataSource** member variable to a Player (see Figure 18.3).

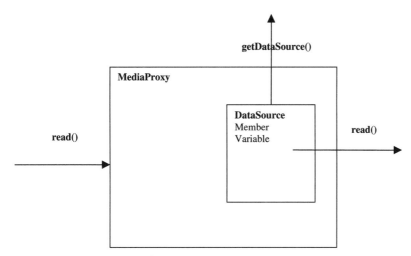

Figure 18-3 Composition of a **MediaProxy**.

Once your **MediaProxy** is connected to a **Datasource**, you can perform transformations on the data. For instance, the RTP **MediaProxy** discussed in Chapter 20 translates RTP-specific streams into general-purpose streams that any **MediaHandler** can decode. In this chapter, we will create TextProxy, a **MediaProxy** that converts a single stream of MCML text into multistream output that the MCML **MediaHandler** we created in Chapter 15 understands.

Single Stream Approach

TextProxy requires a new **DataSource** we will call Single Stream. (It is found in **DataSource.javafile**.) Unlike the original Caption **DataSource**, Single Stream combines all of the timing and textual information into one stream (see Figure 18.4).

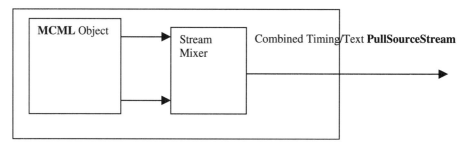

Figure 18–4   Overview of output streams provided by the Single Stream **DataSource**.

Core Tip

The Single Stream **DataSource** *must be given the generic class name* **DataSource** *rather than* **SingleStreamDataSource** *because JMF expects all* **DataSources** *it looks up in the protocol prefix list to be named* **DataSource**. *If you are constructing the* **DataSource** *object manually and are not using the Manager to create it, there are no naming restrictions on* **DataSources** *(see Listing 18.1).*

Listing 18.1 There are no name restrictions on the **Data-Source**'s class name if the Manager is not used to create the **DataSource**.

```
MCMLTextDataSource  mcmldatasource = new MCMLTextData-
Source( timebuffer, textbuffer, filetime );
```

The Single Stream **DataSource** is stored in a package entitled **core-jmf.media.protocol.*caption2***. This package name alerts the JMF Manager that the package contains a **DataSource** that processes files using the **_caption2_** protocol.

Single Stream parses a modified version of the MCML file format—all **<mcml>** and **</mcml>** tags are replaced with **<mcml2>** and **</mcml2>**. This minor change lets us reuse the existing MCML parsing engine by changing a constant string in **mcml2.java**.

```
public static final String MCML_TAG = "mcml2";
```

Single Stream's **getContentType()** method lets the Manager or other JMF objects query the MIME type associated with the MCML file. If the file contains valid MCML tags, **getContentType()** will return "**caption2.mcml**".

The primary change in the **SingleStreamDataSource** can be found in the **getStreams()** method. Unlike the Caption **DataSource** that must create two **PullSourceStreams** in the **getStreams()** method, Single Stream creates only one output stream (**CombinedSourceStream**) in the **getStreams()** method (compare Listings 18.2 and 18.3).

Listing 18.2 Single Stream **DataSource getStream()** creates only one stream.

```
public PullSourceStream[] getStreams()
{
  pullStreams = new PullSourceStream[1];

  textdata = new CombinedSourceStream(istream);
  pullStreams[0] = textdata;

  return pullStreams;
}
```

Listing 18.3 Caption DataSource **getStream()** creates two streams.

```
public PullSourceStream[] getStreams()
{
  pullStreams = new PullSourceStream[2];

  textdata = new TextSourceStream(istream);
  timedata = new TimeTextSourceStream(istream);

  //streams[1] = new TextTimingSourceStream(istream);
  pullStreams[0] = timedata;
  pullStreams[1] = textdata;

  return pullStreams;
}
```

The **CombinedSourceStream** constructor melds the timing information and textual output of the MCML parser into a single string object (see Figure 18.5).

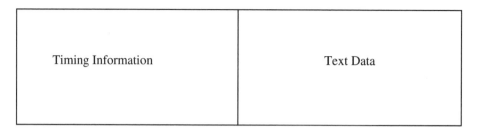

Figure 18-5 Layout of timing and textual information in output stream produced by **CombinedSourceStream**.

Since the timing and textual information are mixed into the same stream, **CombinedSourceStream** offers two methods that a **Media-Proxy** or **MediaHandler** can use to separate the streams: **getTiming-Length()** and **getContentLength()**. The **getTimingLength()** method returns the length of the timing portion of the combined stream, while the **getContentLength()** method reports the length of the textual portion of the stream.

MediaProxy Responsibilities

Every **MediaProxy** contains at least two methods: **setSource()** and **getDataSource()**. The **setSource()** method is part of the **Media-Handler** interface and the TextProxy implementation only accepts **Data-Source**s that stream the "**caption2.mcml**" content type. If the Manager calls **setSource()** with a different type of **DataSource**, TextProxy will throw an **IncompatibleSourceException**.

Once the **DataSource** is verified, TextProxy calls the **readSingleStream()** method to validate the stream's contents. First, **readSingleStream()** retrieves the output stream emitted by the Single Stream **DataSource** and casts this stream to a **CombinedSourceStream**.

```
pullstreams =  dataSrc.getStreams();

mcmlstream = (interactivejava.media.protocol.caption2.Com-
binedSourceStream) pullstreams[0];
```

Next, **readSingleStream()** calls the **CombinedSourceStream** custom methods, **getTimingLength()** and **getContentLength()**, to determine the size of the timing and textual information, respectively. Buffers are then allocated to store the timing and textual information.

```
textbuffer = new byte[(int) mcmlstream.getTextLength()];
timebuffer = new byte[(int) mcmlstream.getTimingLength()  ];
```

After these buffers are allocated, **readSingleStream()** reads in the time and text buffers and feeds them into a **MCMLTextDataSource** object (see Listing 18.4).

Listing 18.4 Streaming data from an input data source into the **mcmldatasource** member variable.

```
int n = mcmlstream.read(timebuffer, 0, (int) mcml-
stream.getTimingLength());
if (n != -1 )
{
    n = mcmlstream.read(textbuffer, 0, (int) mcml-
stream.getTextLength());
    if (n == -1 )

    {
        String msg = "Can't read text info from
MCML2TextDataSource";
        throw new IOException(msg);

    }

    mcmldatasource = new MCMLTextDataSource( timebuffer,
textbuffer, filetime );

}
else
{
    String msg = "Can't read timing info from
MCML2TextDataSource";
    throw new IOException(msg);

}
```

Every **MediaProxy** must contain a **DataSource** (see Figure 18.3). This **DataSource** is responsible for streaming the content produced by the **MediaProxy** through one or more output streams (see Figure 18.6). Text-Proxy feeds two byte arrays into its **MCMLTextDataSource**, and this **MCML-TextDataSource** creates output streams from each byte array.

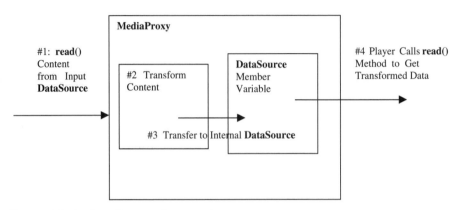

Figure 18-6   Data flow inside a **MediaProxy**.

The **MCMLTextDataSource** is a modified version of the Caption **Data-Source**. Rather than parsing an MCML file, this **DataSource** is supplied with preprocessed MCML content and its only responsibility is to route this content into two separate output streams: **TextSourceStream** and **Time-TextSourceStream** (see Listing 18.5).

Listing 18.5 Creation of output streams in **MCMLTextDataSource**'s **getStreams()** method.

```
textdata = new TextSourceStream(textinfo);
timedata = new TimeTextSourceStream(timeinfo);
pullStreams[0] = timedata;
pullStreams[1] = textdata;
```

Both **TextSourceStream** and **TimeTextSourceStream** are similar to their corresponding classes in the Caption **DataSource**, except they are fed byte arrays rather than having to obtain this information from an **mcml** object (compare Listing 18.6 with Listing 18.7).

Listing 18.6 MCMLTextDataSource's TimeTextSourceStream is supplied with a byte array.

```
public TimeTextSourceStream(byte [] timeinfo)
{
  this.timingInfo = timeinfo;

  // start off at the first text index
  this.index = 0;

  // track the
  this.length = timingInfo.length;

  cd = new ContentDescriptor("text.mcml");
}
```

Listing 18.7 Caption DataSource's TimeTextSourceStream must retrieve timing information from an mcml object.

```
public TimeTextSourceStream(mcml in)
{
    this.dataIn = in;

    this.timingInfo = dataIn.getTimingInfo();

    // start off at the first text index
    this.index = 0;

    // track the
    this.length = timingInfo.length();

    cd = new ContentDescriptor("text.mcml");
}
```

Unlike the Caption **DataSource**, **MCMLTextDataSource**'s **Time-TextSourceStream** uses a byte array to represent the stream. Therefore, we don't have to convert a **String** object to a byte array before we can use **System.arraycopy** to fill the caller's buffer (compare Listing 18.8 with Listing 18.9).

Listing 18.8 `MCMLTextDataSource`'s `TimeTextSourceStream` can directly call `System.arraycopy` without performing any conversions.

```
if (buffer != null)
{
    System.arraycopy((Object) timingInfo, (int) index,
                     (Object) buffer, offset,
                     (int) bytesAvailable);
}
```

Listing 18.9 Caption `DataSource`'s `TimeTextSourceStream` creates a byte array before calling `System.arraycopy`.

```
if (buffer != null)
{
    // extremely inefficient.......
    byte [] temp = timingInfo.getBytes();


    System.arraycopy((Object) temp, (int) index,
                     (Object) buffer, offset,
                     (int) bytesAvailable);
}
```

Besides a **setSource()** method, every **MediaProxy** must contain a **getDataSource()** method. The Manager calls **getDataSource()** to obtain a **DataSource** that will stream content from the **MediaProxy** to another **MediaHandler**. **TextProxy**'s **getDataSource()** returns the **MCMLTextDataSource** member variable we created in the **readSingleStream()** method.

```
public DataSource getDataSource() throws IOException, NoData-
SourceException

    {

return (mcmldatasource);

    }
```

Installation Details

To use TextProxy, you must install the package prefix for both the TextProxy and the Single Stream **DataSource**. Since Single Stream is a **DataSource**, you must install it in the protocol prefix list (see Listing 18.10). Similarly, you must ensure that the Text **MediaProxy** is installed in the content prefix list (see Listing 18.10). Both objects are part of the **interactivejava** package, so you need to install this package name in both the protocol and control prefix lists.

> **Listing 18.10** The `installPrefixes()` method installs the prefixes for both the Single Stream **DataSource** and the Text **MediaProxy**.

```
protected void installPrefixes()
{
   Vector packagePrefix = PackageManager.getContentPrefix-
List();
   String myPackagePrefix = new String("interactive-
java");

   // has this package been installed before?
   if ( packagePrefix.indexOf(myPackagePrefix) == -1 )
   {
       packagePrefix.addElement(myPackagePrefix);
       PackageManager.setContentPrefixList(packagePrefix);

       // write to permanent storage
       //PackageManager.commitContentPrefixList();

   }
   else
   {
      System.out.println("Package already installed....");
   }


   Vector v = PackageManager.getProtocolPrefixList();
   String interactivejavaPrefix = new String("corejmf");
   // has this package been installed before?
```

Listing 18.10 The `installPrefixes()` method installs the prefixes for both the Single Stream `DataSource` and the Text `MediaProxy`. (continued)

```
   if ( interactivejavaPrefix.indexOf(myPackagePrefix)
== -1 )
   {
      v.addElement(interactivejavaPrefix);
      PackageManager.setProtocolPrefixList(v);

      // write to permanent storage
      //PackageManager.commitProtocolPrefixList();
   }
   else
   {
       System.out.println("Package already installed....");
    }

}
```

MediaProxy Management

There are two ways to create a Player that uses a **MediaProxy**: **Manager.createPlayer()** and low-level APIs.

Manager.createPlayer() hides the complexities of **MediaProxy** usage from your application. When you call **Manager.createPlayer()**, the Manager locates and uses **MediaProxy**s if they are required to play the file. For instance, to use a Text **MediaProxy**, you create a **MediaLocator** with the *caption2* protocol (see Listing 18.11). The *caption2* protocol can only be decoded by our Single Stream **DataSource**, so this **MediaLocator** ensures that our Text **MediaProxy** will be used to convert the single MCML output stream into a format that the Caption Player understands.

The **MediaLocator** is passed to **Manager.createDataSource()** to create a **DataSource**. This **DataSource** is then feed into **Manager.createPlayer()** to form a Player.

> **Listing 18.11** Manager methods to create a Player that uses the Text `MediaProxy`.

```
installPrefixes();
MediaLocator mcmlfile = new MediaLocator("caption2:" +
textfile);
try
{
    DataSource src = Manager.createDataSource(mcmlfile);
    player = Manager.createPlayer( src );
    player.addControllerListener(this);
}
catch ( NoDataSourceException e )
{

    System.out.println("Bad data source....");
}
catch ( IOException e )
{
    System.out.println("General I/O error....");

}
catch ( NoPlayerException e )
{
    System.out.println("Can't find a Player....");

}
```

If you don't want to use the Manager to construct a Player that uses the Text **MediaProxy**, you can construct it yourself (see Listing 18.12). First, you create a **MediaLocator** using the *caption2* protocol and attach it to the Single Stream **DataSource** via the **setLocator()** method. Then you connect the **DataSource** via the **connect()** method.

```
textSource = new interactivejava.media.proto-
col.caption2.DataSource(  );
textSource.setLocator ( mcmlfile );
```

After this, you construct a **MediaProxy**, attach the Single Stream **DataSource** to the **MediaProxy** with the **setSource()** method, and retrieve the **MediaProxy**'s DataSource via the **getDataSource()** method.

This **DataSource** is then attached to the Player's **Handler** via **set-Source()** (see Listing 18.12).

Listing 18.12 Manual MCML2 Player construction

```
MediaLocator mcmlfile = new MediaLocator("caption2:" +
textfile);

player = new CaptionMediaHandler();
textSource = new interactivejava.media.proto-
col.caption2.DataSource(   );
textSource.setLocator ( mcmlfile );
try
{
    textSource.connect();
    textProxy = new interactivejava.media.con-
tent.caption2.mcml.Handler(   );
    textProxy.setSource( textSource );
    player.setSource( textProxy.getDataSource() );
}
catch ( IncompatibleSourceException e )
{

    System.out.println("Bad data source....");
}
catch ( NoDataSourceException e )
{

    System.out.println("Bad data source....");
}
catch ( IOException e )
{
    System.out.println("General I/O error....");

}
```

Unless you have custom methods in a **DataSource** or **MediaProxy** that must be called before a Player can be created, you should let the Manager create the Player for you. The Manager is easier to use and can accommodate new Players as they are released.

Core Tip

MediaProxys *are useful if you are writing both the* **DataSource** *and the Player, or if you must interface a Player to an incompatible* **DataSource**. *However, JMF won't let you dynamically insert a* **MediaProxy** *between compatible* **DataSource**s *and Players. Therefore, you can't create a real-time 3-D audio filter that works with existing audio Players. Fortunately, Sun and IBM have promised that JMF 2.0 will give you the ability to attach real-time filters to media streams (see Chapter 21 for more details on real-time filters and JMF 2.0).*

Summary

The **MediaProxy** interface lets you modify the streams produced by a **Data-Source** before it reaches a **MediaHandler**. Every **MediaProxy** contains at least two methods: **setSource()** and **getDataSource()**. The **set-Source()** method attaches an input **DataSource** to the **MediaProxy**.

The **MediaProxy** reads content from the **DataSource** obtained in the **setSource()** method, manipulates the data, and routes the modified data to an internal **DataSource** object. The **getDataSource()** method lets the Manager access this internal **DataSource** so that a **MediaHandler** can read the transformed data and decode it.

We'll explore the role of **MediaProxy**s in greater detail when we examine Sun's RTP architecture in Chapter 20.

REAL-TIME STREAMING

*A Hare one day ridiculed the short feet
and slow pace of the Tortoise, who re-
plied, laughing: "Though you be swift as
the wind, I will beat you in a race."*
Aesop's Fables

Chapter 19

T he multimedia content we've played so far has been retrieved from the local file system or transported over a protocol such as HTTP or FTP. Local storage is the preferred option since it is fast enough to keep the audio and video decoders from underrunning (or running out of data). By contrast, conventional Internet protocols (such as HTTP or FTP) were designed for reliability, and not speed. Thus, you can never be sure if they can supply the decoders with enough data to prevent underruns.

IP Primer

Protocols such as HTTP and FTP are focused on reliability (i.e., ensuring that every packet arrives at its destination). Consequently, they are built on top of the Transmission Control Protocol (or TCP) layer. TCP ensures that each buffer arrives at its destination, and that it arrives in sequence (see Figure 19-1). From a multimedia standpoint, TCP has three significant problems: processing overhead, network transmission delays, and lack of multimedia functionality. The TCP stack is huge and entails establishing a connection between two machines, extensive handshaking, and error detection and recovery.

These extra layers of code steal valuable cycles away from a multimedia decoder and reduce data throughput.

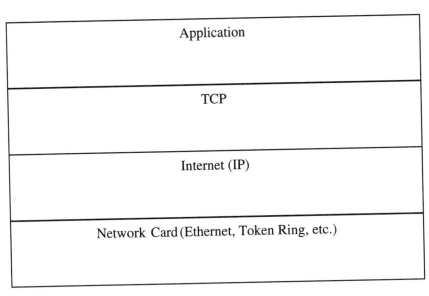

Application
TCP
Internet (IP)
Network Card (Ethernet, Token Ring, etc.)

Figure 19–1   TCP layer.

The second issue with TCP is its reliability. If the network is experiencing errors or is heavily loaded, packets will be lost. When a sender discovers that a packet has been lost, it must retry sending the packet until it is successfully delivered. While this is ideal for file transfers, it's disastrous for real-time streaming since subsequent packets cannot be decoded until the lost packet is successfully received.

The final issue with TCP is that it lacks multimedia features such as multicasting and congestion control. Multicasting refers to the ability to broadcast multiple multimedia streams. Congestion control lets a protocol alter presentation quality when network transmission delays become problematic.

Because of these difficulties, real-time protocols are built on top of the User Datagram Protocol (UDP) layer. UDP is a connectionless and unreliable protocol. Unlike TCP, UDP has no notion of a connection (see Figure 19-2). You can never be assured that the other party is listening or receiving your requests.

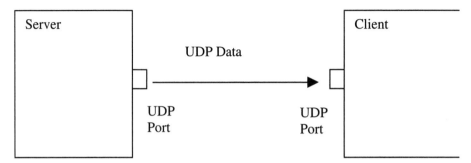

Figure 19–2 Connectionless UDP model. In this illustration, a server application sends packets via UDP to a client machine, but it has no guarantee that the packets were delivered.

UDP is called unreliable because there is no guarantee that any packet you send will arrive at its destination. While this may sound scary, in reality, almost every packet sent via UDP arrives safely. Should a packet get lost, it is up to the receiver to detect the loss and take actions to recover. UDP also does not guarantee that packets will be received in the order they were sent or that a packet isn't a duplicate.

Although UDP seems primitive, it is the ideal platform to build a multimedia protocol since it imposes no overhead and few operating restrictions on applications.

RTP

Unlike general-purpose protocols such as HTTP or FTP, RTP was designed to transport media streams that have strict timing requirements (i.e., a video frame must be played at a specific point in a movie). Every RTP buffer contains a timestamp and a mapping between the timestamp and a globally synchronized clock (the global clock is similar to a JMF Player's **TimeBase**). This time stamp enables you to merge multiple streams from different sources. For example, if you were involved in a multimedia conference and were receiving three different RTP streams, the timestamp would enable your machine to combine the three streams into one entity (see Figure 19-3).

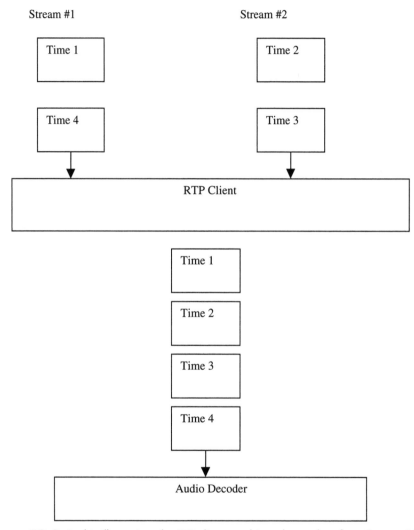

Figure 19–3 In this illustration, the RTP client combines the packets from Stream #1 and #2 into a single stream before it is sent to the audio decoder.

Core Tip

Although RTP is currently unreliable, it does provide the hooks so that you could use it with TCP or another reliable protocol.

Each packet also contains a sequence number. This sequence number lets the receiver detect packet loss since sequence numbers are unique. By contrast, timestamps are not unique since a single timestamp can be used by multiple packets. For example, a video frame may be too large to fit into a single packet and may be split into multiple packets. Each of these packets would have a unique sequence number but the same timestamp since they all should be decoded at the same point in time (see Figure 19-4).

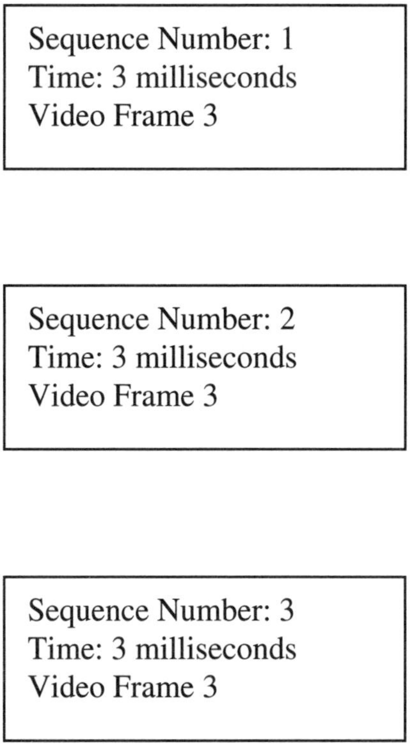

```
Sequence Number: 1
Time: 3 milliseconds
Video Frame 3
```

```
Sequence Number: 2
Time: 3 milliseconds
Video Frame 3
```

```
Sequence Number: 3
Time: 3 milliseconds
Video Frame 3
```

Figure 19-4 Difference between sequence numbers and timestamps in multipacket video. In this illustration, all three packets are part of the same video frame, hence they have the same timestamp. The client is able to distinguish packets via the sequence number.

Since it is UDP-based, RTP must have a mechanism for processing packets that are received out of order. Fortunately, the packet's sequence number lets you know where in the presentation it should be played (see Figure 19-5).

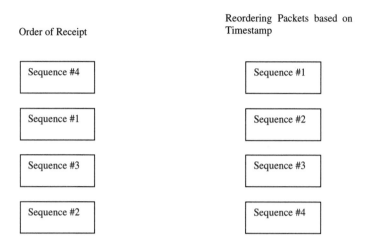

Figure 19-5   Reassembling packets based on sequence numbers.

Class Is in Session

RTP-based media streams are organized into entities called sessions. A session is the exchange of data between two or more participants. For example, if you made an Internet telephone call to your friend, Sue, using RTP, the telephone call would be considered a session and you and Sue would be the participants. If your friends, Doug and Ann, joined the telephone call, there would still be one session, but four participants.

RTP has been designed to deliver real-time media streams with minimal overhead and offers no ability to monitor the quality of the presentation or add and remove participants from a session. Therefore, RTP is combined with the Real-Time Control Protocol (or RTCP). RTCP provides the ability to monitor the quality of the presentation and describe the participants of an RTP session.

RTP Is a Chameleon

Protocols such as HTTP or FTP stream content identified by a single MIME type (i.e., audio/x-wav). This MIME type restricts the stream from transporting another MIME type such as video, text, or even a different audio format. By contrast, RTP streams can interleave numerous media types at any position in a stream. Since a stream is heterogeneous, each RTP packet contains a payload number that identifies the packet's media format (see Table 19.1). Each payload is associated with an encoding name that describes the type of content it contains.

Table 19.1 Potential RTP Payload Types (See Appendix B for descriptions of the encoding names.)

Payload Number	Encoding Name	Audio/Video Data
0	PCM	Audio
1	1016	Audio
2	G726-32	Audio
3	GSM	Audio
4	G723	Audio
5	DVI4	Audio
6	DVI4	Audio
7	LPC	Audio
8	PCMA	Audio
9	G722	Audio
10	L16	Audio
11	L16	Audio
12	QCELP	Audio
14	MPA	Audio
15	G728	Audio
16	DVI4	Audio
17	DVI4	Audio
18	G729	Audio
19	CN	Audio
25	CelB	Video
26	JPEG	Video
28	nv	Video
31	H261	Video
32	MPV	Video
33	MP2T	Audio/Video

Table 19.1 Potential RTP Payload Types (See Appendix B for descriptions of the encoding names.) (continued)		
34	H263	Video
dyn	RED	Audio
dyn	MP1S	Video
dyn	MP2P	Video
96–127	dynamic	Application Specific

The ability to interleave encoding types within a stream enables servers to dynamically switch audio and video CODECs based on network performance (i.e., if the network is sluggish, the server may switch from PCM to a compressed audio format like TrueSpeech).

Besides the payload number, packets contain data frames (see Figure 19-6). Frames divide a packet into logical units, and there are always an integer number of frames in a packet. The size of a frame depends on the payload number and is media-specific (i.e., a video payload might define a frame to contain a square 16x16 pixels wide, while an audio frame might be 10 milliseconds of data) (see Figure 19-6).

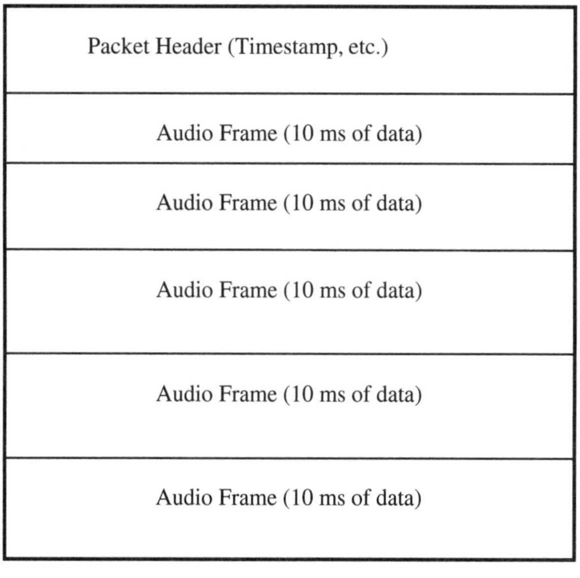

Packet Header (Timestamp, etc.)
Audio Frame (10 ms of data)
Audio Frame (10 ms of data)
Audio Frame (10 ms of data)
Audio Frame (10 ms of data)
Audio Frame (10 ms of data)

Figure 19–6   Audio frames inside an RTP packet. Each frame contains 10 milliseconds of data.

RTSP

The Real-Time Streaming Protocol (RTSP) gives you command and control over multimedia streams. Because RTSP is a higher-level protocol than RTP, it enables applications to request a media stream from a server or join multimedia conferences. Furthermore, RTSP lets media servers alert client applications that members have joined or left a conference.

Like UDP, RTSP is connectionless. Every stream is identified by a session id. However, RTSP control requests (see Table 19.1) are transmitted over a reliable protocol such as TCP. Control requests use a reliable protocol since they are compact and do not contain multimedia data (i.e., no real-time decoder is depending on data packets from a control request). Control requests also are sent over reliable protocols since the loss of a single control request could disrupt the presentation.

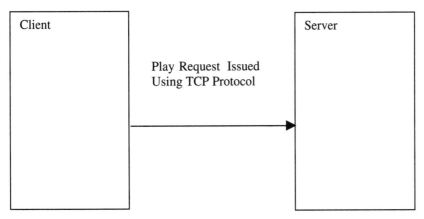

Figure 19-7 RTSP control request using reliable protocol.

Core Tip

RTSP also comes in an unreliable flavor called RTSPU. Although most RTSP applications use TCP, it is possible to send RTSP messages via UDP.

Table 19.2 Common RTSP Control Requests

RTSP Control Request	JMF Counterpart	Explanation
DESCRIBE	`DataSource.getContentType()`	The DESCRIBE request retrieves a description of the media stream.
SETUP	`Manager.createPlayer()`	The SETUP request informs the server of the transport protocol(s) for the media streams.
PLAY	`start()`	The PLAY request tells the server to start sending data.
PAUSE	`stop()`	The PAUSE request stops the stream.
TEARDOWN	`close()`	The TEARDOWN request stops the stream delivery and releases all resources associated with the stream.

As Table 19.2 reveals, RTSP messages are similar to the methods exposed by a JMF Player. In fact, RTP session creation and destruction parallels the steps necessary to create and destroy a Player (see Table 19.3).

Table 19.3 Sample RTSP Session

RTP Action	JMF Counterpart
The client obtains a DESCRIPTION of the media from the server.	No equivalent
The client issues a SETUP request indicating that it wants to use RTP to transport the media.	`Manager.createPlayer()`
The client issues PLAY to start playback.	`Player.start()`

Table 19.3 Sample RTSP Session   (continued)

The client issues PAUSE to pause or stop playback.	`Player.stop()`
When the presentation is complete, the client sends a TEARDOWN message to terminate the RTSP session.	`Player.deallocate();` `Player.close();`

RTSP was designed to interoperate with HTTP as the designers expected many RTP applications to be launched from a Web page or an HTTP-based program. For example, when you click on RTSP content on a Web page, the HTTP server returns the MIME type associated with the file. The browser finds the appropriate RSTP client application and points it at the RTSP server (the MIME type is similar to the information returned by the RTSP DESCRIBE message). RTSP does not require HTTP, and the same content can be played by a dedicated RTSP application without browser intervention.

Although RTSP uses an HTTP-like syntax, there is one significant difference between the two protocols: RTSP provides a separate protocol to transport media streams, whereas HTTP uses TCP for both control requests and media stream transportation. A separate protocol ensures that media streams are transported in the most efficient manner. Normally, RTSP uses RTP for media transport, but other protocols can be substituted based on the particular circumstances (see Figures 19-8 and 19-9).

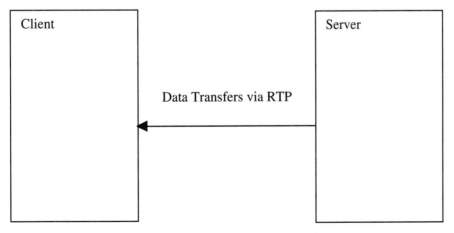

Figure 19–8   RTSP using RTP to transport data. Multimedia data may be transmitted via unreliable protocol. It is the client's responsibility to handle data loss.

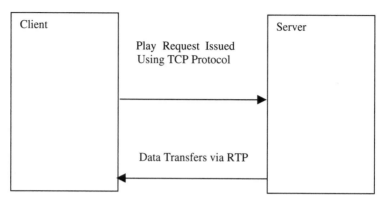

Figure 19-9   RTSP has reliable control request, but unreliable data transport.

Core Tip

We've only scratched the surface of multimedia protocols. Additional sources of information can be found in my Internet protocols article:

> http://www.zdnet.com/pcmag/issues/1604/pcmg0032.htm

or the following Web sites:

> http://www.cs.columbia.edu/~hgs/rtp/faq.html

> http://search.ietf.org/internet-drafts/draft-ietf-avt-profile-new-04.txt

RTP payload information:

> http://www.isi.edu/in-notes/iana/assignments/rtp-parameters

Are You for Real?

If you need to add real-time streaming to your JMF application, there are two alternatives: RealNetwork's JMF client and Sun's RTP Player.

RealNetworks' RealAudio and RealMedia formats are the dominant real-time streaming formats on the Internet. RealNetworks is a major backer of the proposed RTSP standard, and they use RTSP to control multimedia streaming. Therefore, it was a huge boost to JMF when RealNetwork announced that they would be releasing the RealMedia JMF Player.

RealNetworks' JMF Player is built on top of the native RealMedia RTSP and RTP services (see Figure 19-10). Since they provide native clients and servers for a multitude of platforms (i.e., UNIX, Linux and Windows NT/9x), you can run the RealMedia JMF Player virtually everywhere JMF runs.

RealMedia Player
Real Native Libraries (RTSP + RTP)

TCP	UDP

Internet (or IP)
Network Hardware

Figure 19–10 RealMedia JMF architecture.

To develop with the JMF RealMedia Player, you'll need to download and install the RealMedia SDK (it is also included on the book's companion CD). Installing the JMF portions of the SDK is not an automated process, but the following steps will install the JMF Player on your machine:

1. Update your **CLASSPATH** environment variable to include **rjmf.jar** (the RealMedia JMF classes).
2. Configure the protocol and content prefixes with **RJMF-Config**.
3. Verify correct installation of the protocol and content prefixes.

Core Tip

If you have a beta version of the Real JMF SDK installed on your machine, uninstall the beta SDK and beta Real Player. When these items are completely removed, install the production-level Real Player and use the Player's Check Updates *option to download the latest JMF runtimes.*

If you have Netscape installed on your machine, the Player will download the latest `rjmf.jar` *file into Netscape's* `java/classes` *directory. However, it does not update the SDK's* `rjmf.jar`*. As a result, you should copy the new* `rjmf.jar` *file to your SDK's* `java\lib` *directory.*

The first step in installing the RealMedia JMF Player is to add `rjmf.jar` to your **CLASSPATH** (this file is located in the **rmasdk\jmf\lib** directory). Once `rjmf.jar` is in the **CLASSPATH**, you must run **RJMFConfig** to alert the JMF subsystem that RealNetwork's JMF Player can be found in the **com.real** package (see Figure 19-11).

```
java com.real.util.RJMFConfig

RMA JMF Config V1.0
RMA JMF has been configured.
```

Figure 19–11   `RJMFConfig` invocation. When successful, `RJMFConfig` will display the last two lines.

After **RJMFConfig** runs, start the JMF configuration application (**JMFConfig.class**) and inspect the *Content Handler Prefixes* and *Protocol Handler Prefixes*. If you see **com.real** in both of these fields, your Player has been installed successfully (see Figure 19-12). If these packages are not there, it is likely that `rjmf.jar` is not in your **CLASSPATH**.

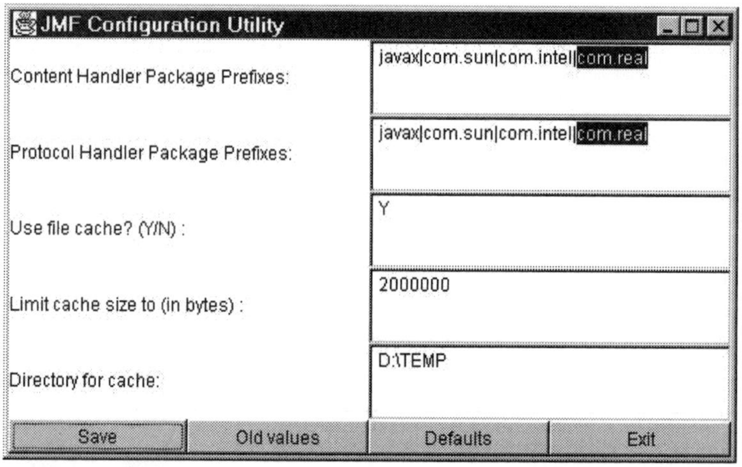

Figure 19–12   Example of successful addition of com.real package to JMF.

Core Tip

*If you have multiple JMF runtimes on your machine, **RJMFConfig** will only update the protocol and content prefixes for the active JMF runtime (see Listing 19.1). You must either manually add* **com.real** *prefix to the appropriate* **jmf.properties** *file, or sequentially run **RJMFConfig** for each JMF runtime (this is the preferred method).*

Listing 19.1 **jmf.properties** file with **com.real** prefix successfully installed.

```
#JMFProperties
content.prefixes=javax|com.sun|com.real|com.intel
cache.limit=2000000
cache.dir=C:\TEMP
cache.use=Y
defaultfont.name=Helvetica
protocol.prefixes=javax|com.sun|com.real|com.intel
```

Once the Real Player is installed, you'll discover that it shields you from the complexities of RTP and RTSP programming. All that is necessary to play a RealMedia file is to create a Player with a RealMedia URL and call the Player's **start()** method. As a result, any JMF application can instantly play RealMedia files.

Additions

Although you can use the generic Player interface to play a RealMedia URL, the Real Player offers custom methods that give you finer control over real-time streaming. We'll explore these methods in RealChooser: a RealMedia file chooser.

This RealMedia file viewer only supports files with valid RealMedia extensions (.ra, .rm, and .rt). Once you select a file, RealChooser will create a Player to preview the file. After the Manager creates the Player, we check to see if it is an instance of **com.real.media.RMPlayer** (see Listing

19.2). Never assume that the Manager will create an instance of a particular Player type since it may find a different Player to play the file than the one you expect.

Listing 19.2 Illustration of detecting a RealMedia Player.

```
// we must use a MediaLocator and not a URL since
// the current Real Player chokes on URL objects.

String mediaFile = "file:///" + f.getPath();
MediaLocator mrl = new MediaLocator(mediaFile);
player = Manager.createPlayer(mediaURL);

if ( player instanceof com.real.media.RMPlayer)
{
    rmPlayer = ( com.real.media.RMPlayer ) player;
}
```

Core Tip

The JMF Manager lets you construct a Player with either a **MediaLocator** *or a URL. If your Real Player is Version 6.0.3.134 or older, the Manager can construct the Real Player via a File URL object, but the Player never progresses beyond the* **Realized** *state. By contrast, if you create the Real Player with a* **MediaLocator**, *it always is able to* **realize**, **prefetch**, *and* **start** *successfully.*

Fortunately, RealNetwork has fixed this bug in their latest JMF Player. As a result, if you need to create a Player from a File URL, be sure to download the latest Real Player.

In general, you should use a **MediaLocator** *rather than a URL since* **MediaLocator***s do not require a protocol handler to be installed. By contrast, if you pass a URL without an associated protocol handler to a Player, it will fail.*

The first unique feature the RealMedia Player provides is the ability to pause a JMF stream via the **pausePlay()** method. As we discussed in Chapter 14, most multimedia APIs offer both pause and flush functionality. If you flush an Internet-based multimedia stream, it may take a while to refill the stream over a slow connection. Consequently, the Real Player gives you finer granularity over stopping: **pausePlay()** pauses a stream, while **stop()** flushes it. Since **pausePlay()** is asynchronous, you detect its completion via **RMPauseEvent**. To resume playback after pausing the stream with **pausePlay()**, call **beginPlay()**.

The next custom feature that the RealMedia Player offers is the **RMOnPosChangedEvent**. This event is similar to the **PositionAdviseEvent** we created in Chapter 15. Unlike our **PositionAdviseEvent**, the RealMedia Player automatically sends this event to client applications. Furthermore, you cannot let the Player know how frequently you want the messages—it always sends them to you in 100 millisecond intervals.

After you detect the **RMOnPosChangedEvent**, you can retrieve the media time by calling **getPositionInNanos()** (see Listing 19.3). Although **getPositionInNanos()** is an acceptable API, if the Real Player was consistent with JMF design principles, **RMOnPosChangedEvent** would return a **Time** object rather than the custom **getPositionInNanos()** method.

Listing 19.3 Detecting the **PositionAdviseEvent**.

```
else if (event instanceof RMOnPosChangedEvent)
{

  RMOnPosChangedEvent rmposadvise = (RMOnPosChanged-
Event)event;

  if ( rmposadvise.getPositionInNanos() > PREVIEW_TIME)
  {
    rmPlayer.pausePlay();
  }

}
```

Core Tip

When I contacted RealNetwork about the apparent inconsistency in the **RMOnPosChangedEvent**, *they immediately recognized this oversight and updated this event to return a* **Time** *object. Consequently, the latest Real Players let you use* **getPositionInNanos()** *or obtain a* **Time** *object.*

RealChooser combines **pausePlay()** and **RMOnPosChangedEvent** to enhance RealMedia file previewing. A previewer should only provide a snapshot of the media file and shouldn't play the whole file or stream. Since

JMF didn't offer position advise capabilities, we had no mechanism to monitor progress in our previous file choosers, so we played the entire file.

Fortunately, when we play RealMedia content, we can monitor media position via the **RMOnPosChangedEvent** (see Listing 19.3). When the media time exceeds our predefined stopping point (in this example, the **PREVIEW_TIME** constant), we pause the stream with **pausePlay()**.

Core Tip

The RealMedia Player's **ControlPanel** *contains heavy buttons. As a result, it will create problems if you use it with lightweight swing components (see Figure 19.13). If you intend to use it with a Swing application, you should follow the guidelines we suggested in Chapter 8.*

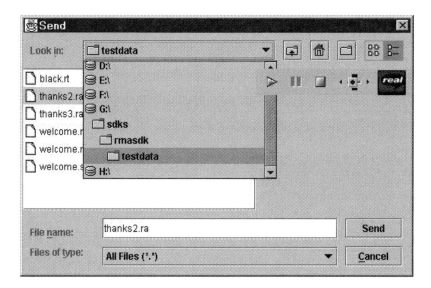

Figure 19–13   Illustration of heavy real components overwriting light swing components.

Besides **pausePlay()** and **RMOnPosChangedEvent**, the Real Player gives controls over multistream presentations with varying picture sizes via **setStickySize()**. It also provides events to monitor volume changes.

Core Tip

The current version of the Real Player will not allow you to make it a master Player (i.e., it doesn't support **addController()** *and* **removeController()**). *As a result, it is not possible to combine it with the Caption Player or with another Real Player.*

Summary

Real-time streaming protocols focus on speed and efficiency and are less concerned with reliability. Two protocols currently dominate multimedia streaming: RTP and RTSP. RTP and its companion protocol, RTCP, focus on media streaming ,while RTSP adds higher-level control APIs.

RealNetworks' G2 JMF Player lets us control RTSP streams. In the next chapter, we'll examine Sun's solution to real-time streaming.

A REAL-TIME HYBRID

So because you are lukewarm-neither hot nor cold-I am about to spit you out of my mouth.
Revelation 3:16 (NIV)

There was a little girl,
Who had a little curl,
Right in the middle of her forehead.
When she was good,
She was very, very good.
But when she was bad,
She was horrid.
Henry Wadsworth Longfellow,
There was a Little Girl

Chapter 20

RealNetwork chooses to implement their real-time streaming solution as a JMF Player with real-time streaming enhancements. By contrast, Sun's RTP architecture combines an RTP **DataSource** and RTP **MediaHandler** with a special **MediaProxy** called the RTP Session Manager (see Figure 20-1). Since both solutions conform to JMF specifications, existing JMF applications can use them without modification.

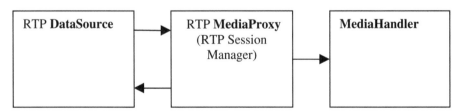

Figure 20-1 RTP Session Manager architecture.

Sun's and RealNetwork's products differ in other areas too. For instance, Sun's RTP runtime is pure Java, while RealNetwork's product uses native RTP and RTSP libraries.

The major difference between the solutions is that the RealPlayer API is entirely contained within the context of the JMF Player architecture. By contrast, the RTP Session Manager is a strange hybrid: It exists both inside and outside JMF (i.e., it has APIs you can call without creating a **Player** or a **DataSource**). Because of its hybrid nature, Sun has not integrated the RTP Session Manager documentation with JMF documentation. Rather, they created a separate set of HTML documents that are listed next to the main JMF documentation (see Figure 20-2). Unfortunately, these RTP documents are unclear in several areas and fail to describe the interaction between certain RTP components.

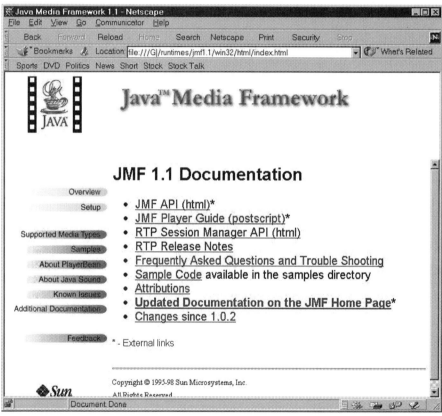

Figure 20-2   The RTP documentation is separated from the JMF documents.

Sun's RTP solution supports both hardcore RTP developers and programmers who want to play RTP content without delving into RTP details. If you are writing an RTP-specific application, the **RTPSessionManager** API offers you details about the session such as number of participants and reception quality. However, if you are writing a general-purpose application, you can let JMF construct the RTP Player and deal with RTP-related issues for you.

Core Tip

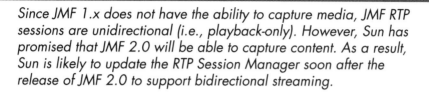

Since JMF 1.x does not have the ability to capture media, JMF RTP sessions are unidirectional (i.e., playback-only). However, Sun has promised that JMF 2.0 will be able to capture content. As a result, Sun is likely to update the RTP Session Manager soon after the release of JMF 2.0 to support bidirectional streaming.

Yet Another Manager?

The RTP Session Manager (**RTPSessionManager**) is responsible for controlling one RTP session. Each session may contain one or more participants, and every participant may receive one or more streams (see Figures 20-3 and 20-4).

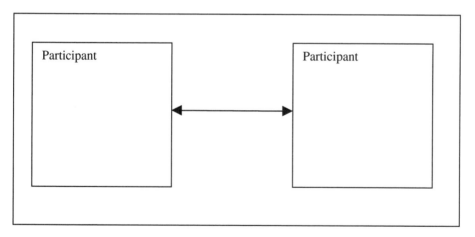

Figure 20–3   RTP session with two participants and one stream.

To decode a stream, the **RTPSessionManager** creates a special RTP **DataSource** called **RTPSocket**. **RTPSocket** extends the **RTPIODataSource** interface to provide RTP-specific functionality. Unlike most **DataSources**, an **RTPIODataSource** has both an output and input stream (see Figure 20-5). The output stream is a conventional **PushStream** that transmits RTP packets. You can grab a reference to the output stream by calling the **RTPIODataSource getOutputStream()** method or the parent **DataSource's getStreams()** method.

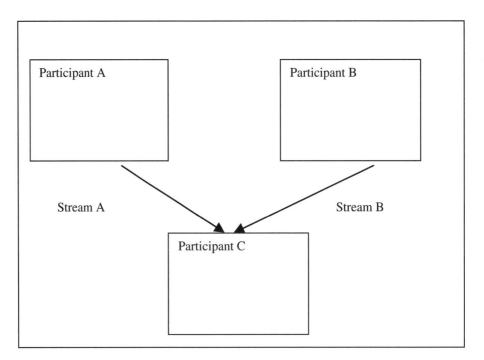

Figure 20–4   RTP session with three participants and two streams. Participant C is responsible for merging the streams for the other two participants.

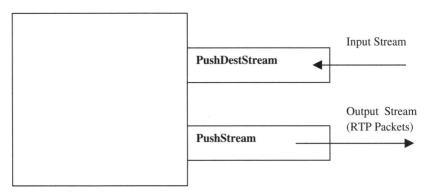

Figure 20–5   **RTPIODataSource** input and output streams.

The input stream is an instance of **javax.media.rtp.PushDest-Stream**. It enables the **RTPSessionManager** to send outbound RTP packets to other participants in the session. Unlike a **PushSourceStream** that streams content through its **read()** method, a **PushDestStream** transmits content through its **write()** method.

Core Tip

*It is surprising that Sun chose to place **PushDestStream** in the **javax.media.rtp** package rather than **javax.media.protocol**, since all protocol-related classes belong in **javax.media.protocol**. One potential explanation is that **PushDestStream** is a transitional object that needs further refinement before it can be placed in **javax.media.protocol**. Another reason might be that it is an RTP-specific class that was never intended for general-purpose usage.*

*Regardless of the reason **PushDestStream** ended up in **javax.media.rtp**, it is possible that an interface similar to **PushDestStream** will be used for media capture in JMF 2.0, so you should become familiar with semantics of **PushDestStream**.*

RTPSocket also implements the **DataChannel** interface. **Data-Channel** contains one method, **getControlChannel()**, which gives you access to another **RTPIODataSource** object that is used to transmit RTCP messages. Since every **RTPIODataSource** has an input and output stream, the **RTPSessionManager** uses this object to send and receive RTCP messages.

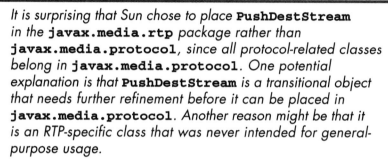
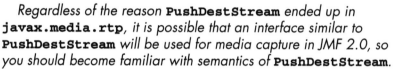
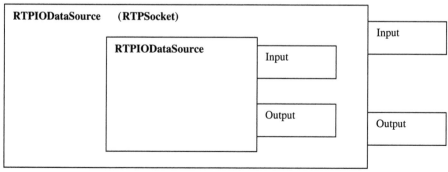

Figure 20–6 **RTPSocket** has both a control **RTPIODataSource** and media **RTPIODataSource** objects.

Core Tip

Sun has chosen a strange design for **RTPSocket**: *a* **DataSource**
that contains a **DataSource** *(see Figure 20-6). They believe this
design clearly delineates the roles of the control and data transfer
objects. However, the contained* **DataSource** *is used for RTCP
messages and is more like a peer than a child.*

A pure object-oriented design for **RTPSocket** *would use two
output streams and two input streams. One output stream would
handle control messages and the other would transmit data.
Similarly, one input stream would accept RTCP messages and the
other would receive a media stream.*

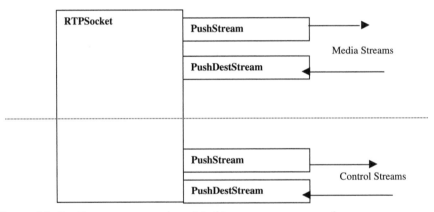

Figure 20–7   Clearer conceptual model of how **RTPSocket** works.

Once the **RTPSessionManager** creates the **RTPSocket**, it requests
that the JMF Manager create a Player to process the content streamed
through the **RTPSocket**. The JMF Manager searches through the content
prefix list for **MediaHandler**s that can accept RTP content.

The Manager finds only one object that will accept the streams produced
by RTPSocket: **RTPSessionManager**. Normal JMF Players consist of a
MediaHandler connected to a **DataSource**. However, as we discovered
in Chapter 19, a **MediaProxy** (or **MediaProxy**s) can be inserted between
a **DataSource** and a **MediaHandler**. **MediaProxies** are used to transform (or manipulate) data before it is sent to the final **MediaHandler** for
decoding. The **RTPSessionManager** is a **MediaProxy**, and it transforms

the RTP packets emitted by the **RTPSocket** into a linear stream of bytes that a conventional JMF **MediaHandler** can understand.

The **MediaProxy** portion of the **RTPSessionManager** consists of three logical components: an RTP Protocol Handler, a **Depacketizer**, and a **DePacketizedDataHandler** (see Figure 20-9). The RTP Protocol Handler parses the raw RTP packets, reassembles an entire frame from individual RTP packets, and removes RTP-specific details from the packets via a **Depacketizer**.

The **Depacketizer** transforms the packet-based output of the **RTPSocket** into a linear byte stream that a JMF **MediaHandler** is able to process. Sun provides a default **Depacketizer** that can handle the payload types listed in Table 20.1.

Table 20.1 Payload Types Supported by Sun's RTP Runtime

Media Type	Win32 RTP	Solaris RTP
H261	X	X
JPEG	X	X
H.263	X	X
G711(PCMU)	X	X
GSM	X	X
DVI (8, 11.025, 22.05, 44.1 kHz)	X	X
G723	X	X

The **DePacketizedDataHandler** receives frames from the **DePacketizer** and alerts the **MediaHandler** that is connected to the **MediaProxy** of the availability of data.

When the Manager discovers that **RTPSessionManager** is a **MediaProxy** and not a **MediaHandler**, it calls **RTPSessionManager**'s **getDataSource()** method to obtain a **DataSource**. The Manager obtains the content type of the **DataSource** and attempts to find a **MediaHandler** to support the content type in the content prefix list. For example, if the **RTPSessionManager** discovers that the stream contains video, it's **getContentType()** method will report **rtp/video** to the Manager.

```
<package-prefix>.media.content.rtp.audio.Handler
<package-prefix>.media.content.rtp.video.Handler
```

Figure 20-8   An RTP-compatible `MediaHandler` informs the Manager that it supports `content.rtp.video` and `content.rtp.audio` by storing its package prefix in the content prefix list.

The Manager then attempts to find a compatible **MediaHandler** for the **MediaProxy**'s Push **DataSource**. Since an RTP stream can contain a multitude of payloads, the **MediaHandler** cannot rely on the **DataSource**'s **getContentType()** method to reveal the stream's content type. Rather, the **MediaHandler** uses the **RTPControl** interface surfaced by all RTP **DataSources** to find out what payloads are in the stream.

The **MediaHandler** calls **RTPControl.getEncodingList()** to obtain an array of known media types (or **BaseEncodingInfo** objects) that will be transmitted in the stream. The **MediaHandler** then verifies that it can decode the media types contained in this array. If it can't handle the payloads indicated by **RTPControl.getEncodingList()**, it throws an **IncompatibleSourceException**.

Core Tip

Writing an RTP **MediaHandler** *is a significant undertaking. Unlike a conventional* **MediaHandler** *that only supports one media format, RTP streams may contain numerous payloads (see Table 19.1). In fact, a stream may contain media types beyond those described by* **RTPControl.getEncodingList()**. *As a result, a robust RTP* **MediaHandler** *should at least be able to decode all of the media types the Sun RTP* **MediaHandler** *decodes, plus whatever unique payload you need to decode.*

Once a **MediaHandler** is connected to the Push **DataSource**, it calls the **DataSource**'s **setTransferHandler()** method to have the **Data-Source** notify it when data becomes available (see Chapter 12 for a detailed description of how **setTransferHandler()** operates). When one or more frames of data become available, the Push **DataSource** interrupts the **MediaHandler** and the **MediaHandler** calls the **DataSource's** **read()** method to obtain content. The **MediaHandler** then decodes the buffer returned by **read()** and plays the frame(s) (see Figure 20-9).

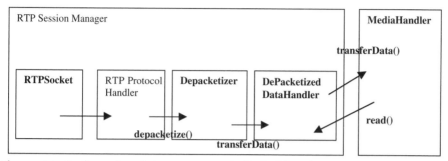

Figure 20–9 Illustration of data movement in Sun's RTP architecture.

Since RTP streams can dynamically change media types, the **MediaHandler** must be able to detect when a frame uses a different payload. It monitors payload changes by querying the **RTPControl.getEncoding()** method. **getEncoding()** returns the encoding associated with the buffer the **MediaHandler** is decoding. Another method of detecting payload changes would be to listen for the **PayloadChangeEvent** in a **RTPSessionManager** listener.

Core Tip

DirectShow also permits filters to dynamically switch payloads (or media types). However, the DirectShow API is more elegant. Rather than assuming the target (or renderer) filter can handle the new payload, the source filter negotiates with the target filter before switching to the new payload. As a result, the target filter knows about the change before it happens, thereby alleviating the need to poll for payload changes.

Peering Inside a DePacketizer

Since RTP streams may contain proprietary protocols that the default **Depacketizer** cannot understand, the **RTPSessionManager** lets you install additional **Depacketizers**. Custom **Depacketizers** are installed in the prefix protocol section of the **jmf.properties** file and the **Depacketizers** package must be in the following format:

```
<rtpdepacketizer.prefixes>.encodingname.DePacketizer
```

Where **<rtpdepacketizer.prefixes>** is your package name and *encodingname* is the name of your payload.

To install a custom **Depacketizer**, you must perform the following actions:

1. Create a **Depacketizer** based on **javax.media.rtp.session.depacketizer.RTPDe-Packetizer**.
2. Store the **Depacketizer** in a package using **<rtpdepacketizer.prefixes>.*encodingname*.DePacketizer**, the naming convention.
3. Add your package prefix to the **jmf.properties** file via **setProtocolPrefixList()**.
4. If you want the changes to be made permanent, call **commit-ProtocolPrefixList()**.

Once your package is installed, your RTP application should call **RTP-SessionManager.addEncoding()** to dynamically bind (or tie) the encoding name of your package to an RTP payload number (see Listing 20.3). When the **RTPSessionManager** detects a packet with the payload number you specified in Step 3 above, it searches the prefix list for **Depacketizer**s that are compatible with the payload. If your package is installed correctly, the **RTPSessionManager** will load and instantiate your **Depacketizer**.

The **RTPSessionManager** then calls the **Depacketizer**'s **setTransferHandler()** method to inform it that it must stream the depacketized data buffers into the **DePacketizedDataHandler**. When a packet is received, the RTP Protocol Handler calls the **Depacketizer**'s **depacketize()** method with a **RTPPacket** object. The **depacketize()** method is responsible for parsing the packet and assembling media frames (each packet will contain an integer number of frames) (see Figure 20-10).

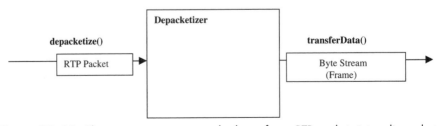

Figure 20-10   The **depacketize()** method transforms RTP packets into a linear byte stream.

For each frame that is decoded, the **Depacketizer** calls the **transferData()** method to alert the **DePacketizedDataHandler** that a frame of media has been successfully parsed. The **DePacketizedDataHandler** in turn calls the **MediaHandler**'s **transferData()** method to inform it that a frame of data is available for processing (see Figure 20-11). The **MediaHandler** calls back into the **DataSource** provided by the **RTPSessionManager** to obtain the frame of data, then it decodes the frame.

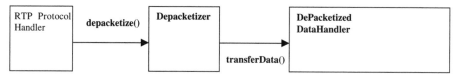

Figure 20–11 **Depacketizer** architecture.

The Easy Route

Most programmers only want to play RTP content and don't want to be bothered with RTP semantics or use RTP-specific APIs. As a result, Sun provides a convenience RTP **MediaLocator** object that lets you construct an RTP Player with minimal fuss. First, you create a specially formatted RTP URL:

rtp://*ipaddress*:*port*/*mediatype*

where ***ipaddress*** is the address of the RTP server, ***port*** is the port that sends RTP packets and ***mediatype*** is the type of media that the server will be transmitting. ***mediatype*** must be either **audio** or **video**.

The RTP **MediaLocator** is then passed to the Manager's **createDataSource()** method to create an **RTPSocket** (see Listing 20.1).

Listing 20.1 Use of a **MediaLocator** to create a **DataSource**.

```
if ((mrl = new MediaLocator("rtp://129.144.251.255:49150/
audio")) == null)
{
     System.err.println("Can't build MRL for " +
filename);
}
     // create a datasource based on the RTP URL
rtpsource = Manager.createDataSource(mrl);
```

For custom payloads, you will need to inform the **RTPSessionManager** about the exact type of payload you intend to stream so that it knows how to depacketize it. For instance, if you intend to stream DVI audio using an undefined payload number, you must tell the **RTPSessionManager** exactly what type of DVI audio you plan to stream.

Since the Manager created a **DataSource** for us, we don't have direct access to the **RTPSessionManager**. However, we can call the **DataSource**'s **getControl()** method to obtain an **RTPControl** object (see Listing 20.2). We've previously used **RTPControl** to determine the payload types that a stream contains, but it is also used to inform the **DataSource**, or **RTPSessionManager**, of expected stream payloads.

Listing 20.2 Obtaining the **RTPControl** interface from an RTP **DataSource**.

```
private static final String rtpcontrol =
"javax.media.rtp.RTPControl";

RTPControl control = (RTPControl)
rtpsource.getControl(rtpcontrol);
if (control == null)
{
        System.out.println("Can't get an RTPControl
interface");
}
```

RTPControl's **addEncoding()** method uses a **BaseEncodingInfo** object to describe an encoding to the **RTPSessionManager.** You should call this method with every custom encoding type you stream. **BaseEncodingInfo** defines the following characteristics of a packet:

- **payloadtype**: The RTP payload number.
- **encodingname**: A descriptive name that identifies the content in the **Payloadtype**. If this is a payload defined in the RTP Specification, this name must match the **Encodingname**s listed in Table 18.1 If it is a custom **Encodingname**, it should match the **Encodingname** of a **Depacketizer** installed in the system.
- **encodingrate**: The clock rate associated with the RTP timestamps. Audio clock rates directly equate to the sampling rate.
- **channels**: Number of audio channels.

- **sampleSize**: This audio attribute defines the size of an audio sample and will vary between audio CODECs.

- **codecString**: CODEC-specific information that varies between media types.

Listing 20.3 shows you how to create a 44-kHz **IMA ADPCM BaseEncodingInfo** object and dynamically bind it to the **RTPSessionManager** via the **addEncoding()** method.

Listing 20.3 Use of **addEncoding()** to dynamically bind an encoding type to a payload.

```
BaseEncodingInfo info = new
BaseEncodingInfo( 96,  // payload type 96 is a dynamic pay-
load number
                    // designed for custom datatypes
           "dvi",// we will be streaming dvi audio
           44100,// clock rate is 44 kHz
           1,     // mono audio
           4,     // IMA ADPM uses 4-bit compressed
samples
           null); // no CODEC specific setup string......

     control.addEncoding(info);
```

Core Tip

If you are using only predefined payloads found in Table 18.1, you do not need to dynamically bind your payloads to the **RTPSessionManager**. *As a result, if you stick with vanilla encoding types that the* **RTPSessionManager** *understands, your JMF application or applet does not need to call an RTP-specific API.*

After you've bound custom encoding types to a payload number, you can ask the JMF Manager to create a Player from your RTP **DataSource** (see Listing 20.4).

Listing 20.4 Creating a Player from an RTP **DataSource**.

```
// Create a Player based on the rtp data source.....
rtpPlayer = Manager.createPlayer(rtpsource);
```

Once the Player is created, you can either treat it as a conventional JMF Player, or you can enhance it with the RTP-specific methods found in **RTP-Control**. For example, **RTPControl.getReceptionStats()** reports how many packets arrived out of sequence, have been lost, or are duplicates.

Core Tip

If you give a JMF Player an invalid **MediaLocator***, it will throw an exception before it completes realization. While the RTP Player will throw an* **IOException** *if you give it an invalid IP address or port, it will* **realize** *regardless of whether the session address is an active session. However, the Player will not* **prefetch** *until the session begins to transmit media streams. As a result, do not assume that because your Player has* **realized** *that you're connected to a legitimate RTP session.*

Dumping Out RTP Statistics

We will illustrate the use of the **RTPControl** interface in **RTPDumper**: a JMF application that dynamically displays RTP session statistics in a **JTextArea**. **RTPDumper** extends **JFrame**. Its **ContentPane** contains stream playback controls and session statistics. **RTPDumer** requires one command line argument: the RTP server URL.

```
RTPDumper rtp://192.168.8.43:49150/audio
```

The initial action we take in the **RTPDumper** constructor is to create a **MediaLocator** based on the command line argument. Since a **MediaLocator** is not RTP-specific, **RTPDumper** can play any content supported by JMF. However, if you load non-RTP media, **RTPDumper** will alert you that RTP-specific features will not be available.

Core Tip

If you decide to base your RTP programs on Sun's RTP samples rather than **RTPDumper***, you should be aware that they use undocumented APIs (such as* **PlayerWindow***) contained in* **com.sun.media.ui***. Since this package may not exist in every JMF runtime, your application will not be pure if you use it.*

The samples also warn you that the source code is confidential and proprietary. Although it is likely that Sun forgot to remove this warning, these statements are disconcerting.

We then construct a **DataSource** from the **MediaLocator** and obtain an **RTPControl** from the **DataSource** (see Listing 20.2). If we can't obtain an **RTPControl** control from the **DataSource**, we know that we aren't playing RTP content and write a warning message to standard output.

After we have a valid **DataSource**, we request that the Manager create a JMF Player from the **DataSource**. If no exceptions are thrown, we attach a listener to the Player and **realize()** the Player. Our last task in the constructor is to create an **RTPStats** object. **RTPStats** extends the **Thread** object and it queries the **RTPControl** object on a periodic basis for session status and writes this status information to the **JTextArea** of the application's **ContentPane**. Although the thread is created in the constructor, we do not start it until the realization process is completed, since no data has been transmitted.

```
statthread = new RTPStats( log, rtpcontrol );
```

When the **RealizeCompleteEvent** arrives at our listener, we check to see if the Player has visual and **ControlPanel** components. If it does, we add them to the **ContentPane** and start the **RTPStats** thread.

```
statthread.start();
```

Core Tip

During the development of **RTPDumper**, *my* **RTPStats** *object had a bug that prevented it from running on a separate thread. As a result, my* **ControllerListener** *held the Player's thread hostage forever when the* **RealizeCompleteEvent** *was received. Although the conventional audio and video players were able to continue functioning and repainting despite this bug, the RTP Player refused to repaint when the window was resized.*

After some debugging, it appears as if the JMF 1.0.2 RTP Player does not use a dedicated thread to report events. Rather it calls your listener on a worker thread. By contrast, the other Players use dedicated event threads to communicate with listeners.

As you learned in Chapter 14, if the **ControllerListener** *takes a long time to process the event, the Player's worker thread is* *suspended until the* **ControllerListener** *completes its task. If the* **ControllerListener** *is hung, then the Player is hung. This real-life example illustrates why robust* **MediaHandlers** *must create a dedicated event thread and cannot rely on programmers to write efficient listeners.*

Once a Player is realized, the user controls the starting and stopping of the Player. However, you'll see that the RTP session statistics constantly change even if playback is paused. These updates occur because RTP is a Push **DataSource** and streams are being transmitted regardless of whether the **MediaHandler** chooses to play them.

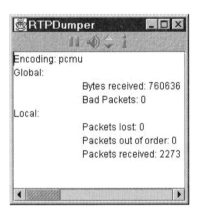

Figure 20–12   **RTPDumper** displaying session statistics.

The **RTPStats** thread wakes up every 500 milliseconds and queries the **RTPControl** object for the following items: encoding information, global reception statistics, and general RTP statistics (see Listing 20.5).

Listing 20.5 Obtaining status information from **RTPControl**.

```
GlobalReceptionStats globalstats =
rtpcontrol.getGlobalStats();
RTPReceptionStats stats = rtpcontrol.getReceptionStats();
BaseEncodingInfo encoding = rtpcontrol.getEncoding();
```

The **RTPStats** only cares about the name of the encoding, and it obtains this information via **BaseEncodingInfo.getEncodingName()** method. If you are using **vat** (an audio RTP tool) to transmit the audio stream, it streams PCM by default, so **getEncodingName()** will return "lpcm" (linear PCM). If you modify **vat** to send **IMA ADPCM** or another audio compression format, the **BaseEncodingInfo** will immediately detect this change and **getEncodingName()** will report the name of the new encoding (i.e., "**dvi4**").

```
String encodingname = encoding.getEncodingName() + "\n";
```

RTPStats queries the global statistics object for the total number of bytes received in this session and the total number of bad packets detected.

```
String bytesreceived = "\tBytes received: " + global-
stats.getBytesRecd() + "\n";
String badpackets = "\tBad Packets: " + globalstats.getBadRT-
Pkts() + "\n";
```

Finally, **RTPStats** queries the RTP statistics object for the number of packets received and the number of packets that were lost or received out of order.

```
String packetslost = "\tPackets lost: " + stats.getPDUlost()
+ "\n";
String outoforder = "\tPackets out of order: " +
stats.getPDUMisOrd() + "\n";
String packetsreceived = "\tPackets received: " +
stats.getPDUProcessed() + "\n";
```

Find an RTP Server to Test on

One of the most challenging tasks a novice RTP programmer faces is finding an RTP server on which to test applications. Although public RTP servers may occasionally surface on the Internet, once people find out about them, they become so heavily burdened that they are rapidly removed. As a result, most RTP servers are used on private networks in schools or businesses where quality of service can be guaranteed.

Another source of RTP servers is the MBone. The MBone, or IP Multicast backBone, is designed to efficiently transmit and replicate multimedia conferences over an optimized IP network. If you have access to the MBone, Sun's JMF RTP Player can join any active session, since all MBone sessions are RTP-based.

Warning

The IP addresses provided by the Sun RTP Player and sample RTP applets are for illustration purposes only and are not valid for development or testing. Most people assume that since the samples are shipped with JMF, they should be functional. Consequently, you can waste hours trying to connect to a phantom server.

In fairness to Sun, they suggest that you change the IP addresses in the samples to a different server. However, they never explicitly mention that the addresses in their samples are not accessible outside the Sun firewall.

Since most people don't have access to a public server or to the MBone, they must simulate one. To simulate a server, you'll need at least two machines. One machine will be a server and it will run software that will stream audio and video streams to the client machine. We will use the freeware tools **vat** and **vic** to stream audio and video RTP content to our client machines.

On the server machine, you start **vat**, the audio tool, with the following parameters:

```
vat -r ipaddress/port number
```

where **-r** tells **vat** to use RTP version 2 headers that are compatible with JMF, and the **ipaddress** is the address of the machine you are streaming content to (i.e., your client machine). For example, the command below causes **vat** to send a continuous audio stream to port **49150** on IP address **129.44.8.63**.

```
vat -r 129.44.8.63/49150
```

Core Tip

vat *(an audio conferencing tool) and* **vic** *(a video conferencing tool) were written by the Network Research Group of the Lawrence Berkeley National Laboratory.* **vic** *and* **vat** *are bidirectional conferencing applications, since they can capture and send streams to other participants and receive streams.*

You can download **vic** *and* **vat** *documentation, source and binaries for Windows, and several flavors of UNIX at http://www.nrg.ee.lbl.gov/*

Additional RTP server tools can be found at following Web sites:

IP/TV – Precept Commercial RTP server/client for Windows:

    http://www.precept.com

ShowMe TV - Sun Microsystems Commercial RTP server/client for Solaris/SPARC:

http://www.sun.com/products-n-solutions/sw/ShowMe/index.html

Your client machine will run the JMF RTP applets and applications. As a result, you must modify the HTML files to point to the local machine (or client) IP address and not the server's address. Although this may initially seem contradictory, the session address used by the **RTPSessionManager** is the destination address (i.e., client machine) of the RTP data packets. The local machine, via the **RTPSessionManager**, will automatically send RTCP packets to all senders for the given session. (see Figure 20-13).

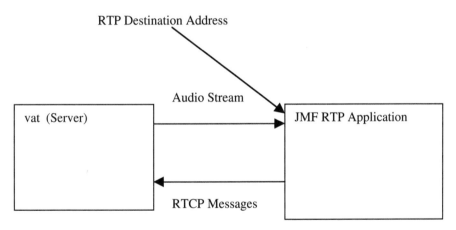

Figure 20–13 Illustration of RTP server simulation setup.

The Hard Way

If you need access to low-level RTP information that is unavailable in **RTP-Control**, you do not have to rely on JMF to create the **RTPSessionManager** for you. Rather, you can construct the **RTPSessionManager** yourself by following these steps:

1. Create the **RTPSessionManager**.
2. Add a listener to the **RTPSessionManager**.
3. Initialize the RTP session.
4. Start the RTP session.

5. Create an RTP **DataSource** after the receipt of a **NewRecvStreamEvent**.

6. Create a Player from the **DataSource** constructed in Step 5.

An RTP session is created when a local participant creates an **RTPSessionManager** (see Listing 20.6). It is crucial that you immediately add yourself as a listener to the **RTPSessionManager**. If you wait too long to add the listener, you will miss vital events.

Listing 20.6 Initializing the Session Manager.

```
// create the new RTPSessionManager
samplesessionman = new RTPSessionMgr();

// ALWAYS add yourself as a RecvStreamListener to listen to
// RecvStreamEvents for RTPRecvStreams of this session
// fa
samplesessionman.addRecvStreamListener(this);
```

Once you've created the **RTPSessionManager** object, you must initialize and start the session (see Listing 20.7).

Listing 20.7 Starting the Session Manager.

```
// get the local IP address
      RTPSessionAddress localhost = new RTPSession-
Address();

try
{
      destaddr = InetAddress.getByName("rtp://
192.168.8.43:49150/audio");
}
catch (UnknownHostException e)
{
      System.err.println("bad host " + e.getMessage());
}


RTPSessionAddress sessaddr = new RTPSessionAddress
(destaddr,
                                             port,
                                             destaddr,
                                             port +1);
      String cname = mymgr.generateCNAME();

      // we send the email, name, cname and tool in the
SDES items
```

Listing 20.7 Starting the Session Manager.   (continued)

```
        RTCPSourceDescription[] userdesclist = new
RTCPSourceDescription[4];
        int i;
        for(i=0; i< userdesclist.length;i++){
            if (i == 0){
                userdescriptionlist[i] = new
RTCPSourceDescription(RTCPSourceDescription.SOURCE_DESC_
EMAIL,

                                    "interactivejava@php-
                                        tr.com",
                                    1,
                                    false);
                continue;
            }
            if (i == 1){
                userdescriptionlist[i] = new
RTCPSourceDescription(RTCPSourceDescription.SOURCE_DESC_
NAME,

                                    "MyUserName",
                                    1,
                                    false);
                continue;
            }
            if ( i == 2){
                userdescriptionlist[i] = new
        RTCPSourceDescription(RTCPSourceDescrip-
tion.SOURCE_DESC_CNAME,

                                    cname,
                                    1,
                                    false);
                continue;
            }
            if (i == 3){
                userdescriptionlist[i] = new
RTCPSourceDescription(RTCPSourceDescription.SOURCE_
DESC_TOOL,

                                    "JMF RTP Player v1.0",
                                    1,
                                    false);
                continue;
            }
        }// end of for

// call initSession() and startSession() on the RTPSM.
try
{
        mymgr.initSession(localhost,
                userdescriptionlist,
                    0.05,
                    0.25);
```

Listing 20.7 Starting the Session Manager.   (continued)

```
        mymgr.startSession(sessaddr,ttl,null);
}
catch (RTPSessionManagerException e)
{
    System.err.println("InitSession err:" + e.get-
Message());
}
catch (IOException e)
{
    System.err.println("StartSession err:" + e.get-
Message());
}
```

At some point after you've started the **RTPSession**, you'll receive a **NewRecvStreamEvent** on your **RTPSessionManager** listener. This event arrives when the **RTPSessionManager** detects a new stream. Since this stream is controlled by an RTP **DataSource**, you can retrieve this **DataSource** from the **NewRecvStreamEvent** object's **getData-Source()** method. The **DataSource** can then be used to create a Player (see Listing 20.8).

Listing 20.8 Creating a **DataSource** and Player upon receipt of **NewRecvStreamEvent**.

```
if (event instanceof NewRecvStreamEvent)
{
    RTPRecvStream stream = null;
    try
    {
        // get a handle over the RTPRecvStream
        stream =((NewRecvStreamEvent)event).getRecvStream();

        // retrieve an RTP datasource from the stream
        DataSource dsource = stream.getDataSource();

        // create a player by passing datasource to the
Media Manager
        newplayer = Manager.createPlayer(dsource);
    }
    catch (Exception e)
    {
        System.err.println("Can't create a player from get-
RecvStream()");
    }

}// instanceof newRecvStreamEvent
```

This process is dramatically more complex than relying on JMF to construct an RTP session for you. Unless you are writing an RTP-specific application and need access to APIs not available in **RTPControl**, use a **MediaLocator** to create the Player.

Summary

Sun and RealNetwork chose dramatically different approaches for their real-time streaming solutions. RealNetwork's G2 JMF player is a JMF-only API with enhancements for RealMedia content. By contrast, Sun's RTP solution is a hybrid: part of it (the RTP **DataSource** and **MediaHandler**) exists in JMF, and the other portion (the **RTPSessionManager**) lives outside of JMF.

Although Sun believes this is the correct architecture, I think it creates needless confusion for RTP programmers (i.e., they must learn two APIs: JMF and the **RTPSessionManager**). It is preferable to have either a JMF-only solution or a self-contained RTP API that is completely separate from JMF (this separate API could use JMF for media transport, but the programmer would not have to be aware of the implementation details). When this mixed programming model is combined with sketchy documentation and samples that have confidentiality warnings, you get the distinct impression that the RTP API needs additional refinement.

WHERE IS JMF HEADED?

*"We seek him here, we seek him there,
Those Frenchies seek him everywhere.
Is he in heaven?–Is he in hell?
That demmed, elusive Pimpernel"*
Baroness Orczy, *The Scarlet Pimpernel*

The future ain't what it used to be.
Yogi Berra

Chapter 21

Throughout this book, we've bumped into a few bothersome limitations in JMF 1.0.x. The most irritating of these restrictions include the inability to run JMF applications on non-Win32 or Solaris platforms, difficulty installing JMF runtimes on client machines, lack of access to low-level sound routines, no CODEC architecture, and no media capture support. Fortunately, Sun is aware of these limitations and has outlined a series of exciting multimedia releases and APIs to address these issues.

JMF 1.1 Provides Immediate Relief

The initial product in the pipeline is JMF 1.1, which contains the first pure Java JMF release. Since it is 100% pure Java, you can run it on platforms that currently have no supported JMF runtimes such as Linux, HP/UX, andOS/2.

This pure Java runtime is not a stripped down subset of earlier JMF 1.0.x native Win32 or Solaris runtimes. Rather, Sun has written a number of pure Java audio and video CODECs that support the majority of audio formats and the most popular QuickTime and video for Windows video file formats (see Table 21.1).

Unfortunately, the pure Java iteration is missing processor-intensive CODECs such as MPEG-1 audio and video. This omission may be due to a phased release schedule or a need for additional performance tuning.

Even when processor-intensive pure Java CODECs are finished, they will never approach the performance of hand-tuned, native assembly instructions that exploit the multimedia capabilities of modern processors (i.e., Intel's MMX™ or Motorola's AltiVec™ instruction sets). Therefore, for the foreseeable future, processor-intensive CODECs will be written in native code.

MIDI support is also missing from the first pure Java release. Sun's explanation for this omission can be found in the following paraphrased statement from the known problems section of the JMF 1.1 beta documentation:

> *Note: The All-Java version of JMF does not include JavaSound. Audio is played through the existing audio programming interfaces in JDK.*

Since JavaSound is required for MIDI synthesis, and there is no pure Java alternative for it, Sun probably decided not to support MIDI until JavaSound became universally supported.

By contrast, if JavaSound is not installed on a given JDK, JMF digital audio Players can fall back to the old **sun.audio** package for audio streaming. This is why the pure version of JMF supports a plethora of audio formats even on non-JavaSound-enabled JVMs.

Although pure Java is Sun's long-term strategy, the company remains cognizant that native code is necessary to boost performance. Consequently, they coined the phrase "performance pack." A performance pack is a euphemism for inserting JNI code into strategic portions of the pure Java JMF runtime to turbocharge performance. Sun has released both Win32 and Solaris performance packs, but has not published any guidelines on how to create a "performance pack" for other platforms.

Table 21.1 File Formats and Multimedia CODECs Supported by Pure JMF 1.1 and Performance Packs

Media Content	Pure Java	Win32	Solaris
AIFF (.AIFF) Audio	x	x	x
G.711 mono	x	x	x
IMA4 ADPCM	x	x	x
u-law 8-kHz mono	x	x	x
8/16-bit mono/stereo linear	x	x	x

Table 21.1 File Formats and Multimedia CODECs Supported by Pure JMF 1.1 and Performance Packs (continued)

Media Content	Pure Java	Win32	Solaris
AVI (.AVI) – Audio			
8/16-bit mono/stereo linear	x	x	x
DVI ADPCM compressed	x	x	x
G.711 mono	x	x	x
GSM mono	x	x	x
u-law 8-kHz mono	x	x	x
AVI (.AVI) – Video			
Cinepak	x	x	x
Indeo (iv31 and iv32)		x	x
JPEG (411, 422, 111)		x	x
GSM (*.GSM)	x	x	x
GSM mono audio			
MIDI (*.MIDI)			
Type 1 & 2 MIDI audio files		x	x
MPEG 1 (*.MPG)			
Audio: MPEG-1, Layer 1 & 2		x	x
Video: MPEG-1		x	x
MPEG Audio (*.MP2)			
Audio: MPEG-1, Layer 1 & 2		x	x

Table 21.1 File Formats and Multimedia CODECs Supported by Pure JMF 1.1 and Performance Packs   (continued)

Media Content	Pure Java	Win32	Solaris
QuickTime (*.MOV) - Audio			
8/16-bit mono/stereo PCM	x	x	x
G.711 mono	x	x	x
GSM mono audio	x	x	x
IMA4 ADPCM	x	x	x
Ulaw	x	x	x
QuickTime (*.MOV) - Video			
Cinepak	x	x	x
H.261		x	x
H.263	x	x	x
Indeo (iv31 and iv32)		x	x
JPEG (411, 422,111)		x	x
Raw		x	x
RLE		x	x
SMC		x	x
RMF (*.RMF) - Audio		x	x
RTP - Audio			
4-bit mono DVI 8/11.05/ 22.05/44.1kHz	x	x	x
GSM mono	x	x	x

Table 21.1 File Formats and Multimedia CODECs Supported by Pure JMF 1.1 and Performance Packs (continued)			
Media Content	*Pure Java*	*Win32*	*Solaris*
G.723 mono	x	x	x
G.711 mono	x	x	x
RTP - Video			
JPEG (411, 422, 111)		x	x
H.261		x	x
H.263		x	x
Sun (*.AU) - Audio			
8/16-bit mono/stereo PCM	x	x	x
G.711 mono	x	x	x
u-law 8 kHz mono	x	x	x
Vivo (*.VIV) - Video			
Audio: G.723.1	6.4 kbps only	x	x
Video: H.263	x	x	x
Wave (*.WAV)			
8/16-bit mono/stereo PCM	x	x	x
G.711 mono	x	x	x
GSM mono	x	x	x
DVI ADPCM	x	x	x
u-law 8-kHz mono	x	x	x
MSADPCM			

Although every JMF runtime supports the same Player API, as Table 21.1 indicates, each runtime may support a different number of media types. Therefore, before you create your media files, be sure to pick a format that is supported by the JMF runtimes on your target platforms.

Pure Java, Speed Demon?

My first question after downloading the JMF 1.1 package was "how much slower will the pure version of JMF be than the native version?" To my surprise, not only was the pure Java release faster in core processing than the native 1.0.2 release, but it is often faster than the native 1.1 release. (See tables 21.2 and 21.3 for detailed performance comparisons.)

Part of the reason for this performance improvement is that Sun has been optimizing the 1.1 code base. The other performance factor is JNI overhead. As Chapter 10 revealed, there is a significant performance hit when Java code calls a JNI method and when JNI code calls back into the JVM. Since a native JMF runtime makes frequent JNI calls, it incurs a performance penalty that a pure JMF runtime does not experience. Whatever the explanation, the pure JMF 1.1 is a testament to the potential of Java multimedia.

Core Tip

These performance numbers only apply to Player creation and destruction and playing primitive data types such as PCM .WAV files or Cinepak .AVI files. Native video and audio CODECs used during playback are considerably faster than their pure Java counterparts (in general, by a factor of 2:1). As a result, native CODECs can achieve higher frame rates with less impact on the CPU than the equivalent Java CODEC.

On a fast machine, enough bandwidth is available that the difference between a Java CODEC and a native one is barely noticeable. As a result, you will see Java versions with less processor-intensive CODECs, such as AC-3 or MPEG-2 audio, in the near future. However, it will be years before the average machine is capable of running a data-intensive MPEG-2 video CODEC.

Table 21.2 Performance Comparison of JMF Releases for a .WAV file

Intel (NT 4.0 400 MHz Pentium II)

Command	*JMF 1.0.2*	*JMF 1.1 (Pure)*	*JMF 1.1 (Native)*
`Manager.createPlayer()`	1823	370	1603
`prefetch()`	871	671	751
`stop()`	20	261	50
`deallocate()`	20	10	20
`close()`	30	10	90

Intel (Win98 400 MHz Pentium II)

Command	*JMF 1.0.2*	*JMF 1.1 (Pure)*	*JMF 1.1 (Native)*
`Manager.createPlayer()`	600	380	
`prefetch()`	940	660	
`stop()`	60	280	
`deallocate()`	0	0	
`close()`	50	50	

Table 21.3 Performance Comparison of JMF Releases for a .MOV file

Intel (NT 4.0 400 MHz Pentium II)

Command	*JMF 1.0.2*	*JMF 1.1 (Pure)*	*JMF 1.1 (Native)*
`Manager.createPlayer()`	1783	1041	671
`prefetch()`	1602	1252	1152
`stop()`	20	671	540
`deallocate()`	40	10	20
`close()`	80	20	20

Table 21.3 Performance Comparison of JMF Releases for a . MOV file   (continued)

Intel (Win98 400 MHz Pentium II)

Command	JMF 1.0.2	JMF 1.1 (Pure)	JMF 1.1 (Native)
`Manager.createPlayer()`	550	330	490
`prefetch()`	1530	1100	1100
`stop()`	0	660	600
`deallocate()`	50	50	0
`close()`	60	60	60

Solaris (Ultra Sparc 10, 300 MHz)

Command	JMF 1.0.2	JMF 1.1 (Pure)
`Manager.createPlayer()`	359	354
`prefetch()`	474	462
`stop()`	17	142
`deallocate()`	10	9
`close()`	23	17

Core Tip

Pure Java JMF Players use heavy visual and `ControlPanel` components. Consequently, they have the same problems with light Swing components as native JMF runtimes (see Chapter 8 for more information on using JMF with Swing). This is surprising since the pure runtimes should not be dependent on native multimedia subsystems that require heavy components to function.

JMF 1.1 also contains a hidden gem: server-specific runtimes that solve many of the installation woes associated with getting the JMF runtime on a client machine. As Chapter 2 revealed, installing JMF on a client is a tedious process, and it varies between each JMF runtime OEM.

By contrast, the Web server version of JMF 1.1 is browser-friendly. It allows you to squeeze out all the unnecessary methods from the bloated **jmf.jar** library and create a custom JMF runtime that contains only the methods your applet needs to run. When the client machine encounters this applet, the server will download the slimmed-down version of the **jmf.jar** file and then initiate playback.

To create the slim JMF runtime, use the **com.ibm.jmf.util.customizer.JMFCustomizer** utility (**customizer.jar** must be in your **classpath** for this command to work). This utility lets you select the methods that will be stored in your custom JMF runtime (see Figure 21.1). We will use the **JMFCustomizer** to create a custom runtime called "**alohajmf.jar**" for the AlohaJMF applet that we created in Chapter 6.

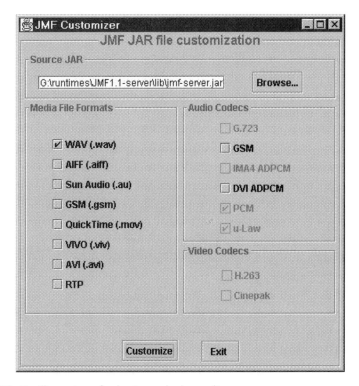

Figure 21-1   Illustration of selecting only the audio components necessary to run the AlohaJMF applet.

Core Tip

Be sure that your **classpath** *points to Swing 1.0.3 libraries before trying to run the* **JMFCustomizer***. The* **JMFCustomizer** *requires a different version of Swing than the one we use in Core JMF (i.e., the 1.0.3 version versus the 1.0). Normally, this would not cause a problem, since Swing is backwards-compatible. Unfortunately, between the 1.0.x and 1.1 releases, Sun had to change the package name of Swing to javax.swing.* from com.sun.swing. Consequently, the* **JMFCustomizer** *will not run with the 1.1 version of Swing.*

Once you've created the custom runtime, simply add an **archive=** parameter to your **APPLET** tag. This **archive=** parameter tells the client browser where it can locate the jar file that contains the code necessary to play the selected .WAV file (see Listing 21.1).

Listing 21.1 Illustration of applet tag that uses the **archive=** parameter to speed up downloading.

```
<APPLET code=AlohaJMF.class
height=200
width=320
archive="alohajmf.jar">
<PARAM NAME="file" VALUE="aloha.wav">
</APPLET>
```

When users encounter JMF applet pages on the Web, they no longer must endure a 800K+ download of the **JMF.JAR** file. Instead, they can hear audio or see video after downloading a **custom JAR** file of only 255 Kbs.

Will We See a Shipping Version of JavaSound in Our Lifetimes?

The second product in the JMF pipeline is the highly publicized JavaSound. We've mentioned JavaSound several times throughout this text as the magical elixir that may cure many of JMF's woes. Typically, when a product receives this much hype and is delayed for an extended period, you will be disappointed when you get your hands on the real thing.

Sun raised expectations for JavaSound by promising programmers direct access to the digital audio streams being fed into its audio mixer and also finer control over MIDI messages and synthesis. In fact, in Sun's JavaSound FAQ, they raise the bar for JavaSound with the following paraphrased statement:

> *Java Sound uses a sophisticated 32 channel audio mixer and advanced MIDI engine that is accessible with a new JavaSound API.*

Will JavaSound give us the low-level access to a digital audio mixer that we crave? Can it provide high-quality, cross-platform MIDI synthesis? Since Java-Sound has not been released even in early access form, it's tough to conclusively answer these questions. However, the details Sun has shed on JavaSound lead me to believe that while JavaSound will not be a cure-all, it will address glaring holes in the JMF architecture.

JavaSound is composed of an audio renderer, MIDI renderer, **TimeBase**, and a renderer device. The audio renderer mixes multiple digital streams, and provides gain control of each stream. Unlike a JMF Player, you can stream digital audio data directly to JavaSound without using a file. As a result, you will be able to stream from memory buffers that you allocated to the JavaSound audio renderer. The ability to stream audio from memory will let you write performance-sensitive applications such as audio conferencing or games.

Core Tip

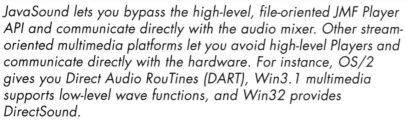

JavaSound lets you bypass the high-level, file-oriented JMF Player API and communicate directly with the audio mixer. Other stream-oriented multimedia platforms let you avoid high-level Players and communicate directly with the hardware. For instance, OS/2 gives you Direct Audio RouTines (DART), Win3.1 multimedia supports low-level wave functions, and Win32 provides DirectSound.

The primary difference between JavaSound and these competitors is that JMF and non-JMF applications can use JavaSound without conflicts. All of these solutions exhibit problems if you try to mix high-level and low-level functions. By contrast, JavaSound is able to simultaneously support JMF and native JavaSound clients.

The JavaSound MIDI renderer's most notable feature is realistic MIDI synthesis that sounds identical on all platforms. The MIDI synthesizer is able to create identical sounds on each platform because it does not rely on the underlying operating system's MIDI device driver. Rather, it uses a technique called wave table synthesis to convert the MIDI data into digital audio content that can be played on any PCM-capable audio device.

Core Tip

A wave table synthesizer stores sampled digital audio representation of all notes used by every instrument in the device. For every note in the MIDI file, the wave table synthesizer finds the matching sampled audio information and inserts the digital audio into the output stream. The resultant digital audio stream is then played through an audio renderer.

If you are a MIDI aficionado, JavaSound gives you access over individual tracks in a MIDI file and control over MIDI channels effects such as **programChange**, **muting**, **afterTouch**, **noteOn**, **noteOff**, etc. Unfortunately, JavaSound was not designed to communicate with external synthesizers, so you can't send these effects outside your computer.

The final component of JavaSound is the renderer device. This object is responsible for taking the final output from the JavaSound mixer and streaming it to the audio hardware.

Will JMF 2.0 Lead Us to the Holy Grail?

Although JavaSound and JMF 1.1 contain new functionality, they do not alter JMF's basic architecture. As a result, many of the weaknesses in JMF remain. For instance, the release will not enable you to create custom CODECs, insert digital audio effects (such as echo), or capture (i.e., record) media. Rather than attempting to hack this functionality into the JMF 1.x code base, Sun and its partner, IBM, intend to incorporate these functions into JMF 2.0.

The most exciting part of JMF 2.0 will be its "Snap-In" API. Although the details are sketchy, "Snap In" will not only permit you to write a single

CODEC object and reuse it in multiple players, but you will have real-time access to media streams (see Figure 21.2).

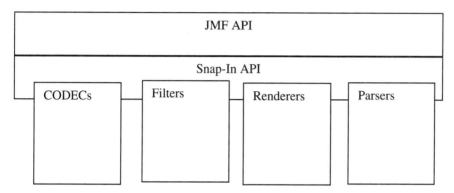

Figure 21–2   JMF 2.0's "Snap-In" architecture.

Real-time access means you can monitor data as it is being transferred from the **DataSource** to the presentation engine (or renderer). Typically, objects that perform real-time modifications to a stream are called signal processing filters. These filters receive one or more input streams, run an algorithm on the data, and route the transformed data to one or more output streams.

One example of a digital audio filter is a noise filter. This filter attaches itself to an audio stream and removes frequencies above those attainable by the human voice. The resultant audio stream sounds "cleaner" since extraneous noise is removed. Other possible audio filters could include reverb, echo, and delay. Signal processing is not limited to the audio realm. You can also attach filters to video streams to map an image onto a three-dimensional surface, such as a cube or pyramid.

The possibilities for video or audio filters are virtually limitless. The only potential roadblock is performance: Java may not be fast enough to implement a processor-intensive real-time filter (see Figure 21.3). For instance, certain types of filters consume so many MIPS that they barely can be considered real-time, even when they are handcrafted in assembly language. As a result, it is difficult to imagine that a Java version will be able to perform adequately. We will have to wait until the release of JMF 2.0 to see if this performance concern is warranted.

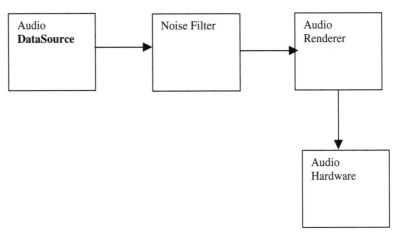

Figure 21-3   How a real-time noise filter would work.

Core Tip

The latest information on the JMF 2.0 architecture can be obtained from the following Web sites:

> *http://www.software.ibm.com/net.media/stds.html*
>
> *http://java.sun.com/products/java-media/jmf/index.html*

An additional benefit of the "Snap-In" API is the ability to reuse parsers (such as our MCML parser) and formatters with multiple renderers. If the "Snap-In" lives up to these lofty goals, JMF will have met and exceeded the native functionality provided by most operating systems.

Core Tip

Most multimedia platforms do not give you real-time access to media streams since they are difficult to design and require sophisticated algorithms to dynamically insert and remove filters from a media stream.

One of DirectShow's compelling advantages over JMF (and virtually all other competing multimedia platforms) is the ease with which you can insert filters in a media stream. Other solutions, such as SPI on OS/2, contain the building blocks necessary for real-time filters, but they have cumbersome interfaces or large buffering requirements that make signal processing impossible.

Although JMF 2.0 is overflowing with new functionality, it remains backwards-compatible with the JMF 1.0 API. Consequently, all our existing JMF programs will run without modification. Although our Players will continue to run in the JMF 2.0 world, it is likely that we will need to rewrite our Players to take advantage of the "Snap-In" API.

Summary

Although the first release of JMF provides a robust environment for creating multimedia applications, we encountered several limitations as we developed the programs in this book. Sun recognizes these problems and plans a continuous stream of updates that should not only address these weaknesses, but also provide exciting new capabilities. If Sun and its partners deliver on their promises, JMF will become an even more exciting platform for creating multimedia applications and applets.

COPING WITH
JMF ERRORS

*The man who makes no mistakes does not
usually make anything.*
**Bishop William Conner Magee,
Bishop of Peterborough (1868)**

To err is human, to forgive is divine.
**Alexander Pope,
*Essay on Criticism***

APPENDIX A

E rror handling is the most neglected part of programming. It's fun to create new programs, but tedious to walk through each line of code and ensure that you've handled every possible error scenario.

A Different Mindset

C or C++ multimedia APIs return error codes for each method or API that you call. As a result, you must check the return code for each call to ensure that it succeeded. Since every call can return a variety of errors, your code rapidly becomes spaghetti-like as you add if/then/else statements to cover each scenario (see Listing A.1).

Furthermore, C/C++ error checking is done on the honor system; the compiler does not force you to validate return codes. As a result, if you forget to check a function's return code or willfully decide to ignore errors, potential error conditions will go unhandled.

Listing A.1 Conventional C++ multimedia error checking.

```
int x = OpenAudioHardware();

if ( x == NO_HARDWARE )
{
      printf("no audio device is available")
}
else if ( x == NO_DSP )
{
      printf("no DSP resource exists")
}
else if ( x == NO_MICROCODE )
{
      printf("audio setup files missing")
}
else if ( x == INTERNAL_ERROR )
{
      printf("driver had an internal error")
}
```

JMF does not rely on methods returning errors. Rather it uses exceptions and events to notify you of error conditions. The advantage of throwing an exception in an error condition is that the compiler will force the programmer to write a corresponding catch block to handle the error (see Listing A.2).

Listing A.2 JMF exception handling example for connecting a **DataSource** to a Player.

```
try
{
    textSource.connect();
    player.setSource( textSource );
}
catch ( IncompatibleSourceException e )
{

    System.out.println("Bad data source....");
}
catch ( IOException e )
{
    System.out.println("General I/O error....");

}
```

Core Tip

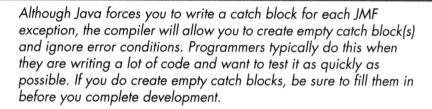

Although Java forces you to write a catch block for each JMF exception, the compiler will allow you to create empty catch block(s) and ignore error conditions. Programmers typically do this when they are writing a lot of code and want to test it as quickly as possible. If you do create empty catch blocks, be sure to fill them in before you complete development.

Cross-Platform Exceptions

If you are accustomed to the multitude of error return codes in MCI or DirectShow, you will be shocked at the dearth of errors in JMF. In fact, Sun has defined only five exceptions that a Player can throw (see Figure A.1).

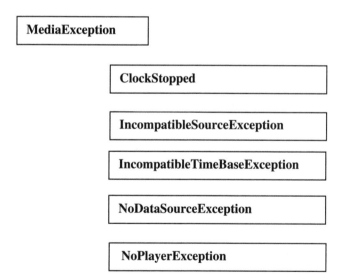

MediaException

ClockStopped

IncompatibleSourceException

IncompatibleTimeBaseException

NoDataSourceException

NoPlayerException

Figure A-1 `MediaException` hierarchy.

Although the exception model simplifies error handling, it complicates debugging and makes it difficult to display an understandable error message. For example, in Listing A.3, if the **createPlayer** call fails, we will catch it in the **NoPlayerException** handler. However, the exception does not tell you why the call failed. By contrast, MCI or DirectShow offers detailed error codes that alert you to the specific reason the call failed (i.e., device overload, hardware malfunction, etc.).

Listing A.3 If an error is thrown, very little information is available to help determine why the call failed.

```
try
{
  player = Manager.createPlayer(mrl);
}
catch (NoPlayerException e)
{
  System.out.println(e);
}
```

Another factor to consider is that each JMF runtime is tailored to a specific platform, and as a result, will throw exceptions at different times. For instance, the MIDI Player for one JMF runtime may use a hardware clock for its **TimeBase**. As a result, it will throw an **IncompatibleTimeBase-Exception** exception if you try change its **TimeBase**.

By contrast, the MIDI Player on another JMF runtime may use the system time clock as its **TimeBase**. Since this Player is not as concerned about timing accuracy, it will permit you to chase its **TimeBase**. Therefore, although both Players were capable of throwing an **IncompatibleTimeBase-Exception**, only one did. Therefore, you should code according to the specification and not the behavior of a Player on a given runtime.

JMF's Tonsils

For decades, doctors believed that the tonsils were nonessential and could be removed without affecting the patient. Today, we know that the tonsils do serve a purpose and doctors are hesitant to remove them without cause. Similarly, most programmers treat **MediaError** exceptions as nonessential and ignore them (see Figure A.2 for a listing of **MediaError**s). In fact, Sun even counsels programmers not to catch these exceptions in it documentation!

This counsel is given because these exceptions are thrown due to programming bugs (i.e., calling **deallocate()** while the Player is started). While it is true that most of these errors should be caught in your initial testing phase, it is possible that a **MediaError** will be thrown in some remote scenario. If you follow Sun's suggestion, this exception will not be caught and your application may terminate. As a result, you should always catch every exception that may be generated no matter what counsel someone may give you (see Figure A-2).

MediaError

StopTimeSetError

NotRealizedError

NotPrefetchedError

ClockStartedError

Figure A-2 **MediaError** hieraarchy.

Listening for Errors

Besides exceptions, JMF may communicate error conditions via events (see Figure A.3). Unfortunately, unlike an exception, the compiler will not force you to update your listener to monitor error events. Therefore, you are responsible for inserting the appropriate error event check into your listener (see Listing A.4). If you forget to listen for these events, your Player may die and your application will be unaware of it.

Listing A.4 Example of listening for an error event

```
if (event instanceof ControllerErrorEvent)
{
    // this error event is terminal for the player.
    player = null;
}
```

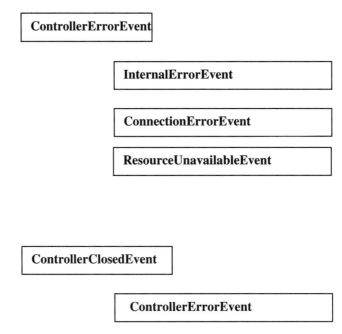

Figure A–3 Error event hierarchy.

Generating Errors in Players

If you are creating a **Player**, you should handle error conditions in the following manner:

1. When an error is encountered, prefer exceptions to C-style error return codes.
2. If a method throws an error, be sure that the method declaration makes callers aware of this.

```
public void setSource(DataSource src) throws IOExcep-
tion, IncompatibleSourceException
```

3. Be sure to give a descriptive reason for any exception you throw. For instance, when the caller catches the **Clock-**

StartedError, they may not be able to understand why it occurred if you throw it like this:

```
if ( state == Controller.Started)
{
    throw new ClockStartedError("illegal method
call");
}
```

By contrast, if you throw the exception with a detailed explanation, it will be obvious to the caller why the exception was thrown.

```
if ( state == Controller.Started)
{
   throw new ClockStartedError("illegal method call—
clock in Started state");
}
```

THE CONFUSED WORLD OF MULTIMEDIA FILE FORMATS

*'I don't think they play at all fairly,' Alice
began, in rather a complaining tone, 'and
they all quarrel so dreadfully one can't
hear oneself speak–and they don't seem to
have any rules in particular; at least, if
there are, nobody attends to them–and
you've no idea how confusing it is all the
things being alive.*

Lewis Caroll, *Alice in Wonderland*

*"Come, let us go down and confuse their
language so they will not understand each
other." That is why it was called Babel—
because the LORD confused the language
of the whole world.*

Genesis 11:7,9 (NIV)

APPENDIX B

F ew people consider the ramifications of selecting an audio or video file format. However, if you want your JMF application or applet to be platform-independent, you must be diligent in your selection of multimedia content. The selection process is especially difficult because there are radical variations in file format and COmpressors/ DECompressors (CODEC) support in each JMF runtime.

Why Is This Process So Complex?

Multimedia compression algorithms are constantly evolving in order to improve audio-visual quality or enable real-time streaming over the Internet. While these advances are essential, they have created a confusing jumble of acronyms, incompatible file formats, and compression algorithms.

This appendix summarizes the essential features of the major multimedia CODECs and file formats so that you can intelligently choose the file formats and compression techniques to use in your JMF applications.

Audio Compression

Chapter 1 revealed that uncompressed audio files are stored in a format called Pulse Code Modulation (PCM). Uncompressed PCM has the highest fidelity sound, but its excessive storage requirements make it unrealistic for most applications. Therefore, programs rely on compression algorithms to conserve space. The most common techniques are μ-law, A-law, ADPCM, MPEG-audio, and AC-3.

ADPCM or (Adaptive Delta Pulse Code Modulation). ADPCM algorithms attempt to predict where the next sample point will occur. Since a prediction typically requires 1–4 bits of storage, as compared to 16-bits for PCM, ADPCM can achieve 4x or higher compression ratios.

G.726. The International Telecommunication Union (ITU) defines how ADPCM data should be encoded for transmission over networks. G.726 supports 2-bit, 3-bit, 4-bit, and 5-bit sample sizes running at 16, 24, 32, and 40 kbs/second respectively. You may also see these algorithms described as G.721 and G.723 in older documents. G.726 combined the older G.721 and G.723 standards into a single ADPCM standard. As a result, the ITU has reused G.721 and G.723 for different audio algorithms.

Core Tip

The ITU standards mentioned in this appendix are preceded by G. This G is an abbreviation for Series G Recommendations: Transmission systems and media, digital systems, and networks. Series G defines standards that relate to the transmission of multimedia content over a network—exactly the area served by JMF.

IMA (DVI) ADPCM. IMA ADPCM algorithm compresses 16-bit samples into 4-bit entities. This algorithm was originally designed for Intel's Digital Video Interactive (DVI). Before DVI became defunct, the International Multimedia Association (IMA) adopted the algorithm as a preferred compression technique. The primary advantage of IMA ADPCM is that it can be implemented in software on low-end processors. Unfortunately, this simplicity means that IMA ADPCM does not sound as good as processor-intensive algorithms, such as MPEG.

Microsoft ADPCM. Like IMA ADPCM, Microsoft ADPCM uses 4-bit samples and can be implemented in software. The sound quality is marginally better than IMA ADPCM.

μ-law, A-law (G.711). These are companding algorithms (i.e., they use logarithmic scales that are heavily weighted to capture the frequencies of human speech).

Motion Pictures Expert Group (MPEG) Audio. MPEG is a family of standards that cover a variety of audio/visual technologies. The MPEG audio algorithms take advantage of peculiarities in human hearing (or perception) to strip out redundant or unnecessary information. There are three popular MPEG audio compression techniques (or layers). Each is based on perceptual encoding, but the higher numbered layers use more complex algorithms to increase compression ratios or improve audio quality.

> Layer 1: Based on frequency masking (i.e., removal of unused frequencies).
>
> Layer 2: Improves the filtering features of Layer 1.
>
> Layer 3: Improved filtering plus Huffman encoding. This layer is used to compress most MPEG audio content on the Internet and can be found in .mp3 files.

Dolby Digital (or AC-3). AC-3 (Audio Code Number 3) is an audio compression algorithm that was designed to compress up to six audio channels for home theatre systems. It is the preferred audio compression technology for advanced multimedia platforms, such as DVD and Laserdisc.

While it is theoretically possible to use MPEG to compress multichannel audio, audiophiles point out that MPEG was never designed to properly handle multichannel compression and creates unforeseen side effects.

Linear Prediction Coder (LPC). LPC attempts to model the human vocal cord with a set of mathematical equations. These equations are then used to synthesize speech. Although LPC tries to model the human voice, it often yields a mechanical or metallic sound

Code Excited Linear Prediction (CELP). CELP uses similar mathematical modeling techniques as LPC; however, it also computes the difference between the model and the original audio content. These differences (or codes) are used by the decompressor to enhance the LPC mathematical model. Consequently, the resultant sound is much closer to the original.

Because the calculation of these codes is processor-intensive, CELP requires more processing resources than LPC and vastly more than an ADPCM algorithm. Despite its smaller size, a properly written CELP algorithm can sound as good as an ADPCM bitstream, but with a lower data rate.

Global System for Mobile Communications (GSM). GSM is a variant of LPC called RPE–LPC (Regular Pulse Excited–Linear Predictive Coder) and it is a preferred format for the digital cellular phone industry. It has a data rate of 13.2 kbs/sec at 8000 samples/sec. Although GSM has excellent sound quality, it requires extensive processing resources.

TrueSpeech (or G.723.1). G.723.1 dominates the Voice over IP (VoIP) market and is heavily used in speech-centric applications. The TrueSpeech algorithm can operate at different rates where higher data rates result in improved sound fidelity. The G.723.1 flavor of TrueSpeech operates at 6.3 or 5.3 Kbps. This rates balances audio fidelity, while minimizing data transmission requirements.

G.729. G.729, also called CS–ACELP (Conjugate–Structure Algebraic Code Excited Linear Prediction). It provides the same audio quality as a 32 kbps ADPCM CODEC, but operates at 8Kbps.

G.728. G.728 is a low-delay code excited linear prediction (LD–CELP) algorithm. All compression algorithms introduce delays as they compress PCM data. Low-delay algorithms minimize this impact by operating on very small buffer (or frame) sizes.

Audio File Formats

Chunk-Based Audio File Formats

Although Electronic Arts is currently a large game development company, they began as a small, but innovative, multimedia developer for the Commodore Amiga platform. One their inventions was the Interchange File Format (IFF). IFF files consisted of chunks, or logical divisions in the file. These chunks enabled an audio file to contain a variety of media types and attributes for these media types.

Core Tip

Unlike the narrowly focused .WAV or .AIFF formats, IFF files may contain audio, video, image, or virtually any multimedia content. Image applications such as DeluxePaint used IFF to store graphics, while presentation programs used it for audio. Although IFF is the oldest chunk-based file format, it remains one of the most flexible formats.

Apple leveraged IFF's chunk concept to create the Apple Interchange File Format to store audio content. Similarly, IBM and Microsoft used chunks in their Resource Interchange File Format (RIFF).

RIFF audio files use a .WAV extension. Each chunk in a .WAV file may contain a different audio compression type or attributes such as musical lyrics. Applications detect the type of data in a chunk by examining the chunk header. Chunks enable .WAV files to incorporate new compression technologies as they are released.

Microsoft reused the chunk concept in its video file format (.AVI). Chunks let .AVI developers mix video and audio compression technologies in a single file and permit .AVI to support new compression technologies.

Core Tip

Chunks are superior to CODEC-specific file formats. However, they are not as elegant as Quicktime's track concept. Tracks permit an application to easily control disparate media types. By contrast, chunks were designed to separate data and are not as flexible in controlling multiple media types.

Miscellaneous Audio Formats

.mp2. These files are compressed with a MPEG I Layer II CODEC.

.mp3. These files are compressed with a MPEG I Layer III CODEC. The files may optionally contain ID3 tags, which let content creators attach information to an MPEG audio file. ID3 version 1 defines fixed-size tags that describe a limited set of attributes (such as artist, album, song, year of publishing, and music genre). By contrast, ID3 version 2 offers variable sized tags (similar in concept to chunks) to represent embedded pictures, detailed copyright information, and synchronized lyrics.

Core Tip

The International Standards Organization (ISO) has recently approved the Mpeg IV (.mp4) standard. Mpeg IV is targeted at streaming over networks and the Internet. As a result, it has a higher compression ratio than MPEG I. Due to algorithmic advancements, it also provides higher quality at the lower data rates.

Musical Instrument Digital Interface (MIDI). MIDI files store representation of musical notes and do not contain sampled audio. A synthesizer transforms these notes into digital audio streams. Since each note can be represented in a few bytes, MIDI files are extremely small in comparison to .wav or .au files. Unlike other multimedia formats, MIDI defines a message format that can be used by nonmultimedia applications. For instance, you could use MIDI messages to communicate with a robot.

Rich Music Format (.rmf). RMF provides high quality audio with minimal bandwidth requirements to facilitate audio streaming over the Internet. An RMF file contains CD-quality digital samples of the instruments required for playback along with MIDI-like representations of the notes played by these instruments. Consequently, RMF files have much of the flexibility of a sampled digital audio file with considerably less bandwidth requirements.

http://www.headspace.com/beatnik/rmf/index.html

Module Format (.mod). MOD files are similar in concept to RMF files, since they store instrument samples and instructions on how to manipulate these samples. However, unlike RMF files, .mod files are not based on MIDI, nor can they be converted into MIDI files. Like IFF, these files originated on the Amiga system and there are no JMF Players that support them.

Sun/Next Audio Formats (.au). The .au file format originated on UNIX and is a popular Internet audio format. Because most of the Internet .au files contain µ-law audio, many people assume that .au files may only contain µ-law data. In reality, .au files contain a header that describes their content, so they can support a variety of audio compression formats.

Video CODECs

Cinepak. A proprietary video CODEC originally designed by SuperMac for Quicktime in the days of x386 and 68030 processors. It is based on a Vector Quantization (VQ) algorithm. Although it used to be a superior CODEC, it is not up to the quality standards of modern CODECS, such as MPEG-2.

H.261. H.261 is an ITU video coding standard designed to exploit ISDN data rates of 64Kbt/second. Since all H.261 content is transmitted in multiples of 64Kbt/second, H.261 is nicknamed *px64Kbt/s*. H.261 was the first CODEC based on Discrete Cosine Transform (DCT) with Motion Compensation later popularized by MPEG.

H.263. H.263 is an ITU video conferencing CODEC that refines the H.261 and MPEG-1 standards and is specifically designed for low data rates. Like H.261, H.263 uses Discrete Cosine Transform (DCT) with Motion Compensation to compress video content.

Indeo (Intel Video). A CODEC developed by Intel. It was originally designed to exploit the power of the Intel processors (486 and later). Indeo has about the same quality level as Cinepak.

MPEG

MPEG video content can be stored in *system* (or interleaved audio and video) streams or *elementary* streams that separate audio or video streams. Either *system* or *elementary* streams can be placed in Quicktime, .AVI, or other audiovisual formats.

MPEG-1. MPEG-1 is based on the DCT technology pioneered in H.261 and is popular in the Far East, where it is used in VideoCDs. Most processors are powerful enough to decode MPEG-1 in software.

MPEG-2. MPEG-2 is based on the MPEG-1 DCT algorithms, but is tailored for platforms such as DVD or Digital Broadcast Satellite that demand broadcast-quality digitally encoded audio and video. MPEG-2 has higher data rates than MPEG-1 and requires high-end Pentium II or RISC processors to decode in software.

Run Length Encoding (RLE). A simple compression technique that attempts to identify compressable sequences of video or audio content.

Video File Formats

.MOV or Quicktime. Apple's track-based multimedia file format (.MOV) that may contain an arbitrary number of audiovisual CODECs. Apple has enhanced and refined this format over the years and Quicktime has been chosen by ISO to store MPEG IV content.

Audio/Visual Interleaved Format (.avi). A RIFF-based video file that contains audio and video chunks.

RealVideo G2. RealNetwork's video CODEC, optimized to transmit video over the Internet.

VideoNow (.vivo). A video format that is designed to stream content over a network.

SAMPLE CODE

Delightful task! To rear the tender thought,
to teach the young idea how to shoot.
James Thomson, *The Seasons, Spring*

APPENDIX C

A   All of the source code described throughout Core JMF is available in the source directory of the CD that accompanies this book. The source directory is composed of subdirectories, each of which contains the source files described in a particular chapter. The overview below will guide you through the contents of the source directory.

Chapter 1: Multimedia Evolution

Backdoor

- applet sample fileinputstream (backdoor.java)
- html sample (backdoor.html)

Screendoor

- applet sample using URL (screendoor.java)
- html sample (screendoor.html)

Chapter 6: AlohaJMF: A JMF Applet

AlohaJMF

- AlohaJMF.java (applet source)
- Page1.htm

AlohaJR

- AlohaJR.java (applet source)
- Page1.htm

Chapter 8: Multimedia Swing Set

- JMFFileChooser.java (illustrates how to create custom JMF FileChooser)
- MultimediaFileView.java (displays audio icons)
- MultimediaFilter.java (filters out nonmultimedia files)
- MultimediaPreview.java (previews audio content).

Chapter 9: The Next Generation: Java-Beans and JMF

- JumpingBean.java (sample JMFBean)
- JumpingBeanBeanInfo.java (multimedia bean properties)
- MultimediaFileView.java (displays multimedia icons specified by the bean)
- MultimediaFilter.java (filters out nonmultimedia files)
- MultimediaPreview.java (previews audio content).

Chapter 10: Going Native

BeanBridge.cpp (sample C++ source to launch JVM and use JMFFi-leChooser)

Chapter 13: The Multimedia Caption DataSource

- TextSourceStream.java (**PullSourceStream** sample that outputs timing info)
- TimeTextSourceStream.java (**PullSourceStream** sample that outputs timing info)
- DataSource.java (MCML **DataSource**)
- mcml.java (mcml parser)
- *.mcml (sample caption files)

Chapter 15: The CaptionMediaHandler

- AlohaJMF.java
- CaptionControlPanelComponent.java (GUI controls for Player)
- CaptionPrefetch.java (prefetch thread)
- CaptionRealize.java (realize thread)
- CaptionStart.java (start thread)
- CaptionStop.java(stop thread)
- CaptionVisualComponent.java (output class for Player)
- Handler.java (core Player methods)
- SendThread.java (event thread class)

Chapter 16: Grapling with the CD

- AlohaJMF.java (sample class to control the CD Player)
- CDAudio.java (JNI interface class to CD device)
- CDMediaHandler.java (core Player methods)
- CDPrefetch.java(prefetch thread)
- CDRealize.java (realize thread)
- CDStart.java (start thread)
- CDStop.java (stop thread)
- MCIHack.java (java thread to work around Win32 MCI bugs)

- PositionAdviseEvent.java
- SendThread.java (event thread class)
- CDControlPanelComponent.java (GUI controls for Player)
- cdcontrol.cpp (JNI routines to control the CD)
- *.mak (makefiles for specific platforms)
- *.mcml (sample caption files)

Chapter 17: The Ultimate Synchronization: the Marriage of Players

- SyncTest.java (synchronizes CD and caption Players)
- *.mcml (sample caption files useful in synchronization)

Chapter 18: Meddling in a Player's Business with a MediaProxy

- AlohaJMF.java (sample class to control **MediaProxy**)
- CombinedSourceStream.java (**PullSourceStream** sample that outputs both text and timing info)
- DataSource.java (single output stream MCML **DataSource**)
- mcml.java (mcml parser)
- mcml2.java (mcml parser—single output stream)
- MCMLTextDataSource.java (converts single stream MCML input into two stream output needed by **Player**)
- playersrc/CaptionControlPanelComponent.java (GUI controls for Player)
- playersrc/CaptionPrefetch.java(prefetch thread)
- playersrc/CaptionRealize.java (realize thread)
- playersrc/CaptionStart.java (start thread)
- playersrc/CaptionStop.java(stop thread)
- playersrc/CaptionVisualComponent.java (output class for Player)
- playersrc/Handler.java (core Player methods)
- SendThread.java (event thread class)

- TextSourceStream.java (**PullSourceStream** sample that outputs text info on byte input stream)
- TimeTextSourceStream.java (**PullSourceStream** sample that outputs timing info on byte input stream)
- *.mcml (sample caption files)

Chapter 19: Real-Time Streaming

- MultimediaFileView.java (RealMedia/audio icon viewer)
- MultimediaFilter.java (filters out nonmultimedia files)
- MultimediaPreview.java (previews RealMedia content)
- RealFileChooser.java (illustrates how to use the RealNetwork's JMF API)

Chapter 20: A Real-Time Hybrid

- RTPDumper.java (illustrates how to use the **RTPSessionManager**)
- RTPStats.java (rtp statistics class)

INDEX

warrant that the SOFTWARE will meet your requirements or that the operation of the SOFTWARE will be uninterrupted or error-free. The Company warrants that the media on which the SOFTWARE is delivered shall be free from defects in materials and workmanship under normal use for a period of thirty (30) days from the date of your purchase. Your only remedy and the Company's only obligation under these limited warranties is, at the Company's option, return of the warranted item for a refund of any amounts paid by you or replacement of the item. Any replacement of SOFTWARE or media under the warranties shall not extend the original warranty period. The limited warranty set forth above shall not apply to any SOFTWARE which the Company determines in good faith has been subject to misuse, neglect, improper installation, repair, alteration, or damage by you. EXCEPT FOR THE EXPRESSED WARRANTIES SET FORTH ABOVE, THE COMPANY DISCLAIMS ALL WARRANTIES, EXPRESS OR IMPLIED, INCLUDING WITHOUT LIMITATION, THE IMPLIED WARRANTIES OF MERCHANTABILITY AND FITNESS FOR A PARTICULAR PURPOSE. EXCEPT FOR THE EXPRESS WARRANTY SET FORTH ABOVE, THE COMPANY DOES NOT WARRANT, GUARANTEE, OR MAKE ANY REPRESENTATION REGARDING THE USE OR THE RESULTS OF THE USE OF THE SOFTWARE IN TERMS OF ITS CORRECTNESS, ACCURACY, RELIABILITY, CURRENTNESS, OR OTHERWISE.

IN NO EVENT, SHALL THE COMPANY OR ITS EMPLOYEES, AGENTS, SUPPLIERS, OR CONTRACTORS BE LIABLE FOR ANY INCIDENTAL, INDIRECT, SPECIAL, OR CONSEQUENTIAL DAMAGES ARISING OUT OF OR IN CONNECTION WITH THE LICENSE GRANTED UNDER THIS AGREEMENT, OR FOR LOSS OF USE, LOSS OF DATA, LOSS OF INCOME OR PROFIT, OR OTHER LOSSES, SUSTAINED AS A RESULT OF INJURY TO ANY PERSON, OR LOSS OF OR DAMAGE TO PROPERTY, OR CLAIMS OF THIRD PARTIES, EVEN IF THE COMPANY OR AN AUTHORIZED REPRESENTATIVE OF THE COMPANY HAS BEEN ADVISED OF THE POSSIBILITY OF SUCH DAMAGES. IN NO EVENT SHALL LIABILITY OF THE COMPANY FOR DAMAGES WITH RESPECT TO THE SOFTWARE EXCEED THE AMOUNTS ACTUALLY PAID BY YOU, IF ANY, FOR THE SOFTWARE.

SOME JURISDICTIONS DO NOT ALLOW THE LIMITATION OF IMPLIED WARRANTIES OR LIABILITY FOR INCIDENTAL, INDIRECT, SPECIAL, OR CONSEQUENTIAL DAMAGES, SO THE ABOVE LIMITATIONS MAY NOT ALWAYS APPLY. THE WARRANTIES IN THIS AGREEMENT GIVE YOU SPECIFIC LEGAL RIGHTS AND YOU MAY ALSO HAVE OTHER RIGHTS WHICH VARY IN ACCORDANCE WITH LOCAL LAW.

ACKNOWLEDGMENT

YOU ACKNOWLEDGE THAT YOU HAVE READ THIS AGREEMENT, UNDERSTAND IT, AND AGREE TO BE BOUND BY ITS TERMS AND CONDITIONS. YOU ALSO AGREE THAT THIS AGREEMENT IS THE COMPLETE AND EXCLUSIVE STATEMENT OF THE AGREEMENT BETWEEN YOU AND THE COMPANY AND SUPERSEDES ALL PROPOSALS OR PRIOR AGREEMENTS, ORAL, OR WRITTEN, AND ANY OTHER COMMUNICATIONS BETWEEN YOU AND THE COMPANY OR ANY REPRESENTATIVE OF THE COMPANY RELATING TO THE SUBJECT MATTER OF THIS AGREEMENT.

Should you have any questions concerning this Agreement or if you wish to contact the Company for any reason, please contact in writing at the address below.

Robin Short
Prentice Hall PTR
One Lake Street
Upper Saddle River, New Jersey 07458

About the CD

What's Included

All source code described throughout *Core Java Media Framework* is available in the source directory on the CD. The source directory is composed of subdirectories, each of which contains the source files described in a particular chapter (see Appendix C for detailed directory contents).

The CD also contains RealPlayer® G2, a JMF Player. To install on Microsoft Windows 95®, Windows 98®, or Windows NT®, run the setup program in the real\g2player subdirectory. For QuickTime® users, Whipped Butter, a JMF runtime, is available in the quicktim subdirectory. This directory contains the Macintosh runtime (WB1.1(Mac).hqx), the Win32 runtime (WB1.1(Win).zip), and associated documentation (WBDocs.zip).

System Requirements

The CD-ROM is a standard ISO 9660 CD formatted with RockRidge and Joliet extensions.

Installation instructions, copyright notices, license agreements, and system requirements are provided for each program as appropriate.

Use of the *Core Java Media Framework* CD-ROM is subject to the terms of the License Agreement following the index in this book.

Technical Support

Prentice Hall does not offer technical support for any of the programs on the CD-ROM. However, if the CD is damaged, you may obtain a replacement copy by sending an email describing the problem to:

disc_exchange@phptr.com